"*The Lions of Iwo Jima* is a powerful, gut-wrenching account of one of the bloodiest battles of World War II. A tale of courage, heartbreak and the power of the human spirit to overcome adversity, this outstanding book is also a reminder that we must never forget that the price of war is paid for by the sacrifices of gallant warriors like those of Combat Team 28."

—Carlo D'Este, author of *Patton: A Genius For War*
and *Eisenhower: A Soldier's Life*

"This riveting and memorable account of the horrors and heroics of Iwo Jima is much more than another war story. It is about courage, grief, sacrifice and, most of all, about honor."   —Tom Brokaw, NBC News

"A competent account of the key World War II battle . . The authors work hard to include anecdotes, colorful characters and philosophical musings, so military buffs will have no trouble finishing the book."   — *Kirkus Reviews*

"*The Lions of Iwo Jima* captures in stark detail the incredible trial by fire of Combat Team 28 in the Marine Corps' most challenging battle of the Pacific War. It shows what Americans can do when the chips are really down."

—Dan Rather

"A great work that recaptures one of the most ferocious battles in human history. The seizure of Mt. Suribachi has been an inspiration to all Marines. *The Lions of Iwo Jima* tells the rest of the story of the famous Flag Raising, Combat Team 28's five-week battle against an enemy who preferred death to surrender on the most heavily fortified island in the world. I have walked the volcanic ground upon which they fought. I now fully appreciate how and what CT 28 accomplished. BRAVO ZULU/well done!"

—H. C. "Barney" Barnum, Colonel of Marines (ret),
Medal of Honor Recipient

"*The Lions of Iwo Jima* is, above all, a story of the indomitable resolve of Marines in battle. Colonel Liversedge emerges as one of the great combat commanders in Marine history. His example led his men to countless acts of breath-taking courage and sacrifice for their brother Marines and for America."   —General James L. Jones, 32nd Commandant of the
Marine Corps and Supreme Allied Commander Europe

"General Haynes and James Warren have written a brilliant firsthand account of the legendary battle that defined the US Marine Corps. As a student of the battle who has walked the black sand beaches of Iwo many times, I was fascinated by the detail and riveting description of every action. This is a must-read for all those who want a grunt's-eye view of ferocious combat in an epic battle."

—Zinni (USMC-ret)

"This is the most comprehensive documentary of the battle for Iwo Jima. History has yet to understand the immense implications this epic struggle had for the strategic air campaign that finally broke the will of Japan's leadership. The vivid personal accounts of Fred Haynes and others make it a living history that is both painful to read and inspiring to contemplate."

—Jack Lambert, author of *The Pineapple Air Force: Pearl Harbor to Tokyo*

"General Fred Haynes and James Warren claim that the Marines and Sailors of Combat Team 28 comprised one of the finest fighting units in the history of American arms. After reading this remarkable book, you have to believe they are exactly right."

—General Carl Mundy, 30th Commandant of the Marine Corps

"The high drama of heroic character in action elevates this factual retelling of the Battle of Iwo into a seamless, rhythmic classic in the literature of twentieth-century warfare. To read *The Lions of Iwo Jima* is to realize that out of the chaos of the Marines' months-long struggle for the island (to borrow a phrase from a William Butler Yeats poem), a terrible beauty is born."

—Mary Hayden, Ph.D., Professor Emeritus, American and British Literature, University of California

"*The Lions of Iwo Jima* is a superb addition to the history of Iwo Jima. Aside from offering fresh insights into the flag raisings on Mount Suribachi, Warren and Haynes offer a graphic and moving portrait of the terrible fighting that followed. Especially noteworthy is the firsthand account of one of the toughest fights within the battle our Marines fought on Iwo Jima—the battle of Bloody Gorge—a desperate last-ditch killing spree that would require the entire 5th Division and all of her heavily bloodied combat teams nine continuous days and nights of violent death."

—Colonel John Ripley (USMC-ret), hero of *The Bridge at Dong Ha*, and former Director of Marine Corps History

"*The Lions of Iwo Jima* is a first-class piece of history writing. It recounts in powerful detail the experiences of a great unit of Marines in the Corps' most costly battle. It's also a memoir by a Marine at the center of the storm. The story of Combat Team 28 surely confirms the importance of good leadership and the role of the human will in combat."

—General Alfred Gray, 29th Commandant of the Marine Corps

Also by James A. Warren

American Spartans: The U.S. Marines:
A Combat History from Iwo Jima to Iraq

Portrait of a Tragedy:
America and the Vietnam War

THE LIONS OF IWO JIMA

THE LIONS
OF IWO JIMA

★

Major General
FRED HAYNES (USMC-ret)

and JAMES A. WARREN

A John Macrae/Holt Paperback
Henry Holt and Company · New York

Holt Paperbacks
Henry Holt and Company, LLC
Publishers since 1866
175 Fifth Avenue
New York, New York 10010
www.henryholt.com

A Holt Paperback® and ⑰® are registered trademarks
of Henry Holt and Company, LLC.

Distributed in Canada by H. B. Fenn and Company Ltd.

CT 28 logo courtesy of the U.S. Naval Institute

Library of Congress Cataloging-in-Publication Data
Haynes, Fred.
     The lions of Iwo Jima / Fred Haynes and James A. Warren. —1st ed.
       p. cm.
     Includes bibliographical references and index.
     ISBN-13: 978-0-8050-9017-8
     ISBN-10: 0-8050-9017-7
     1. Iwo Jima, Battle of, Japan, 1945—Personal narratives, American.
2. United States. Marine Corps. Marines, 28th.   3. Haynes, Fred.
I. Warren, James A.   II. Title.
     D767.99.I9H38 2008
     940.54'2528—dc22   2007042245

Henry Holt books are available for special promotions
and premiums. For details contact: Director, Special Markets.

Originally published in hardcover in 2008 by
John Macrae Books/Henry Holt and Company

Maps by James Sinclair

Designed by Victoria Hartman

Printed in the United States of America

3   5   7   9   10   8   6   4   2

The entrance to the War Memorial Chapel in the National Cathedral in Washington is guarded by two oak railings bearing the following inscription: "In remembrance of more than 600 members of the 28th Marines (Reinforced) fallen during the assault on Mount Suribachi and the seizure of Iwo Jima, 1945. 20th Anniversary, 19 February 1965." To them, and to all the other gallant warriors who fell on Iwo Jima, we humbly dedicate this book.

CONTENTS

THE LIONS OF IWO JIMA

PREFACE

arch 8, 2006. Two men stand just above a long crescent beach on a small volcanic island 650 miles south of Tokyo. It is about seventy degrees Fahrenheit, a beautiful day to explore hallowed ground. A seven-knot wind blows out of the south. The surf gently breaks on Green Beach, Iwo Jima, where, sixty-one years earlier, the forty-five hundred Marines of Combat Team 28 landed. Their mission: to seize a 554-foot mountain—Mount Suribachi—that dominated the full length of the beach and then to join with seven other combat teams to wrest the entire island from its twenty-two thousand defenders. Iwo Jima in February 1945 was the most densely fortified piece of real estate on earth.

The sound of the surf is broken only by the occasional plaintive cry of a seabird. The younger man wears a Marine-issue bush hat and carries a small tape recorder. The older one, slightly stooped, holds a cane in one hand and gesticulates toward the shoreline below. The two men gaze from north to south along the beach.

To the north, a natural quarry looms over the beach. In the center, there is nothing but the terraced beach of black sand. To the south, rising up like the head of some primordial sea creature, is the mountain. Dusty green foliage obscures cave entrances at the mountain's base. Even from a distance of four hundred yards, the craters of countless large-caliber projectiles are visible on the mountain's face.

The older man is a retired major general in the Marines named Fred Haynes, this book's senior author. He was one of a small number of men in Regimental Combat Team 28 (CT 28) to survive the entire battle without a single wound, and one of a handful of regimental staff officers responsible for planning the assault on Mount Suribachi. He speaks to the man in the bush hat, his coauthor, James A. Warren, a military historian who has written, among other books, a history of the Marines. Fred begins:

I'd recently received my regular commission as a Marine, and had worked harder in preparing for this operation than for anything I had done before in my twenty-four years. I had been in the Corps for two years but had never seen combat. I felt something similar to how I'd felt back home in Plano, Texas, just before a big high school football game. It's difficult to describe, really. My brother, Doc, used to call it "feeling heavy in the pants." It was an odd mixture of anticipation and excitement, mixed with fear of what I might run up against and some apprehension as to how I'd respond under what was sure to be heavy fire. Of course, we'd used live fire in countless training exercises. But that was meant to reproduce the sights and sounds of combat and instill in us a measure of the seriousness of our job. It wasn't meant to kill people—unlike the fire we were about to receive on the beach at Iwo Jima.

The first unpleasant surprise was the black, volcanic sand. Your feet sank deep into it with each step, and it was all but impossible to gain traction. Enemy fire at that point was heating up—the big stuff was joining the chorus of mortar and small-arms fire we'd been taking since the first amphibious tractors came ashore at 0900. It was bedlam in every direction, real pandemonium front, rear, and on both flanks.

I flopped down on the second of the beach's three terraces next to a warrant officer named Joe Bush, who commanded our rocket section.

Joe and I started to dig in right there, in part because the fire was increasing and in part because we needed to gain our bearings before moving forward—something we knew we had to do, and fast. I didn't know where our command post (CP) would be, as I could find neither Colonel Liversedge nor Lieutenant Colonel Williams. We needed one of them to set up the CP to run the fight.

Anyway, Joe and I were there not more than a minute or two when a few rounds from a Japanese machine gun went stitch-stitch-stitch, about a foot and a half in front of us. My first thought was, "Isn't this strange . . . they're shooting at us." But this wasn't exactly true—they were just firing in every direction, and these particular rounds, well, they came pretty close to severing our heads. I thought of Kipling's old ballad, Gunga Din:

> It was "Din! Din! Din!"
> With bullets kickin' dust-spots on the green.

I also remember thinking that maybe I'd made the wrong career move. I'd been active in the church around that time and had thought about joining the priesthood. I soon had other causes for concern. Colonel Williams had suggested I get a couple of extra sandwiches from the ship's galley the previous night, as we weren't likely to get anything decent by way of chow on the first day ashore. So I did just that, but the sandwiches were lost somewhere on the beach, probably not far from where those machine-gun rounds landed.

The next thing that happened was very grim, but it was the sort of event that was happening up and down that beach all day, and although I wasn't aware of it at the time, it turned out to be a gruesome metaphor for the entire thirty-six-day battle. An artillery round must have blown a couple of Marines to bits to our left, and a foot and a part of a calf, with legging and combat shoe attached, landed just a few meters away. I told one of our runners, a former Trappist monk novitiate named Len Bulkowski, "Take that over to the regimental surgeon at the aid station. Maybe he can match it to a casualty."

Fred Haynes pauses for a moment and takes a long, hard look up and down the beach, and then faces south, to the mountain. He spoke slowly, a slight hint of emotion in his Texas drawl:

The intensity of the combat on Iwo was governed by the very close confinement of the battlefield and the sheer density of the fortifications on the island. Within a couple of days on that little rock—Iwo Jima is only about eight and a half square miles—we had one hundred thousand men trying with the utmost resolve to kill one another. That's more than ten thousand men per square mile!

The Marines had been in some horrific fighting and suffered heavy casualties in World War I and on island battlefields in the Pacific in World War II, but what happened on Iwo was beyond description. It was a close-in slugging match of Marine infantry against hundreds of mutually reinforcing, heavily fortified positions manned by soldiers who preferred death to surrender, even when surrounded and with no hope of escape.

It was a battle of Marine flesh against Japanese concrete in a very real sense. This slugging match went on day after day for five weeks. We had trained hard for close to a full year as a combat team. That's about double the time a typical Marine unit would spend in preparation for an operation in World War II.

We knew our business. The Japanese surely knew theirs. It's hard for me to imagine now how anybody got out alive, when you consider the sheer density of shells flying around that island hour after hour, day after day. By the time we reached the final pocket of Japanese resistance in Bloody Gorge near the north end of the rock, a month after we had landed, virtually all the guys who'd done the frontline fighting in taking Mount Suribachi were dead or wounded. The replacements were doing most of the fighting by then, and they were really getting plastered. Some of the Marines who had been in it from the beginning stopped caring about safety. They were too tired to care. And yet, they refused to quit. It was not uncommon for wounded men up there in that deep gash in the earth to refuse evacuation or to escape the hospital after sustaining two or even three wounds in order to rejoin their buddies still on the line. The thought of being killed in combat was for many of our Marines preferable to leaving their buddies to carry on without them.

There was never anything quite like Iwo Jima in the annals of American arms before, and with any luck, we won't see anything like it again.

As Haynes talks, an active-duty Marine and decorated veteran of the Iraq war, Col. Stacy Clardy, walks below the general with a former Combat Team 28 machine gunner, Gordon Schnulle of Elgin, Illinois, who is reading from a sheet of paper the names of fifteen Marines from his hometown who fought on Iwo Jima. Five of these men lost their lives there. Colonel Clardy snaps to attention. Other visitors to the landing beaches quietly gather black volcanic sand into plastic ziplock bags.

Though the detritus of battle is plentiful here, beach sand is the only souvenir that the Japanese, to whom the island was returned in 1968, allow visitors to remove. Spent shells and even live rounds can be found if one wanders just a short way off the paths and roads or enters the many caves, tunnels, and underground barracks that housed thousands of Japanese soldiers.

The mood on the beach is solemn and elegiac. The plaintive calls of gulls and the lapping of the waves are the only sounds one hears.

INTRODUCTION

Many military historians today regard the attack on the island fortress of Iwo Jima as the supreme test of the amphibious assault in the annals of war. Three reinforced divisions of Marines and their supporting forces, some 110,000 men in all, not counting the massive numbers of men manning the ships and planes surrounding the island, assaulted the Japanese on February 19, 1945. From its formal inception in October 1944, the operation to wrest Iwo Jima from its defenders was considered by American planners to be potentially the most difficult mission in the 170-year history of the Marine Corps.

The campaign itself, fought between February 19 and March 26, 1945, proved the planners entirely correct. The battle, in the end, took thirty-six days of unceasingly ferocious combat. Most of the killing was at close range by infantrymen and demolitions men wielding rifles, flamethrowers, and explosive charges designed to blow up gun emplacements and the underground tunnels and caves that comprised the Japanese defensive system. One-third of the nineteen thousand Marines who were killed in World War II died on

Iwo Jima. Operation Detachment, the official name of the operation, was the sole campaign in the Pacific in which total American casualties exceeded those of the Japanese.

The fortifications on the island were the most elaborate encountered by Allied infantrymen in the Pacific. Because Iwo Jima was so small and the combatants so numerous, the battlefield was intensely cramped. During the first two weeks of the fight, there was no safe place, no "rear area" that could not be reached by Japanese guns. The Japanese fighting positions ranged from one-man spider holes to pillboxes, dug-in tanks, blockhouses, trenches, and interconnected cave openings. They were scattered throughout the island, but camouflage rendered the vast majority undetectable.

The commander of the Japanese forces was a superb professional soldier. A lieutenant general, Tadamichi Kuribayashi was a fifth-generation samurai and a gifted defensive strategist. He had long admired the United States and believed the decision to initiate war against the Americans a grave mistake. Nonetheless, for eight months before the invasion, Kuribayashi drove his garrison at a furious pace. They prepared a lethal system of interlocking defenses across the entire island. More than nine hundred major gun emplacements and several thousand individual fighting positions were supplied by a network of underground barracks and storehouses, connected by eleven miles of tunnels.

The Japanese garrison on Iwo waged one of the greatest campaigns of static defense in the history of war, exacting—and paying—an enormous price in blood. Avoiding the large-scale, costly banzai attacks that had featured prominently in earlier battles, the Japanese instead chose to adhere, as a V Amphibious Corps (V Corps or VAC, the senior military command echelon on the island) report put it, to a "well coordinated plan by a commander who has prepared his defensive positions and utilized the terrain to the best tactical advantage in order to conserve his force, inflict heavy casualties on the enemy, and delay the capture of this strategic island. . . . Each Jap defender was given the mission of killing 10 Americans before dying himself."[1]

"The gravity of the coming battle filled me with apprehension," wrote Lt. Gen. Holland "Howlin' Mad" Smith, who, in leading the Marines in their drive across the Pacific, had become a symbol of the Corps' fighting spirit.[2] Smith had predicted at least fifteen thousand casualties among the landing force. Before the landing, the V Amphibious Corps believed the enemy bastion on Iwo to number about fourteen thousand men. In fact, there were close to twenty-two thousand defenders.

The Americans suffered twenty-eight thousand casualties, while fewer than two thousand Japanese survived the battle. "I was not afraid of the outcome. I knew we would win," wrote Smith. "We always had. But contemplation of the cost in lives caused me many sleepless nights. My only source of comfort was in reading the tribulations of leaders described in the Bible. Never before had I realized the spiritual uplift and solace a man on the eve of a great trial receives from the pages of that book."[3]

"Great trial" indeed. On Iwo Jima, there would be no flanking attacks or amphibious assaults behind enemy lines designed to crack the thick belt of defensive positions from the rear. There could be no end run around the enemy. The island was too thickly fortified to undertake such maneuvers, which have traditionally limited both casualties and the duration of large battles. For the assault troops, Iwo Jima was from beginning to end a matter of frontal assault against an enemy who resisted attacks almost to the last man.

Beginning on December 8, 1944, and continuing for the next seventy-four consecutive days, the island was bombarded by B-24 Liberators of the 7th Army Air Force. The island received by far the heaviest preinvasion bombardment of the Pacific War, yet an official intelligence report issued two weeks before the battle confirmed that the daily bombings only served to slow down the furious pace with which Kuribayashi and his men were digging in and building new positions.

Photographic evidence of the bombings between December 3 and January 24, an American intelligence report made clear, had "not prevented the enemy from improving his defensive position, and as of 24 January 1945, his installations of all categories of [fortifications] had notably increased in number. The island is now far more heavily defended by gun positions and field fortifications than it was on 15 October 1944, when initial heavy bombing strikes were initiated."[4]

It was Adm. Ernest J. King, commander in chief of the U.S. Fleet, who proposed the strategic directive to the Joint Chiefs of Staff (JCS) that led to the island's seizure. On October 2, 1944, he issued a directive indicating that the Navy lacked the resources to sustain the provisionally scheduled invasions of Formosa and China. The JCS had envisaged constructing air bases on both to conduct a massive strategic bombing campaign against Japan proper.

King argued that the Navy did, however, have sufficient resources to take intermediate air bases on the islands of Iwo Jima and Okinawa, and that their seizure would greatly enhance the strategic bombing of the Japanese home islands from bases already established in the Marianas. Gen. Henry "Hap" Arnold, who led the Army Air Forces, ardently supported the directive. Iwo Jima, in particular, could be used as a base for long-range P-51 fighter escorts for the massive B-29 Superfortress raids designed to destroy Japan's capacity to make war. The island was equidistant from Tokyo and the B-29 air bases on Guam, Tinian, and Saipan. It already had two airfields suitable for use by fighters.

The capture of Iwo would eliminate the two-hour warning of impending attack from the island's radio station. With fighter escort protection and without the fuel-wasting dogleg around the island, the B-29s could fly in low over their critical targets in Japan.

On October 3, the JCS accepted King's proposal. There was a secondary reason for taking the island: Japanese bombers flying from Iwo had already succeeded in destroying more than a dozen B-29s on American airfields in the Marianas. If the Japanese opted to replenish their air armada on Iwo Jima, most of which had been destroyed by American air raids, they could continue to punish American air bases and their most precious assets —the Superfortresses themselves. The JCS also saw Iwo Jima as a staging area for the invasion of the home islands and an air base from which American planes could cut off shipping in the Sea of Japan.

Once the strategic bombing campaign began in November 1944, the wisdom of the decision to take the island was confirmed in a compelling, unanticipated way. Far too many B-29s returning from the raids on Japan were ditching into the sea, often with the loss of all hands on board. With Iwo Jima in American hands, the damaged Superfortresses could land on the island for repairs and then fly back to the Marianas. Possession of Iwo's airfields gave Army Air Forces general Curtis LeMay, who commanded 21st Bomber Command in the Marianas, and his B-29 crews an enormous boost in morale. More than twenty-two hundred B-29s landed on Iwo Jima by war's end. Not all of these crews would have been lost at sea. Some landings were for training purposes only. But it seems reasonable to assume that several thousand American lives were saved because of tiny Iwo Jima's airstrips. Moreover, the long-range P-51 fighters that were placed on the island made an important, if largely unheralded, contribution to the destruction of enemy airpower in Japan proper.

Recently a historian and active-duty Marine captain, Robert S. Burrell, has published several controversial articles and a book arguing that "the irony is that the battle's impact on the history of the Corps far surpasses any strategic relevance capturing the island may have served."[5] Implicitly, Burrell suggests that the cost in blood of taking the island was too high, given its strategic contribution to the defeat of Japan, and that the decision to take Iwo Jima was essentially a strategic miscalculation.

Captain Burrell's work, we believe, sheds far more heat than light. It relies too heavily on hindsight and on a tenuous foundation of cherry-picked information and analysis unavailable in the fall of 1944. The capture of Iwo did, in the end, greatly enhance the strategic bombing of the home islands. That bombing campaign was clearly decisive in Japan's defeat, for it threatened to destroy Japanese civilization, and thus paved the way for the decision by Japan's leaders to surrender unconditionally to the United States.

In assessing the strategic impact of taking the island, Burrell ignores the *moral element* of strategy deemed so vitally important by Carl von Clausewitz, the legendary Prussian philosopher of war. By "moral," Clausewitz posited immeasurable, nonmaterial factors such as morale, willpower, and a nation's unity of purpose in carrying on despite extreme adversity. Here, we believe the effect of Iwo Jima on both nations was profound.

The loss of the island, the first piece of Japanese soil invaded and the first target in the inner defensive ring protecting the home islands, stunned the Japanese people, for they viewed it as the gateway to Japan itself. Its loss led the Imperial Japanese Army to conclude that though they might fight on, there was no way they could successfully repulse additional amphibious assaults by the Americans. Further, the stoicism and courage of the Marines, symbolized in the iconic Joe Rosenthal photograph of the second flag raising on Mount Suribachi, gave the war-weary American public a much-needed boost when morale was clearly low, providing a palpable sense of optimism that the defeat of the Japanese was inevitable.

Historians are in general agreement that the high casualties sustained on Iwo Jima and Okinawa were a critical factor in President Harry Truman's decision to try to end the war by means other than an invasion of the Japanese home islands. Military historian John Keegan puts the projected casualty figure for the invasion of the island of Kyushu alone—an invasion in which Combat Team 28 was slated to participate—at 268,000 men killed and wounded, a staggering number when one acknowledges that American battle deaths in all theaters in World War II totaled 292,000.

★

IN THE AMERICAN imagination, Iwo Jima joins Lexington and Concord and the Battles of New Orleans, Gettysburg, Belleau Wood, and Normandy as one of a handful of military engagements that transcend the war of which they were a part and that speak powerfully to our sense of national identity. When photographer Joe

Rosenthal captured the stirring image of five Marines and a Navy medical corpsman raising the American flag atop Mount Suribachi, the place of Regimental Combat Team 28 in the annals of American history was assured. *The Lions of Iwo Jima* is the first full history of that Combat Team's costly struggle on "Hell's Volcano."

The story of the flag raisings—there were in fact two such events—has generated an enormous body of writing and, recently, a major feature film. It beckons to us today, reminding us of the sacrifices men and women have had to make in perilous times. But very little is known about the unit's fate after the flag went up.

The Lions of Iwo Jima seeks to recapture the experiences of the 4,500 Marines of Combat Team 28, placing particular focus not just on the opening struggle to seize Mount Suribachi, but on the monthlong assault *after* the famous flag raising. During the fight against the main belt of enemy defenses, amid the lethal tunnel and bunker complexes of Hill 362A and Nishi Ridge, CT 28 sustained a devastating number of casualties among its junior officers and seasoned noncoms. Once those objectives were secured, the Team, its assault units increasingly manned by replacements with limited infantry training, struggled forward against hundreds of well-prepared defenses, yard by yard, north toward Kitano Point. With the help of the remnants of CT 26 and CT 27, CT 28 cleared out the last bastion of organized resistance on the island, hidden in a deep gash in the volcanic earth christened "Bloody Gorge."

The gorge measured only seven hundred yards in length and between two hundred and five hundred yards in width, yet it took the exhausted Marines nine days of brutal combat in the worst terrain on the island to clear out the labyrinth of subterranean defenses there. The last phase of the battle lent credence to General Smith's assertion that Iwo Jima was "troglodyte war on a primitive level with modern refinements that burned men to ashes, blasted through concrete masses, split the earth with seismic effect . . . entomb[ing] thousands alive."[6]

Hill 362A, Nishi Ridge, and Bloody Gorge, each a "battle within the Battle," are remembered only by a few hundred survivors and a handful of military historians. This book aims to remedy that situation.

The question might well be asked: Why another book on Iwo Jima when so many have been written already? Because the complete story of CT 28 has never been told, and its history, we believe, presents a fresh perspective of the battle in which it played such a crucial role.

Earlier histories of the battle offer only bits and pieces of Combat Team 28's campaign, and without exception, they focus on the Team's first phase of the fight, with its two flag raisings. This is not surprising, given the Rosenthal photo's enormous symbolic value, as well as the tactical importance of the first. Suribachi was a fortress unto itself, with multiple levels of tunnels and numerous large-caliber gun emplacements. It completely dominated the landing beaches, with a garrison of more than 1,600 Japanese soldiers capable of raining down all manner of fire upon the Marine invasion force. Suribachi had to be taken fast.

By the time CT 28 had broken through the main defenses on the left flank of the island-wide attack and reached Bloody Gorge, the Team teetered on the verge of collapse. Yet it somehow pressed on until the last enemy defensive positions were reduced. According to "the book," CT 28, with its combat efficiency rated at 40 percent, should have ceased to function as a unit by that point. It was during the fighting in the north that the Team lost most of its key small-unit leaders, including three of the men in the photo of the second flag raising. By campaign's end, more than 70 percent of the Marines who had landed in the unit's three infantry assault battalions were dead or wounded. In thirty-one days of hard fighting on the line, CT 28 advanced 5,600 yards, closed 2,880 caves, killed an estimated 5,210 enemy soldiers, and took 16 prisoners. Total casualties sustained for the 28th Marine Regiment alone, the core infantry unit around which the Team was built, were 89 officers and 2,287 enlisted men killed or wounded. It had gone into the battle with 3,250 Marines.

A single volume, exploring in detail the experiences of one of the eight combat teams to bear the brunt of the fighting, would deepen our understanding of one of the most excruciating ordeals experienced by Americans in arms in the twentieth century. By telling the story of a superbly trained unit of Marines, we hope to illuminate the nature of the Pacific War and the Marine Corps' vital role in that conflict.

Why was CT 28 such an extraordinary outfit? In a sense, the entire book offers readers an extended answer to this question. A short response to the question might be as follows: the men of the regiment lived together "under canvas" in Southern California and Hawaii, away from "mainside" barracks for their yearlong training period. The Team was led by one of the greatest combat commanders in Marine Corps history, Col. Harry Liversedge. Its training regimen in Hawaii was specially designed for assaulting the most densely fortified island in the Pacific War, and that training reflected a large body of hard-won knowledge acquired by Marines who had fought against the Japanese for more than two full years.

Unlike the combat teams of the 3rd and 4th Marine Divisions, who also fought with impressive resolve in Operation Detachment, CT 28, as a unit, had never seen combat. Yet fully 40 percent of the men in the 28th Regiment were combat veterans. Many of these men hailed from the Corps' elite Raider and Paratroop regiments—units that attracted men who were highly motivated and competitive, even by Marine standards, with strong athletic backgrounds.

The Lions of Iwo Jima is a narrative of ground combat, but three of its nine chapters—one on the enemy's mind-set and two on how the adversaries prepared for this epic struggle—provide historical context. It is also a war memoir. Fred Haynes was a twenty-four-year-old Marine officer in the unit's headquarters element. He survived the entire campaign and was in touch daily with the assault unit commanders and many of the troops who fought under them.

As an operations officer, Fred was among the handful of Marines who planned and coordinated the assault on Suribachi, as well as the daily attacks during the subsequent month of punishing combat. An excerpt from the citation for Fred's Bronze Star nicely summarizes his roles in the battle. It was written by Colonel Liversedge himself.

> After rendering outstanding service during the planning phase of this vital operation, Captain Haynes effectively discharged the task of coordinating the regiment's ship-to-shore movement, contributing in large measure to the success of the landing by his excellent work as Tactical Control Officer. Frequently visiting the front lines throughout the entire campaign, he braved heavy enemy fire to obtain valuable tactical information on the disposition of troops and the terrain over which the regiment would attack.

Fred has long been a leading member of the tight-knit community of Iwo Jima survivors and their families. For more than sixty years, he has collected clippings, letters, and unpublished manuscripts from his comrades in CT 28, as well as documents, maps, and official records concerning the battle. These previously untapped sources, in addition to more than one hundred recent interviews with surviving members of the team, ensure that *The Lions of Iwo Jima* offers readers fresh insight into the battle.

Our goal in writing the book has been to reconstruct the world of CT 28 as it prepared for and fought its only battle and to give the reader a vivid sense of the range of experiences and emotions these men endured. Some men, Japanese and Americans alike, were shattered by the life-and-death struggle that raged on day after day. Many more emerged from the battle as stronger, more humane people, their sense of commitment and compassion deepened by the suffering and loss they encountered.

All history is interpretive. The "facts" do not speak for themselves. In the case of a battle as furious and destructive as Iwo Jima, many of the "facts" recorded even in the official Marine Corps documents and histories conflict with one another, and most of the key participants we have written about are long dead. Recollections of individual Marines about the same day or event often differ quite widely.

Indeed, recollections of individuals about the battle tend to morph over time.

Confronted with these realities, we have relied on the professional judgment of a Marine officer who fought in three wars and a military historian who has spent the last twenty years writing about war, and more particularly, the role of the Marine Corps in conflicts since World War II. The movements of battalions and companies, the changes in leadership, the nature of the tactics and the defenses described in the book have, with few exceptions, been corroborated by several reliable sources. Stories of individual experiences in some cases could not be corroborated in the same manner. Yet, taken together, the recollections and reflections of individual participants speak to a truth about the battle, and about the experience of war, that cannot be found in the official histories and reports. Among the thousands of stories and anecdotes we encountered in the research stages of this project, we have steered clear of those for which the evidence was questionable.

A word now about the manner in which we tell this story: Fred's personal recollections and analysis as a participant—the memoir element of the book—are written in the first person and are set off from the main narrative in italics. Quotations taken from interviews or unpublished manuscripts have been edited for grammar and spelling and errors of chronology. A few changes in the order of sentences have been made to eliminate confusion. However, we have not changed the tone or meaning of excerpts from the many unpublished sources that appear for the first time in this book.

★

AS FOR THE men of Combat Team 28, it only remains to say that no earthly language, no rational analysis can explain how these men fought under such horrific conditions, day in, day out, for more than a month. They seemed sustained by a mysterious and transcendent force. These Marines were driven by a powerful desire not to let their buddies down, to get the job done.

This is their story.

1

FORMING UP
AT CAMP PENDLETON

n early February 1944, trainloads of men and matériel for the newly activated 5th Division—the fifth of six divisions created during the war by a Marine Corps that numbered fewer than twenty thousand men on the eve of the conflict—came down the spur of the Santa Fe Railroad into Camp Pendleton. The largest Marine base in the world, Pendleton was the ideal place to organize and train a new division for combat in the Pacific. Men and equipment flowed into the base day and night from Parris Island, Camp Lejeune in North Carolina, and Navy bases and barracks around the world.

The 28th Marines, under Col. Harry Bluett Liversedge, was activated on February 8. The division's three combat teams, CT 26, 27, and 28, would spend close to a full year preparing for their first and only battle. The operations and training officers for CT 28 were the beneficiaries of a wealth of new knowledge and experience gained by the Marine Corps in more than two years of fighting against the Japanese.[1]

Moreover, the Marine Corps that sent CT 28 into this great battle had been remarkably prescient. For twenty years, it had anticipated war against the Japanese. Amphibious warfare had been a Marine Corps' raison d'être since the early 1920s. Between the two world wars, the most imaginative minds in the Marine Corps had fashioned the first coherent doctrine in military history for conducting assaults against defended beaches—a type of operation that the vast majority of military strategists in Europe and the United States felt to be doomed to failure in light of the disastrous campaign waged by the British Commonwealth and French forces against the Turks at Gallipoli in 1915.

The Corps studied the Gallipoli campaign closely and reached a different conclusion. The assault there cost the lives of more than forty thousand Allied troops. It failed not because the Turks were better fighters than the British, Australians, and New Zealanders, but for lack of proper amphibious doctrine and equipment. Particularly glaring problems concerned the absence of specially designed landing craft and adequate supporting fire from ships and aircraft.

It was Maj. Earl "Pete" Ellis, among the Corps' most driven and eccentric officers, who in the early 1920s envisaged the basic outlines of an amphibious war against Japan. Ellis also was among the first strategists to conceive of the amphibious assault as a complex tactical movement, the success of which depended on shock troops with specialized training focused on moving from ship to shore while covered by accurate air and naval gunfire.

In 1934, drawing on the work of Ellis and Maj. Gen. John Lejeune, the Corps published *The Tentative Manual for Landing Operations*. It was the first manual in the history of warfare to lay out systematically the basic principles of bringing combat power from sea to shore. It broke down its subject into six discrete parts: command relationships between the Navy and Marines; naval gunfire support; aerial support; ship-to-shore movement; securing the beach and logistics; and the loading of specialized ships and landing craft in such a manner that the force ashore could get what it needed in the correct sequence. "Combat loading," as this procedure was called, was part art, part science, and if it wasn't executed with meticulous planning based on good intelligence, the chances for a successful invasion of a well-fortified beach were slim indeed.

In the years between the manual's publication and the Battle of Iwo Jima, the senior planners and logistics specialists, headquartered at the Marine Corps Schools in Quantico, Virginia, worked closely with their Navy counterparts to refine procedures, tables of organization, and equipment. Perhaps most importantly, the Marines realized the vital importance of striking the right mix of landing craft and specialized supporting arms to bring combat power from sea to shore. By the time CT 28 began to plan in earnest for the invasion of Iwo—October 1944—the Corps had been able to procure an ample supply of excellent amphibious tracked vehicles, called amtracs or LVTs (landing vehicles, tracked) for short. These LVTs could bring about thirty-five combat-loaded infantrymen across a defended beach effectively. More heavily armored tractors equipped with 75mm cannons, LVT(A)-4s, could provide fire against enemy positions as the troops hit the beach. These amtracs, along with wheeled amphibious trucks (called DUKWs) and a wide variety of other heavy weapons and equipment, were transported to the operations area in large landing ships, such as LSTs, "Landing Ship, Tank" in military parlance.

Personal weapons and communications equipment and procedures had improved over those used in the earlier battles, such as Guadalcanal and Tarawa. So, too, the organization and tactics of tankers, demolitions teams, and infantrymen had been revised and integrated in the light of earlier combat experience.[2]

By the time the 28th Marines were forming up, extraordinary progress had been made in coordinating the movement of troops ashore with supporting air and naval gunfire. By this time, it was widely recognized that large-caliber naval guns had to be used to knock out the largest enemy installations in advance of the landing and that such naval gunfire had to be highly accurate if the operation was to succeed without drastically high casualties.

Leadership was equally important. Weighing in at about 250

pounds and standing six feet three inches tall, Col. Harry Liversedge was a living legend in the Marine Corps. Widely known as "Harry the Horse" for his loping strides, he had set the intercollegiate record for the shot put while a student at Berkeley, where he also starred on the gridiron as a tackle just before World War I. He was the first West Coast player to make Walter Camp's All-American collegiate football team. When the United States entered World War I, Liversedge, a junior at Berkeley, felt the pull of patriotism and adventure, so he joined the Marines. Although he arrived in Europe too late to see combat, he served in postwar northern France and was subsequently selected to join the Navy's team in the 1920 Olympics, where he entered several track and field events. He won a bronze medal in the shot put in the games.

Liversedge served briefly in Haiti and with the 3rd Brigade of Marines in Tientsin, China. He coached the Marine boxing team in China, and upon his return to the large Marine base at Quantico, Virginia, played football for several of the outstanding Marine teams in the 1920s.

He was a modest man, unswervingly decent and utterly fearless in combat. I never heard him say anything that could be construed as self-aggrandizing. I had the opportunity to see him daily throughout the entire time he commanded the 28th Marines. Never once did he show the slightest sign of fear or confusion during the Iwo Jima campaign, despite being surrounded by a great deal of both.

Harry Liversedge may have been modest, but he exuded a quiet self-confidence that was infectious. Liversedge is remembered by the surviving men in the 28th Marines as fearless in combat, but also compassionate and understanding. When two enlisted men were caught by MPs hunting outside the boundaries of their training camp on the big island of Hawaii, Liversedge deliberately pretended to understand that they had fired their rifles inside the camp—a lesser infraction resulting only in additional KP duty.

Toward the brutal climax of the battle for Iwo Jima, when a high-ranking career officer of the 28th Marines was immobilized by exhaustion and could no longer bear to send his battered platoons against enemy emplacements in the rugged northern end of the island, Colonel Liversedge quietly relieved him of his command, assigned a young captain to look after him, and gave him time to rest and regain his composure. The officer in question was put back in command of his unit a few days later.

The relationship between Marine officers and enlisted men was (and is) different than in the other American services. Marine officers tend to be closer to their men, in part because the Corps has always been smaller than the other services and has a more people-centered culture. Liversedge embodied the guidelines set down governing the relations between officers and enlisted Marines by Maj. Gen. John Lejeune in the Marine Corps manual of 1921—guidelines still honored today. "The relation between officer and enlisted men should in no sense be that of superior to inferior nor that of master and servant, but rather . . . should partake of the relationship between father and son, to the extent that officers, especially commanding officers, are responsible for the physical, mental and moral welfare, as well as the discipline and military training of the young men under their command."[3]

A Japanese-language officer who served with Combat Team 28, 1st Lt. John K. McLean, recalled that

> Liversedge was a superb field commander, greatly respected by his troops. Col. Liversedge was never bombastic or flamboyant—no macho displays. He was self-assured and quietly confident, born of his experiences as a successful commander in earlier Pacific battles. He enjoyed the complete respect and confidence of his troops. But there was more to him than that. The colonel had a sense of humanity and a deep regard for his men, which inspired all to perform to the best of their ability.
>
> One day while we were still training in Camp Pendleton, the word was passed that the colonel would hold a troop inspection. I failed to get the word that it would be formal and showed up

without my field scarf [Marine lingo for "necktie"]. To my horror, I saw all the officers were wearing theirs. One asked me, "Where is your field scarf, Lieutenant?" I could have crawled into a hole, certain I would be chewed out royally. Col. Liversedge looked at me for a few seconds, then turned to his officers and said, "Gentlemen, the inspection will be without field scarf!"

I venture to say that there was not a man in the 28th Regiment, from the highest-ranking officer to the lowest private, who would not gladly have followed Col. Liversedge to hell and back. And at Iwo Jima every one of them did.[4]

Harry Liversedge was a man of few words who did not suffer fools gladly. Fair-minded and flexible when solving disputes and personnel problems within the unit, he could on occasion get angry. A lifelong bachelor, he liked a good bourbon and had a passion for playing slot machines. First Lieutenant McLean remembers, "One evening Colonel Liversedge came in and started playing the slot machines, which were in a room adjoining the bar. All of a sudden there was a loud crash. We all raced to the scene of the noise to see what had happened. There stood the colonel. He had thrown the slot machine through the window of the bar."[5]

Liversedge had distinguished himself in combat leading a Marine Raider battalion in the Russell Islands early in the war. His second in command of the 28th Marines, Lt. Col. Robert Hugh Williams, was also a decorated combat leader. Although a study in contrasts, the two men got along very well. Liversedge was a large, hulking man, with a plebian demeanor. He reminded several of his Marines, including Fred, of Abraham Lincoln. Williams was more patrician in manner and outlook than his commander. Although he had grown up on a Wisconsin farm, he was the son of a highly regarded Presbyterian minister and a graduate of The Ohio State University. Unlike his boss, Williams was of average height and build.

Married into a prominent Washington family, Williams also had a keen ear for classical music. A well-published military writer, he possessed a deep understanding of the subtleties of military operations.

He had known from the age of ten that he wanted to be a soldier. A cousin of his in the Lafayette Escadrille in World War I was a major influence on Williams as a teenager. "He loved pageantry," his wife, Alice, wrote in a letter to Fred, "likened himself to Tristram, and believed it was man's God-given duty to improve himself. He considered himself out of place in the 20th century, but he fit the Marine Corps like a glove."[6]

At CT 28's second training ground at Camp Tarawa on the big island of Hawaii, Colonel Williams quietly got together with the captains and majors in the regiment and indicated that he felt we should have "batmen" to clean our tents and uniforms and make up our cots each morning. He suggested that we find a few privates willing to undertake this task and that we pay each one seven dollars a month. So each one of us ended up hiring a young Marine. After a month or so, we quietly dropped the project, without telling anyone up the line.

Williams was a great believer in the value of military tradition. Bob deeply admired Great Britain's Royal Marines, a very small but superb military organization. Williams may very well have adapted some of their tricks of the trade in setting up our training problems. The Royal Marines certainly seemed to influence his bearing, as Bob was always immaculately turned out. Even on Iwo Jima he found time to shave each morning, which was quite striking under the circumstances.

Colonel Williams was particularly fond of swagger sticks. I think he may have slept with one in his rack! One of our officers, Maj. Red Williamson, owned an ancient car that had a rusted-out hole in the floor in front of the right-hand front seat. Colonel Williams usually rode in that position, and one day when we were on our way back to our Pendleton training area from the weekend with our families, his favorite swagger stick evidently fell through that hole. He did not notice it was missing until we arrived at Tent Camp 1. This was a favorite stick of his, made of rosewood with sterling silver tips, with one end having a small Marine Corps emblem. It was not known generally, but the next day we changed the plans for one of the rifle companies, which was scheduled for a ten-mile conditioning hike. Instead of the hike being conducted entirely on the Camp Pendleton ranch, the company was sent out on the Pulgas Canyon Road and then north on Highway 101 and told to keep their eyes open for this highly prized swagger stick. It was found, much to the relief of Colonel Williams and, indeed, to the rest of us who had to ride back and forth with him!

★

LIVERSEDGE'S COMBAT TEAM was assigned to Tent Camp 1 in Las Pulgas Canyon because there was no room in the built-up area of Camp Pendleton to provide the regiment with permanent barracks. The 5th Division's training regimen commenced quickly and efficiently; it had to be built into a formidable fighting machine within six months.

Tent Camp 1 consisted almost entirely of pyramid-style tents, where the officers and men were billeted, and a few wood frame buildings, including an officers' and a noncommissioned officers' (NCO) club, and a couple of office huts. The camp was in the approximate center of the Pendleton Ranch, about four miles from the Pacific Ocean and about the same distance from the areas where training with small arms such as grenades, rifles, pistols, and Browning Automatic Rifles (BARs), as well as indirect-fire weapons such as mortars and artillery, was carried out.

Camp Pendleton had diverse terrain, including rolling hills, mountains, valleys, and steep-sided canyons. It even had rocky areas similar to some of the terrain CT 28 encountered on Iwo Jima. It contained about eighteen miles of Pacific coastline that made for ideal amphibious exercises.

The reinforced 5th Division consisted of about 25,000 Marines. It was commanded by Maj. Gen. Keller Rockey, a veteran of World War I who had been awarded the Navy Cross for valor in France. Marine ground divisions at the time were (and indeed, remain) triangular in nature: three infantry regiments are in a division, three infantry battalions are in a regiment, three companies in a battalion, three platoons in a company, three squads form a platoon, and three fire teams form a squad.

The principal fighting element around which Combat Team 28 was built was the 28th Marine Regiment (approximately 3,250 men). The combat team had a Headquarters and Service Company (320 men), which prepared all orders and coordinated planning, training, and operations, as well as providing logistical support, communications, and medical services for the Team.

The 28th's three infantry battalions (approximately 950 officers and men each) contained three infantry companies, supplemented with 60mm mortar and light-machine-gun units. Attached to each of these battalions and forming the battalion landing teams (BLTs) were platoons or small sections of specialized troops: engineers (46 men per BLT), who dealt with mines and demolitions; forward observer teams (14 men), who controlled artillery fire; a joint assault signal company detachment (18 men), which controlled naval gunfire and air support; and casualty-handling sections (25 men). In addition, a weapons company (175 men) with four 75mm half-tracks, twelve 37mm antitank guns, and heavy machine guns supported all three battalions in the field.

Three other large units rounded out the Combat Team: C Company of the 5th Tank Battalion (16 tanks, 125 men) and C Company of the 5th Pioneer Battalion, for combat loading and unloading and general logistical support (180 men). Finally, the 3rd Battalion of the 13th Marines, an artillery unit with 12 howitzers and 623 men, provided vital fire support.

Thus, the Combat Team was essentially a self-sufficient and highly flexible ground fighting team, although it had to be supported in sustained operations such as Iwo Jima by additional logistical troops, air power, and naval ships and guns. The Marine Corps retained this triangular, flexible structure for its ground units in Korea,

Vietnam, Iraq, and in the many other small operations since World War II for a simple reason: it can be rapidly tailored to fit different operations, and it works well. (A detailed breakdown of CT 28's organization for the invasion of Iwo Jima is included in the appendix.)

On Iwo Jima, much of the fighting tended to break down into discrete firefights by platoon-size units of 40 men—three squads and one platoon leader, typically a second lieutenant. Since the burden of fighting was carried out by the platoons of the infantry assault battalions, we should take a close look at how these units were constructed.

Each rifle platoon contained two rifle squads and one demolition squad. In each of the rifle squads were 13 men—the squad leader and 12 others. These were divided into three fire teams of 4 men each: a team leader, usually armed with an M1 Garand rifle; an automatic rifleman, armed with a BAR (Browning Automatic Rifle); an assistant BAR man who hauled ammo; and finally, another M1 rifleman.

The assault demolition squad also contained three teams of 4 men each, plus a squad leader. Each of these teams had a separate function, however. The team with the general mission of bringing a large amount of fire to bear on a particular target, such as a pillbox or cave, was armed with a bazooka, two BARs, and an M1 rifle. One of the other teams was equipped with two sections of bangalore torpedoes and at least four heavy charges of explosives, usually C2. The last team included two flamethrower-bearing Marines, who, in turn, were covered by two riflemen with M1s. The usual tactic was to pin the Japanese to their pillbox or cave using the bazooka team assisted by the rifle squads, while one, or both, of the other demolition teams would move in for the kill with flamethrowers and explosive charges.

To summarize, each infantry platoon consisted of nine teams of varying specialties that could be used simultaneously or in any desired combination depending on the objective and the terrain. Each of the members of these teams carried at least one weapon other than his specialty, which could include smoke and fragmentation grenades, carbines, or pistols. Machine-gun and mortar sections, controlled by the company commander, reinforced the efforts of each platoon in both offensive and defensive combat.

Combat Team 28 was given a comprehensive training directive almost immediately upon its formation. This directive called for training of the unit at all echelons, from small-arms training for individual Marines, to fire team, platoon, company, battalion, and regimental training operations, in which all units in the Team participated in a series of challenging field problems. Although the Team had yet to be assigned a mission, we trained very rigorously. This was in part because even those of us on the unit's training team who hadn't been in combat knew we faced a formidable, often devious, enemy who fought until annihilated. And of course, Colonel Liversedge had met the Japanese in combat himself. He had a deep respect for their stubborn skill and resolve. Liversedge was determined to prepare his Marines for the extreme physical and emotional trials of combat. His quiet modesty belied a shrewd professionalism and self-assurance. Thus, the training schedule at Pendleton was truly demanding, especially the small-unit training, but there was very little in the way of bitching or resentment among the troops.

Liversedge understood that amphibious combat in the Pacific was especially chaotic, violent, and fast moving. Success depended on the capacity of individual Marines to make quick, intuitive decisions, as well as on the unit's collective strength of will and endurance. This was a view he had learned from his own experience in war as well as from the nooks and crannies of Marine Corps culture over a long and varied career. A passage from today's Marine Corps' bible on how to think about war, entitled Warfighting, *might well have been written by Harry Liversedge:*

> Because war is a clash between opposing human wills, the human dimension is central in war. It is the human dimension which infuses war with its intangible moral factors. War . . . is an extreme trial of moral and physical strength and stamina. . . .

No degree of technological development or scientific calculations will diminish the human dimension in war. Any doctrine which attempts to reduce warfare to ratios of forces, weapons and equipment neglects the impact of human will on the conduct of war and is therefore inherently false.[7]

The Team's master schedule prescribed training of the individual Marines in the first few weeks after the unit formed up. The report of rifles, BARs, carbines, and pistols as well as machine guns and mortars could be heard from all over Pendleton.

The infiltration course was run over and over by each man in the unit. This consisted of crawling with your weapon cradled in your arms over a distance of about one hundred yards. You went through and under barbed wire, while live machine-gun fire was pinging overhead and charges were exploding at various spots to simulate the effects of combat under fire.

Perhaps the most important training the Team undertook, in light of the brutally repetitive combat we endured on Iwo Jima, was the practice assaults on pillboxes and blockhouses. Our engineers built concrete pillboxes of various sizes on the firing ranges. The idea was to concentrate fire on the apertures of these pillboxes, using rifles, BARs, and, occasionally, bazookas. The object was to keep the enemy pinned down, away from his firing ports, while demolitions men would place explosive charges, either by hand or on the end of a pole, into the apertures. The demolitions men would move as close as they could to the enemy position and signal that the fire should be lifted. If the wind was right, smoke from mortars or grenades could also be used to blind the enemy and to make it easier for the demolitions men to place their charges. After the demolitions exploded, a flamethrower man would move into position and squirt the aperture with a shot of live flame. The riflemen involved in the attack would then move forward with grenades and fixed bayonets and finish the job.

When CT 28 went into combat on the north end of Iwo Jima, virtu-

ally every squad conducted these kinds of maneuvers hour after hour, day after day.

★

TO UNDERSTAND THE unique spirit of the 28th Marines, one has to understand something of the history and ethos of the men who were its key leaders, both officers and enlisted men. A great many of these Marines hailed from the recently disbanded Paramarines and Raiders. Officers who joined the regiment from the Marine Corps Schools in Quantico had graduated at the top of their classes and were well acquainted with the latest developments in amphibious tactics and equipment.

The Raiders and the Paramarines were the World War II Marine equivalent of today's special forces, performing long-range reconnaissance, night operations, and hit-and-run raids against enemy units often many times their size and strength. Speed and guile were their trademarks. Both outfits were expert in the subtleties of guerrilla warfare and the tactics of light infantry combat.

Three members of the regiment's senior leadership were drawn from these units. Colonel Liversedge, the commander, had led Raiders. Lieutenant Colonel Williams had commanded Paramarines, and Maj. Oscar Peatross, the "Regimental 3," or top operations officer of CT 28, led a platoon in the Raiders. These three men, along with Fred, the assistant operations officer, bore much of the responsibility for planning and overseeing the training regimen in California and Hawaii. Liversedge, Williams, and Peatross had all been awarded the coveted Navy Cross, the nation's second-highest award for gallantry in combat, in earlier campaigns against the Japanese.

Oscar Peatross was a platoon commander in the much-publicized raid by Evans Carlson's raiders on Japanese forces on Makin Island. An unfortunate combination of poor seas and communications problems put his units' rubber boats ashore unexpectedly behind enemy lines. Nonetheless, the men rapidly adapted to difficult circumstances and acquitted themselves well, ambushing a Japanese patrol. Peatross's Navy Cross citation tells the story:

> When extremely rough seas forced his separation from the rest of the raiding party, Captain Peatross boldly landed his men behind the enemy lines and attacked a superior enemy force. Continuing to harass the enemy's rear, thereby creating confusion in their ranks, Captain Peatross's daring tactics caused one of the enemy's aerial bombing formations to bomb its own troops. In this forceful and courageous engagement he and his group killed or wounded fifteen Japanese. His resourcefulness, leadership and personal valor were in keeping with the highest traditions of the United States Naval Service.[8]

Harry Liversedge commanded the 3rd Raider Battalion in the Russell Islands campaign as well as in the heavy fighting on New Georgia Island. It was in these fights that Liversedge gained a Corps-wide reputation for being unflappable and brilliant in combat. For his leadership on New Georgia, he earned the first of his two Navy Crosses. (His second was awarded for his leadership on Iwo Jima.)

Bob Williams received the Navy Cross for "extraordinary heroism and courageous devotion to duty" during the fight for Gavutu, in which he was wounded. A great many Paramarines who had seen action in the Solomons ended up in the 28th Marines, including three enlisted Marines associated with the two flag raisings on Mount Suribachi: Henry Hansen, who played a key role in raising the first flag; Harlon Block, the Marine at the far right of Joe Rosenthal's photo of the second flag raising; and Ira Hayes, the Pima Indian whose hands are raised toward the flagpole on the far left. In any case, both the personnel and the esprit of these two elite organizations left an enduring mark on Combat Team 28 in training, and on Iwo Jima during the big fight.

The small cadre of the most promising young officers from the Quantico schools had not faced combat themselves, but they had gained reputations for excellent leadership and forward thinking about ground combat tactics. Because they were charged with train-

ing officers for future Pacific battles, they had had extensive expo
sure to the growing body of knowledge about the strengths and
weaknesses of Japanese tactics and the latest adaptations in Marine
strategies, weapons, and equipment. Fred was one of these Marines.
As a platoon leader, he had taught weapons and tactics in addition to
serving as assistant operations and training officer in the officer candidate school during his first span of duty in the Marines.

*Combat Team 28 in effect became a potpourri of Marines of varied
backgrounds. Those of us teaching at Quantico were able to study the
after action reports from many units in the Pacific, Army and Marine
alike, as well as formal studies commissioned by Headquarters Marine
Corps in Washington, and we had good information from the British
and Australians, who, like the U.S. Marines, came to be feared by the
Japanese for both their guts and general fighting skills.*

*But the truth is in CT 28 we learned a great deal through informal
contact with fellow Marines who had seen heavy action out in the Pacific. It was quite an experience. And the people we were training came
from everywhere—they were virtually all reservists. This meant that
they were in for the duration of the war, not professional Marines. They
brought a lot of fresh ideas into the program.*

*And let's not forget, this was not Vietnam. It was not Korea or Iraq.
There was none of the public ambivalence and political hand-wringing
that attended those later wars. Every American back in the early 1940s
was fully committed to the Allied cause. The men who joined the
Marines at this time were not interested in doing their share of the
fighting; they wanted to do more than their share.*

*The interesting thing about CT 28 was that we had all sorts of people
with varied levels of experience who bonded early and worked closely together from the start. Even before the battle, I had a strong sense that I
was part of an exceptional Marine unit, as did most of my comrades.*

The final phase of the master training plan for Combat Team 28 at
Camp Pendleton was a major amphibious landing exercise on the

beaches that form the western boundary of Camp Pendleton. The Pacific Fleet Troop Training Unit (TTU) brought their staff to Pendleton to assist the 5th Division in preparing for amphibious warfare. One of the first steps in this training was to teach the Marines how to climb up and down net-covered towers, similar to the rigs that would be used by transports ferrying the Combat Team into battle.

After completion of TTU training, our entire division embarked for a major amphibious exercise. Troops on both sides used blank ammunition. To add realism, the defending force planted fireworks on the beach. As the assault units reached the barbed wire obstacles and gained a foothold, the defending forces fell back to prepared delaying positions. Unit umpires and division headquarters officers and NCOs controlled the advance of the assaulting combat teams as well as the actions of the defenders.

One of the observers of the final amphibious exercise was none other than Franklin D. Roosevelt, our commander in chief. He was accompanied by his son Col. James Roosevelt, USMC, who, like Oscar Peatross, had been awarded a Navy Cross for the Makin raid earlier in the war.

Soon after completion of this amphibious exercise, Combat Team 28 packed up its gear and equipment and headed by truck and bus to the port of San Diego in late August and September. The Team boarded Navy transports for the six-day sail to the port of Hilo on the Big Island of Hawaii. More training lay ahead. And at long last, in early October, came the big decision. The United States Marines would attack a tiny wedge of volcanic rock in the inner defensive ring protecting the home islands of Japan: Iwo Jima.

2

THE ADVERSARIES
PREPARE FOR BATTLE

he 28th Marines disembarked at Hilo and made their way by truck and narrow-gauge railroad up to the windswept Parker Ranch area where they would complete their training for battle. En route, the leathernecks could see Hawaii's giant volcanic peaks, Mauna Kea and Mauna Loa. The landscape was spectacularly varied—with steep hills, fields of sugarcane, fingers of black lava, and fields of grazing cattle. Their new training ground was a forty-thousand-acre military reservation called Camp Tarawa. It had been named after the 1943 battle for a tiny atoll in the Gilbert Islands, the Marines' first amphibious assault against a well-fortified beach in World War II. The 2nd Marine Division had fought that bloody affair. The Corps had learned many valuable lessons concerning amphibious doctrine and equipment at considerable cost at Tarawa.

The 2nd Marine Division had sailed back to Hawaii to recover and refit after the battle. Its Marines became the first inhabitants of the camp. In the summer of 1944, they had packed their sea bags and sailed from Hilo to fight in the Marianas.

Camp Tarawa and the outlying training areas were all located on the Parker Ranch, at the time the second-largest cattle ranch in the world. The land had been leased to the Marine Corps by Richard Smart, a well-known Broadway actor, whose family had owned the ranch for decades. Smart's spacious ranch house became General Rockey's divisional headquarters.

Here, as at Camp Pendleton, the Team was housed entirely under canvas, with pyramidal tents each holding four to six men. A few Quonset huts and hastily built wooden structures served as NCOs' and officers' clubs and mess halls. Near the center of the training area was a small ranch town, called either Waimea or Kamuela.

The training facilities prepared by the 2nd Division were in the process of being expanded and improved by Marine engineers and Seabees. After we arrived at Camp Tarawa, CT 28—already well prepared for combat—received four additional months of intensive training, focusing on small-unit tactics and innovative amphibious-assault techniques tailored to our impending attack on Iwo Jima and, more particularly, our initial objective: seizing Mount Suribachi.

Kamuela was the home of only four hundred people before the Marines arrived—mainly paneolos and their families. Paneolo was a Hawaiian derivative of the Spanish. In the early days of the ranch, the Parker family had imported a sizeable number of cowboys from Latin America. The town was also home to a few small-business owners catering to the needs of the ranchers. Kamuela was on a line separating two microclimates—one a rain-soaked area of mountain and jungle, the other an arid, open, hilly area. On this lava-covered ground there were excellent ranges for training with heavy weapons of all types, including 105mm howitzers.

Ensign Marvin Veronee, a member of the 5th Joint Assault Signal Company and attached to Landing Team 1/28 as a naval gunfire spotter, recalled the island and the camp:

The big island, Hawaii, is much different from the islands to the northwest. It is very large in comparison, volcanic, with a landscape that varies from lush tropical forests, many square miles of fresh lava flow, high mountains, ranch land, beaches, waterfalls, few towns, and only one city, Hilo. Our camp was built on the Parker Ranch on the edge of the small town of Kamuela. The Kohala Mountains just to the north caught the northeast trade winds and usually were covered in clouds. In the hills and even in our camp, mist, fog, and drizzle were common. A few miles south the land was arid, with cacti and little rainfall. To the west, a dirt road led to the calm waters in the lee of the island with coral reefs off the beach and coconut palms fringing the shore. To the southwest, the paved road to Kona wound through desert ranch country before reaching the coast.[1]

The beaches to the west—about twelve miles from the center of the camp—offered an ideal location to perfect amphibious landing techniques. Many Marines also spent their leisure time near the ocean, swimming and sunbathing, and then heading into the town of Kona for beer and hamburgers.

The presence of the 5th Marine Division transformed little Kamuela from a sleepy, sparse settlement into a twentieth-century American town. Electric generators brought by the Marine Corps allowed settlement houses to be lit by bulbs rather than kerosene lanterns. The Waimea Hotel became a four-hundred-bed hospital with modern medical facilities. A stream nearby, known as the Waikoloa, was dammed, and military engineers constructed reservoirs to supply water to both the division camp and the town. An icehouse was built, where Marine cooks turned out cartons of ice cream for the Marines and the townspeople as well.

Cpl. Wayne Bellamy, a Michigan native who served with both A and B Companies of the 1st Battalion, 28th Marines as a mortarman, recalled the friendly reception from the town's four hundred inhabitants: "The local people in Hawaii accepted the Marines much better than the people in California, who, it seemed, were tired of seeing servicemen. At Pendleton, we had little transport for liberty, and many cars would pass you before you got a ride. This wasn't the case at Camp Tarawa. The people were very congenial. They accepted and appreciated our presence there."[2]

The Marines introduced rodeo to the townspeople. Baseball diamonds were in constant use by a variety of teams drawn from the 5th Division as well as from other services passing through Hawaii. Local entrepreneurs opened makeshift huts and generators to sell burgers, cigarettes, newspapers, and sandwiches. Local teenagers were hired to do the Marines' laundry. Marine "liberty" shoes were shined by teenagers for twenty-five cents a pair.

Small department stores, such as the Chock and Hayashi, were amply supplied with gifts, such as kimonos and Asian fans, that Marines could buy for their mothers, sisters, and sweethearts. And each morning, in connection with "colors," the division band would march through the small town, much to the excitement of the neighborhood kids. Very often, CT 28's mascot, a lion cub named Roscoe, would join the procession, riding on the hood of a jeep with several "lion tenders" along to calm our mascot. Roscoe had initially been purchased for twenty-five dollars by Pfc. Bob Coster of the Headquarters and Service Company from the Los Angeles Zoo as a present for his young son. Bob's wife immediately vetoed the idea. Then Coster brought Roscoe to Tent Camp 1 at Pendleton, and Colonel Liversedge agreed we could keep him as the regimental mascot. The Navy allowed us to take him to Hawaii, provided he went through quarantine on Oahu.

"Roscoe set us apart from the other units in the division. He was a boost to morale," said former Raider Pfc. Robert Snodgrass, a brawny machine gunner in I Company, Landing Team 3/28. "A lion—that'd give any Marine something to talk about. We'd say to guys in other units on the island, 'We got a lion. What do you have, a bunch of jackasses?'"[3]

Several small outdoor theaters were set up in Camp Tarawa for the troops' entertainment. The neighborhood kids would hide in the bushes to watch the latest movies and USO shows. The town and its *paneolos* grew to appreciate the hubbub and excitement. Local families took in Marines for a home-cooked meal, forging fast friendships. Meanwhile, in the rows of tents inside the camp at night, small groups of Marines gathered to shoot craps and play poker. Others formed singing groups.

Among our many music enthusiasts in CT 28, one man stood out: Capt. Joe Cason, the eccentric, highly intelligent adjutant, the "R-1" officer in charge of managing personnel and morale issues for the Team. Cason, like myself, was born and raised in Texas. In civilian life he had studied archaeology at the University of Texas. A member of Phi Beta Kappa, Joe kept his PBK key on his wristwatch band so when he leaned on his elbow it would be visible to all present!

Cason was an insomniac of the first order, an inveterate multitasker long before the term was coined. Joe also imagined himself as a kind of modern-day Nathan Bedford Forrest—the famously daring Confederate cavalry raider—in Marine green. He loved to ride horses bareback.

At Camp Tarawa, we had to view a series of training films, one of which featured staged footage of British troops in the North African desert, marching into battle to the tune of Scottish bagpipes. Cason was captivated by the idea of taking up the pipes himself. He managed to procure a set locally, and in the early evenings, the sound of Cason's pipes wafted about the tent camp.

About three hundred yards from Cason's tent was the home of Roscoe the lion. During Cason's midnight concerts, the lion would let go with a series of violent howls and roars. After a few nights, the noise of the pipes, combined with Roscoe's protestations, began to grate on Marines in the area. Finally a few of us paid a visit to Cason's tent and told him he'd have to practice elsewhere or suffer severe consequences. We had heard quite enough of the bagpipes, and so had Roscoe!

While Cason was torturing poor Roscoe with his pipes, two former Paramarines who had seen heavy combat on Bougainville, Cpl. Mel

Grevich and Pfc. John Lyttle, prepared six custom-built light machine guns. Lyttle recalled the story:

> Mel was my squad leader on Bougainville, where he got an idea for a new, very light, machine gun. Mel was able to take a machine gun from a Navy torpedo plane and convert it to a fast-firing handheld weapon. The project never went anywhere at the time, due to lack of support from our senior officers. While on the big island, however, Mel was able to get support from Lt. Col. Charles Shepard [the 3rd Battalion commander] to procure six of the weapons. I can't recall how or where we got them, but I do recall that Mel was overjoyed, and fell to immediately. He brought the guns to his tent, where we worked on them. I camouflaged them with paint that Mel had shown up with from God knows where. Mel handpicked the men to carry these new "stingers." It was my job to write the name [that each man] chose to call their new stingers. Without exception they were girls' names. Mel's gun was named "Betty Ann."[4]

During the Team's stay at Camp Tarawa, Lieutenant Colonel Williams's patrician demeanor emerged. Major Peatross and I had heard that the pheasant hunting was good on the upper slopes of Mauna Kea. So we got permission from the colonel to draw two shotguns from the quartermaster and a supply of ammunition. The colonel also agreed to let us take a jeep up the Saddle Road and then up a branch road that led up toward the peak. The pheasants were indeed quite plentiful. Peatross and I, being southerners and hunters, had lots of experience with firearms before joining the Marines. We were both good shots, and we brought back a dozen or so birds, much to the delight of the colonel. Williams then announced that our headquarters officers would share a dinner of pheasant under glass. No one knows where the cooks found the glass covers. They may have been bell jars used in chemistry labs. The pheasant dinner was an extraordinary treat after eating standard "slop chute" chow in the camp. However, a couple of the officers boycotted the meal on the grounds that it was "over the top" for Marines to be eating in such formal style in the middle of a wartime field training area.

There were other forms of amusement at night besides eating pheasant. Capt. Aaron Gove Wilkins, a fun-loving Dartmouth grad, had a broad smile and a terrific sense of humor. He was one of scores of high school football players who peopled the ranks of the 28th Marines. Gove had become one of my closest friends when we were at Quantico. One night he came into the tent I shared with Capt. Arthur Neubert, our regimental intelligence officer. Wilkins said, "Hey guys, come over to my tent very quietly. I've got a mouse who breaks wind." So we got a piece of cheese from a box of K rations and very quietly went to Wilkins's tent. We placed the cheese on part of the tent frame toward the corner and sat quietly to see what happened. Shortly after, a mouse in fact did appear and perched itself next to the cheese, tasting it very carefully. Right after his first bite, the mouse broke wind. We could hardly contain ourselves! After a few minutes of enjoying the spectacle, we looked down under Wilkins's cot, and there was a little puppy that he had taken as a pet. We had uncovered the real wind breaker!

Gove Wilkins's humor would show itself when least expected. Capt. Ace Britton, who later commanded Wilkins's A Company after the big battle, was on weekend liberty with Wilkins and several others in L.A. In the bar at the Biltmore, the conversation inevitably turned to women. According to Britton, Wilkins said he'd made the acquaintance of a movie starlet, and he planned to seek her out. After a brief phone call, he told the group that the lady would meet him. "But," she had added, "no funny business."

The group gathered the next morning for brunch and Bloody Marys and a full debriefing of the previous night's activities. Wilkins reported that the starlet did in fact show up—in a full-length mink coat. And, he added, with a big grin, "absolutely nothing on underneath it!"

Captain Wilkins enjoyed himself almost as much as one of the unit's prized possessions, a real character named Louis Boone. Corporal Boone was an Alabama country boy who joined the reconnaissance *platoon of the 28th Marines at about the time he was completing seven years in the Corps. Boone had been promoted to corporal only a few weeks before we left for Hawaii, which gives a clue as to the kind of Marine he was. He seemed always to be in trouble and was strictly a nonconformist. If the uniform of the day was dungarees, you could be sure that he would show up in khakis. If his first sergeant didn't have at least a couple of sea cruises behind him and exceptional command presence, Boone paid him no mind whatsoever. If a regimental order forbade enlisted men from having pistols, Boone would wear a .45 on his hip.*

Every fighting outfit needs to have one Boone. But no more than one, or good order and discipline will suffer. You couldn't help but like the guy. He reflected what a great many Marines would have liked to do but could not, because they had developed inner discipline and respect for authority through their experiences in Sunday school and church, the Boy Scouts, or, of course, in boot camp.

Before we left Camp Pendleton, the officers bought a sizeable amount of liquor out of bond. This meant that we could not open it until we were outside United States jurisdiction. We couldn't drink it in Hawaii. It was kept under lock and key in a cane-board hut in our regimental area at Camp Tarawa. Boone got wind of it. Using his K-bar combat knife, he cut a hole barely big enough to scoot out a single bottle. He got away with four or five bottles of bourbon and proceeded to throw a big party in his tent. Because of all the racket there, a couple of us investigated, and Boone confessed that he had been the guy who'd stolen our firewater. Boone was charged with theft and conduct to the prejudice of good order and discipline. His fellow drinkers were let off with a light warning, as they hadn't been involved in the act of pilfering. Colonel Liversedge decided to delay the court-martial. We would see how well Boone did on Iwo Jima. As we shall learn, he did very well indeed.

Pfc. Robert Snodgrass recalls that on several weekend liberties with members of his machine-gun squad, one of his buddies smuggled out a primitive whiskey still in his seabag. He and several other

Marines would snatch some potatoes and raisins from the mess hall. "We'd go out into the boonies somewhere on the island and make up a mash. We'd shoot us a wild boar. Somebody would shoot the poor, dumb thing with a BAR, and there wasn't that much meat on it, but we had a big old time out there for a couple of days."[5]

★

IN EARLY OCTOBER 1944, the Joint Chiefs of Staff issued a general strategic directive that made the assault on Iwo Jima inevitable: Adm. Chester Nimitz's forces were to seize an island in the Nanpo Shoto group, a long chain of islands stretching more than 750 miles south of Tokyo to within 300 miles of the Marianas. The ideal candidate would have had airfields sufficient to cover American bases in the Marianas and provide fighter cover for the strategic bombing of Japan. Only Iwo Jima fit the bill. Halfway between the Marianas B-29 bases and the major islands of Japan, it already had two operational airfields. Iwo Jima was also part of Tokyo Prefecture; in other words, it was an organic part of the Japanese homeland.

The Japanese recognized Iwo Jima's strategic value just as clearly as the Joint Chiefs and Admiral Nimitz. In the late spring of 1944, the Imperial General Staff (IGS) in Tokyo sent Lieutenant General Kuribayashi, along with thousands of reinforcements, including the elite 145th Infantry Regiment, to Iwo Jima. Kuribayashi's orders were to defend the island for as long as possible. They were to fight to the death.

The IGS conceived of Iwo Jima as a critical base in the inner ring of defenses, meant to serve as a sort of speed bump, slowing down the inexorable American drive toward Kyushu and Honshu. Tokyo wanted Kuribayashi to buy that most precious commodity in wartime. Time to allow the Japanese to prepare defenses and to train civilians in how to resist the impending American onslaught. The IGS also hoped to gain time enough to train hundreds of new kamikaze pilots to fend off the assault on the home islands. Almost all of Japan's few remaining skilled fighter pilots had been shot out of the skies by Americans in the "Great Marianas Turkey Shoot" in June 1944.

Kuribayashi embraced his final mission with energetic resolve. In eight months, the general pushed his garrison to create perhaps the most formidable defensive fortress in the history of warfare. Virtually the entire subterranean defensive network was dug with hand tools. By the time of the American assault, the Japanese had built more than nine hundred major gun installations and several thousand fighting positions along the approaches to the big guns.

Moreover, the major emplacements were concentrated in two defensive belts that stretched across the entire breadth of the island. Mount Suribachi, too, had its own semi-independent system of defenses at the narrow southern tip of Iwo.

The brilliance of Kuribayashi's defensive plan for the island is hard to overestimate. Each of Iwo Jima's cross-island defensive belts contained several "anchor" hills or ridges that had been hollowed out with reinforced caves, barracks, undetectable pillboxes, and blockhouses with multiple entrances. Positions in and around these anchor defenses were connected by subterranean passageways. Kuribayashi had hoped to dig seventeen miles of tunnels, connecting all of his defense sectors deep underground, but our arrival interrupted his work in progress. About eleven miles had been completed when we landed.

The system allowed for the defenders when attacked from one direction to quickly shift to alternative positions; they could then lay down fire on the rear and flanks of the attackers. The approaches to these anchor defenses were also covered by mutually supporting machine-gun nests and riflemen hidden in spider holes.

Kuribayashi's plan for the island's defense was static, for he planned neither organized withdrawals of units in the face of overwhelming American pressure nor large counterattacks. But the annex to his operations order of December 1, 1944, made it clear that he wanted his subordinate commanders to train their men for small-unit counterattacks in front of major defensive positions, with a view to recapturing them from the Americans. Troops should also rehearse moving inside major defensive installations, including Hill 362A and Nishi Ridge, where CT 28 would encounter its fiercest resistance. Dispersal and concealment were emphasized as well. As one of the general's directives put it: "We must strive to disperse, conceal, and camouflage personnel, weapons and matériel. . . . In addition we will enhance the concealment of various positions by the construction of dummy positions to absorb enemy shelling and bombing."[6]

The Japanese engineers put Iwo's broken, contorted terrain to good use. Many of the defensive positions along the western flank, where the 28th Marines fought after taking Mount Suribachi, were clustered around open ground that an attacking force would have to cross to reach the next ridge. This would prove costly for the attacking Marines, particularly in the first two weeks of fighting, when the Japanese still had large-caliber guns on the central plateau.

The defensive system also anticipated that the numerically superior Marine assault force was bound to cut the Japanese communication lines and thus hamper command and control. This was not as serious a problem as it might seem at first glance. Once the battle began, Kuribayashi's lower-echelon commanders were expected to direct the fighting in their areas *independently,* each holding fast to his prescribed defense plan.

Indeed, once the fight was joined, Kuribayashi wouldn't need to issue further decisions. It all came down to holding ground for as long as possible and killing as many Marines as each Japanese soldier could, until he himself met his end.

Admiral Nimitz made a trenchant observation about Kuribayashi's defenses as the battle raged. He said that the Japanese general seemed to have fathomed an undefined principle of strategy: that there was a proper ratio between the area being defended and the number of troops and discrete installations dedicated to its defense. In other words, Kuribayashi had a singular knack for assigning just the right number of troops to each of his major positions, given the nature of the terrain and the role of the position in the overall plan.

As historians Jeter A. Isely and Philip A. Crowl have pointed out, expert observers who had inspected German fortified areas in both world wars testified that they had never seen a position so thoroughly defended as Iwo Jima. Moreover, Kuribayashi's engineers had fortified Iwo "to near perfection. Where terrain dictated a blockhouse or covered emplacement, there it was. Where fields of fire called for mutually supporting pillboxes to protect in turn a heavier defense, they were sure to have been built. Caves were dug to reinforce other defenses."[7]

The Japanese garrison was well supplied with ammunition, foxhole periscopes, and large quantities of mortars and rockets, including 320mm spigot mortars that hurled shells weighing seven hundred pounds into Marine lines. These large-caliber weapons were not very accurate, but they had a powerful psychological effect. The marksmanship of individual Japanese riflemen on Iwo Jima, however, quickly gained the respect of the Marines. "Whenever a man showed himself in the lines it was almost certain death," said one battalion commander on the island.[8]

The Japanese set up an extensive telephone network connecting all defensive sectors to the general's headquarters. They expected that the lines would be cut early on by Marine forces as they fought their way methodically up the island. In the absence of phone lines, runners carried orders and reports from one commander to another via trenches and tunnels. Radios were apparently in short supply, for few were discovered by Marines who entered the tunnel networks.

These factors, in addition to the high level of resolve of the enemy garrison as a whole, explain why it took the Marines so much longer to capture the island than the planners had hoped.

General Kuribayashi was a solemn soldier and a wise samurai. He had never wanted Japan to fight the United States. In 1928 he was assigned to Washington as deputy military attaché. He made many friends in the American military and had come to admire the American people. As he wrote in a letter to his wife before the war began: "The United States is the last country in the world that Japan should fight. Its industrial potentiality is huge and fabulous, and the people are energetic and versatile. One must never underestimate the Americans' fighting ability."[9]

Unlike most of his contemporaries in the Japanese officer corps, Kuribayashi was under no illusion that the mystical Japanese "fighting spirit"—the mantra of the militarists who ran the Imperial General Staff in Tokyo—would compensate for Japan's deficiencies in logistics, its limited industrial production capacity, and its inferior armor and artillery. Unlike most of his superiors, he thought the Americans neither soft nor decadent.[10]

In the years since the end of the war, Kuribayashi has become a cult figure among the Japanese people, and Iwo Jima is thought of in Japan as a kind of Custer's Last Stand. Kuribayashi certainly gained the respect of the Marines who met his forces in battle on Iwo Jima. "Of all our adversaries in the Pacific," wrote Gen. Holland "Howlin' Mad" Smith, "Kuribayashi was the most redoubtable. Some Japanese island commanders were just names to us and disappeared into the anonymity of enemy corpses left for burial parties. Kuribayashi's personality was written deep into the underground defenses he devised for Iwo Jima. . . . As one of my officers fervently remarked, 'Let's hope the Japs don't have any more like him.'"[10]

★

ON OCTOBER 19, 1944, Colonel Liversedge received the tentative plan for the Iwo Jima assault. In light of the ferocious battles fought the previous summer on Guam and Saipan and preliminary intelligence reports on Iwo's defenses, American planners concluded that the impending operation was sure to be extremely difficult—in fact, the JCS reckoned it would prove to be the toughest fight of the Pacific War.

Iwo Jima was far and away the most meticulously planned amphibious assault in the Pacific to date. From the outset it was clear to the V Amphibious Corps (VAC) planners that the top priority in the first phase of the battle was to surround and capture the island's most prominent piece of terrain, 554-foot Mount Suribachi, for its garrison of sixteen hundred troops could rain fire down the full length of the landing beaches. Enemy observers on its crest would have an unimpeded view of the movement of the entire Marine assault force.

The mountain was separated from the main defensive network by a narrow isthmus leading up to the Motoyama plateau and the airfields. Even from a psychological point of view, it was essential that the mountain be taken quickly.

A full regimental combat team would be required to get the job done. Early in December 1944, the senior VAC planners had to decide on the proper team. After close evaluation and study, the mission was given to Col. Harry Liversedge's Combat Team 28.

Long before it crossed the black sands of Green Beach on February 19, 1945, CT 28 had developed a reputation as a Marine unit of exceptional esprit and competence. This reputation was to be confirmed not only by the unit's performance in battle, but also by the opinions of military professionals with firsthand knowledge of the Team's brief but brilliant history. Five CT 28 members—including Harry Liversedge, Oscar Peatross, Robert Carney, Robert H. Williams, and myself— went on to become Marine generals. I am the only one of the five still alive, but I can assure you from conversations with each of these individuals over many years that we all believed CT 28 was a remarkable entity well before the landing. After the war, to put it plainly, we all thought it to be the best Marine infantry unit of its size to have fought in the Pacific.

The Team had trained to a razor's edge even before leaving for

Hawaii. In a very real sense, our objective, with its jumbled and broken terrain, lack of cover, and brilliant defensive layout, demanded a great deal from every man on the team. They gave it everything they had.

I should make it clear that the other seven combat teams who fought on Iwo performed courageously and well. Their ranks were also full of heroes. The troops of the entire assault force, particularly those in the 5th Marine Division, were almost certainly the most rigorously trained and best-conditioned troops to make an amphibious landing in any theater in World War II.

This was the result of both chance and intention. The 5th Division's initial combat operation was to have been an assault on the island of Yap in the western Caroline Islands, slated for the fall of 1944. That operation, however, was scrapped due to a change in strategy. This was a stroke of good luck for us, in light of the formidability of Iwo Jima; it allowed for a longer preparation and planning period than was typical for ground units in World War II. And it was our good fortune to conduct about a third of our training in Hawaii, which offered good stand-ins for Mount Suribachi.

Once we had a clear sense of the nature of our objective, planning and training at all levels was ramped up to an unprecedented level. There was a strong sense of urgency. The assault was likely to be the toughest assignment ever given to the Marine Corps.

Certainly there was no better judge of a World War II infantry unit's capabilities than General Smith, who had commanded both Marine and Army troops in the Pacific. He believed CT 28 was the best prepared of the combat teams slated to land on Iwo's beaches, and said as much:

> The success of our entire assault depended upon the early capture of that grim, smoking rock. For the job [of taking Suribachi], we selected the 28th Regiment, Fifth Division, commanded by Colonel Harry Liversedge—called "Harry the Horse" by his men. Perhaps other officers and other regiments could have done the Suribachi job, but both Harry Schmidt

[commander of all three Marine divisions in the assault] and Major General Keller E. Rockey [commander of the 5th Division, of which CT 28 was a part] felt that Harry Liversedge was the man and the 28th was the regiment. He had a good record in the South Pacific for tackling tough assignments, and although Iwo Jima was no tropical, jungle-covered island, this qualification was vital.[11]

In the wake of the mission assignment, there followed an intense and protracted regimental planning period, which was accompanied by a series of rigorous training exercises geared to perfect the strategy for the assault on the mountain. Combat Team 28 would land on 500-yard-wide Green Beach on the far left of the 3,500-yard landing zone on Iwo's east coast. The Team was to drive immediately across the 750-yard-wide neck of the island, cutting off Suribachi from the body of the island.

After reaching the west coast, the Team's assault battalions were to turn south and seize Mount Suribachi and the remainder of the southern end of the island. Landing Team 1/28 was designated to make the initial crossing. Speed was of the essence. The Team planned to accomplish this maneuver under a rolling barrage of naval gunfire that would move ahead of the assault troops as they fought their way across the narrow neck. This was to be the first such barrage in the Pacific, and it had to be carefully regulated by aerial spotters who could keep track of the infantry's progress and adjust the barrage accordingly.

Landing Team 2/28 would follow 1/28. Once the neck had been crossed, both battalions were to deploy facing Suribachi and prepare to launch an attack on the mountain proper. Landing Team 3/28 would be held in division reserve and brought in during the first day only if heavy casualties prevented LT 1/28 and LT 2/28 from sustaining the attack.

The planning phase, which ran from early November through much of December, was punctuated by continuous liaison between the division's units. The objective of the Team's planning was designated as "Island X." The actual identification of Iwo Jima as the prime objective remained secret until the unit was well out to sea.

The planning and training for the attack on the island was aided immeasurably by photographic reconnaissance. Iwo had been photographed frequently for months at various altitudes with state-of-the-art cameras. The Marine and Navy planning staffs produced a detailed grid map of the island, revealing many of the enemy's primary defensive positions. Individual bombardment ships were assigned targets within specific squares of the grid map.

In Hawaii the engineers and Seabees had built replicas of the Japanese defenses near Mount Suribachi and Green Beach. The assault troops spent hundreds of hours running exercises over terrain on the Parker Ranch that closely resembled Suribachi and its surroundings.

Assault companies conducted multiple practice landings on the beaches of Hawaii and Maui. As machine gunner Bob Snodgrass remembered:

> You'd get all your equipment and your machine guns—I was the big oaf that carried the weapon in my squad—and you'd end up taking about 120 pounds of gear and weapons with you on a twelve-mile march to the beaches, and then you'd practice landings for about three hours. We'd get sunburned and tired and all that stuff, and then you'd load your stuff on your back and start back for camp in the late afternoon. If you fell out and jumped on a truck because your feet were giving you too much pain, and you didn't have a hell of a lot of blisters when you got back to camp, the first sergeant would put you to work cleaning the head [Navy slang for the latrine] with a toothbrush![12]

Sand-table models of the island were modified in light of new intelligence data. Aerial reconnaissance increased as the invasion date approached. The mission and tactics of each company and platoon in the assault were studied by the officers until they had the sequence of the attack and the disposition of the forces deeply ingrained in their minds.

Despite the caliber of intelligence we had during the planning phase, none of us knew the extent to which the Japanese were burrowing into virtually the whole island. The defenders cleverly disposed of huge quantities of excavated soil, presumably by dumping it into the sea at night. The only defenses we were able to detect were blockhouses, those pillboxes not completely camouflaged by sand, trenches that connected fighting positions, and antitank ditches. The labyrinthine tunnels connecting emplacements, the broken terrain features that hid all sorts of weapons from view, and the huge number of caves, both natural and man-made, only became evident as we inched our way forward in the attack.

Nonetheless, Combat Team 28 was indeed in an excellent position to fulfill its mission once it hit the beach on Hell's Volcano. On the slopes of Mauna Kea and within hiking distance of the camp, there were several cinder cones that varied in height from three hundred to five hundred feet above the level of the surrounding lava fields. Here the platoons and companies of the three assault battalions practiced their attack. The primary stand-ins were Pu'u Ula'ula, Pu'u Holo'holo'ku, and Buster Brown.

Liversedge, Peatross, and I worked up a challenging two-day exercise that simulated the landing and rapid movement across a strip of terrain that approximated the width of Iwo Jima's neck. This initial exercise was carried out by the boat teams of the 1st Battalion—absent, of course, the boats—based on the landing plan that was being developed for the operation itself by the divisional staff.

Landing Team 1/28 held an overnight exercise in conjunction with Combat Team 27, which was to land to our immediate right. The landing was made by simulated boat teams, and an attack was conducted against our stand-in for Mount Suribachi. All three assault battalions participated in these exercises.

A series of live-fire exercises with individual platoons and squads sharpened our "fire and movement" tactics for attacking the type of defensive emplacements on the narrow neck of Iwo Jima. We put the platoons through practice assaults, with live flamethrowers and demoli-

tions charges, in addition to rifles and machine guns. These exercises were combined with training films, sand table exercises, and films of actual combat against the Japanese in earlier campaigns. Every Marine in the assault battalions received a very solid grounding in what he would be expected to do in the initial assault.

★

WHILE CT 28 worked tirelessly, practicing assault maneuvers, planning by the senior staff of VAC unfolded at a frenetic pace. Some 800 naval vessels were ultimately involved in Operation Detachment, directly or indirectly. It took 485 ships alone to transport the assault force and its supplies. Adm. Raymond Spruance was the strategic commander for the entire operation, and Vice Adm. Richmond Kelley Turner commanded the Navy's amphibious forces—Task Force 51. He held command over the entire Marine force as well as the Navy until the assault force was ashore, just as he had in earlier campaigns in the Central Pacific theater. Rear Adm. William H. P. Blandy commanded the Amphibious Support Force responsible for executing the naval bombardment plan in addition to overseeing the minesweepers and the Underwater Demolition Teams that conducted close-in reconnaissance of the landing beaches. Maj. Gen. Harry Schmidt directed the V Amphibious Corps—the three Marine infantry divisions and their supporting units.

Only one area of serious disagreement arose between the Marine Corps and the Navy: the crucial issue of the pre–D-day naval gunfire bombardment, designed to knock out the heavy gun emplacements, concrete blockhouses, and pillboxes that constituted the island's primary defenses.

The Marines believed—and indeed, the definitive postwar study of the operation confirmed— that about nine days of preliminary, close-in fire from large rifles (five- to sixteen-inch naval guns) could have knocked out the lion's share of the enemy's main defensive emplacements, leaving the Marines to deal with the machine guns, rifle, antitank, and mortar positions. The planners correctly estimated that these lighter weapons numbered well in excess of ten thousand.

American intelligence before the invasion had identified some seven hundred of the nine hundred primary and secondary heavy-weapons installations. The Japanese were masters of camouflage, and many of these installations had to be uncovered the hard way—by Marines fighting on the ground, drawing their fire.

The Marines well understood before the battle the implications of Admiral Nimitz's observation that "once the landing force was ashore, the compactness of the battlefield and the close proximity of our troops to enemy positions frequently [would deny] us the benefit of adequate naval bombardment."[13] The only supporting weapons that could take out the primary enemy installations efficiently and with no loss of life were the big naval guns of Admiral Blandy's fleet. Marine artillery and tanks didn't pack enough punch, given the fact that most of Kuribayashi's heavy emplacements were protected by reinforced concrete between four and ten feet thick.

The proper time to take out these emplacements, so far as the Marines were concerned, was before the landing. Unfortunately, for a variety of strategic reasons the Navy agreed to only three days of preattack naval bombardment. Why? Admiral Spruance was concerned with the danger of leaving such a large fleet exposed to Japanese submarine or air attack for nine days. American intelligence correctly believed that the enemy had hoarded his aircraft on the home islands and that a full-scale attack, including kamikazes, might endanger the fleet and its capacity to land the Marines successfully.

The Navy also had at its disposal only a limited number of high-explosive shells for the big naval rifles, and the decision was made to save over half of the available supply for the impending battle of the much larger island of Okinawa, slated for April 1.

Finally, Admiral Spruance felt it essential that he use the Navy's most powerful battle wagons, the only vessels with sixteen-inch guns, to provide adequate cover for Adm. Marc Mitscher's Task Force 58—a "covering" attack on key military targets on the Japanese home islands slated to begin simultaneously with the naval bombardment of Iwo Jima. The Mitscher raid, Spruance felt sure, would keep the Japanese air force preoccupied and thus unable to inflict much damage on the huge armada surrounding Iwo Jima.

Mitscher's raid had a broader strategic purpose: it was meant to degrade the enemy's capacity to manufacture planes by bombing aircraft factories near Tokyo, Kobe, and Nagoya. Moreover, it would show that the Navy, not just the Army Air Forces, could and should play a major role in the bombing of the enemy's homeland.

Spruance was convinced that such a diversionary raid was necessary to prevent a massed attack by aircraft or submarines, or both, on the fleet off Iwo Jima. He may very well have been right, but we shall never know.

While argument still lingers concerning the brevity of the preassault bombardment, it must be said that naval gunfire during the invasion and the battle that followed proved indispensable to the success of the operation. Sailors and Marines of the joint assault signal companies (JASCOs), personnel aboard naval gunfire support ships, and airborne and ground spotters who helped the tactical commanders call and adjust naval gunfire and air support performed brilliantly. The JASCO units had been born earlier in the war as a result of ineffective bombardment and coordination in island invasions. By the time that the planning for Iwo Jima was in full swing, the days of pummeling islands with large quantities of area fire and hoping for the best were gone.

Iwo Jima was the first battle in history where there were central fire-support coordination centers both afloat and ashore, and the coordination of various supporting arms was unprecedented.

Once the battle was in full swing, the big guns of the fleet were able to lay down pinpoint fire on Japanese emplacements that could not have been readily destroyed by any artillery piece we Marines had on the island, including the 155mm howitzers. In fact, many of the strongest Japanese gun emplacements remained functional even though hit directly by large-caliber Marine artillery multiple times.

Nowhere in the history of amphibious warfare, write historians Isely and Crowl, "was progress more rapid or decisive than in the field of naval gunfire support. Here again [as with close air support during the war] advances were made not so much as a result of technological improvements in naval guns and shells, but rather because of refinements of established techniques coupled with the assimilation of lessons through experience and a rigorous program of training."[14]

★

WHILE THE AMERICANS thrashed out the tactical planning and logistical details, General Kuribayashi's garrison pressed on relentlessly, digging tunnels and building more gun emplacements and pillboxes. By the time the 28th Marines landed, no less than seventy blockhouses had been built around the base of Suribachi alone. Ultimately, most of these emplacements, some barely visible from as close as twenty-five feet, would be taken by Marines charging forward with flamethrowers and satchel charges, supported by tanks, machine guns, and riflemen. Once silenced, the emplacements had to be blown up, their multiple entrances sealed by Marine engineers to ensure they would not be reoccupied by Japanese lurking in their underground bastions.

Kuribayashi understood that the war was already lost and that his sole job was to ensure that the Americans paid in blood for every inch of ground they gained, and paid for as long as possible, so that his countrymen could prepare for the onslaught against the home islands. The general was steadfast in his refusal to go along with the pleas of his more sanguine officers that he attack the Americans at the beach, engaging them in furious combat and following up with suicidal banzai charges. His subordinates clung to the illusion that somehow the Japanese soldier's fabled "offensive spirit" would cause the Marines to lose heart. Kuribayashi wasn't hearing any of it. Banzai charges, to his way of thinking, would be wasteful and self-defeating, given that protraction of combat was the objective, not victory.

In the pillboxes, blockhouses, and subterranean caverns of Iwo Jima, the general had posted his "Courageous Battle Vows" for all to read and take to heart:

> Above all else we shall dedicate ourselves and our entire strength to the defense of this island. We shall grasp bombs, charge the enemy tanks, and destroy them. We shall infiltrate into the midst of the enemy and annihilate them. With every salvo we will, without fail, kill the enemy. Each man will make it his duty to kill ten of the enemy before dying. Until we are destroyed to the last man, we shall harass the enemy by guerrilla tactics.[15]

★

WHILE THE JAPANESE burrowed in and set up interlocking fields of fire to protect their anchor installations all around the island, Combat Team 28 kept up a busy schedule of small-unit and amphibious training, focusing heavily on the crucial mission of taking a well-defended mountain from its defenders. As this work went on apace, the team grew stronger, more proficient in its fire-and-maneuver tactics and in coordinating supporting arms with ground attacks.

Leaders at all levels gained confidence in themselves and in the men they would lead in combat. Here the green Marines, the men who had never seen combat, benefited enormously from the wisdom and reassuring presence of hundreds of former Raiders, Paramarines, seasoned officers, and noncoms. Everyone—infantrymen, mortar men, demolitions specialists, flamethrower operators, forward artillery observers, the strong-backed men of the pioneer units who bore the brunt of the combat loading and unloading of the amphibious ships— got to know their jobs backward and forward, as well as the jobs of their buddies, on the notion that many of those buddies could be lost soon after the initial landing.

Speed became one of the key elements in exercises that dealt with the assault phase. These exercises emphasized how important it was to get "inside" the decision-making process of the enemy. The officers and noncoms alike stressed the importance of denying the enemy time to react to the Marines' fire-and-movement tactics.

Throughout December, the battalion landing teams worked out the intricate details of coordination with naval-gunfire and close-air-support liaison teams on nearby Maume Beach and on the coast of Maui. Subordinates were given ample opportunity to command squads, platoons, and companies, for combat leaders at all three of these echelons were expected to take heavy casualties, given the grim information provided by the division's intelligence section. In retrospect, considering our losses of junior officers and noncoms, the extra time we invested in leadership training of the subordinates at the company level and lower proved a godsend.

A final set of landing exercises in Hawaii was held for the Combat Team in mid-December. Before heading toward the western Pacific and the big event, the convoy docked at Pearl Harbor. There, wrote 1st Lt. John McLean,

> we took on provisions, additional equipment, and other necessaries for the operation. Officers and men were allowed liberty from time to time, and I was assigned the duty of officer of the deck on several occasions. I remember one evening listening to the haunting strains of Anton Dvorak's "Goin' Home," from the *New World* Symphony, broadcast over our ship's radio. Listening to the melody, I pondered whether I would really be "going home" again or not.[16]

As the flotilla left Pearl Harbor and headed west, Liversedge, Williams, Peatross, and I were on the USS Talledega's flying bridge watching Diamond Head slowly disappear below the horizon. We were silent, absorbed by our own thoughts as to what lay ahead. Liversedge broke the reverie. His words have been deeply embedded in my memory for sixty-two years: "Well, gents, I think we've done all we can to be ready. Above all else, I believe we have faith in ourselves and in each other."

Two days out of Hawaii, a soft-spoken former Mississippi sharecropper, Cpl. William W. Byrd, recalled "looking out across the Pacific Ocean, remembering the last words I had spoken to my dad. As I got on the train in Jackson, Mississippi, he said: 'Take care of yourself, son.' His own dad had said the same thing to him as he prepared to go to France to fight the Germans. I watched as the sun set on the ocean. I can still remember how beautiful that sunset was."

The convoy carrying the 28th Marines sailed from Hilo on January 7. After briefly stopping at Eniwetok on February 5, the entire 5th Division sailed westward to Saipan. After a final practice landing exercise on Tinian in rough weather on February 13, the convoy sailed for Iwo Jima on the sixteenth.

By the time we had finished with the last amphibious exercise on Tinian, an aura of invincibility was everywhere in evidence among the Marines in the unit. Combat Team 28 had trained for close to a full year under realistic combat conditions; it was exceptionally well led, and once we were under way at sea, every man in the unit was showing the pride of knowing he had been selected for the critical mission in the first phase of the assault.

The men of CT 28 possessed another confidence-building asset: they had the moral strength that came with being Marines, with being part of a long and distinguished tradition. Every Marine had been trained first and foremost as a rifleman, and the Corps' unique system of indoctrination and training produced a spirit of camaraderie and brotherhood of remarkable durability. The Marines were, and are today, an organization committed to a demanding warrior code and the acceptance of a set of core values—loyalty, discipline, teamwork, boldness, persistence, courage, and, of course, pride.

The World War II Marine Corps, despite its expansion from fewer than seventy thousand men at the time of Pearl Harbor to close to half a *million by the time of Iwo Jima, retained its elite status and distinctive esprit. We managed to bond hundreds of thousands of young Americans from widely diverse backgrounds into a cohesive, highly disciplined fighting organization.*

Because of Liversedge's shining personal example and quiet confidence and because we had trained together so extensively, Combat Team 28 was an outstanding example of how Marine Corps training methods could meld a large group as varied as the races of the earth into a single fighting organism. And of course, we were deeply engaged, as was the entire country, in a moral crusade as well as a military one.

"We never thought about losing. It was just a matter of how long it would take us to clear out the Japanese," wrote Pfc. Ted White of F Company, a former Paramarine who had seen action on Bougainville and would later become a member of the four-man patrol that preceded the flag-raising platoon to the crest of Mount Suribachi.[18]

The executive officer of Combat Team 28, Lt. Col. Robert Williams, was undoubtedly thinking about his experiences with the Team when, many years after the battle, he wrote about the nature of Marine esprit de corps:

> An individual, although he reflects it if he belongs to a group that possesses it, can never create esprit de corps by himself. He can only contribute to its development in proportion to the forcefulness of his own personality and the extent that it is drawn into the magnetic field of the group.
>
> Pride is its essence, the collective pride of individuals in being members of a group which has, or which believes it has, a special competence surpassing that of other similar groups. The pride is born of a deep conviction, dimly comprehended and seldom articulated, which grows in the hearts of men who comprise a ship's company or a squadron. This is that the whole is greater—much greater—than merely the sum of its parts. A realization emerges, accompanied by a mighty sense of belonging, that the group can perform functions far beyond the aggregate

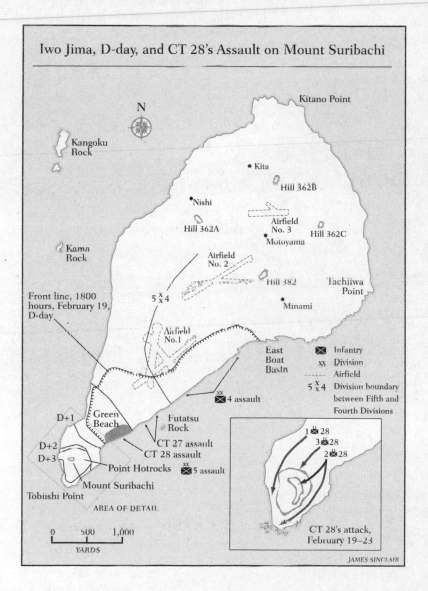

Iwo Jima, D-day, and CT 28's Assault on Mount Suribachi

N

Kitano Point

Kangoku Rock

• Kita

Hill 362B

• Nishi

Airfield No. 3

Hill 362A

Motoyama

Hill 362C

Kama Rock

Airfield No. 2

Hill 382

Tachiiwa Point

5 $\frac{x}{x}$ 4

• Minami

Front line, 1800 hours, February 19, D-day

Airfield No.1

East Boat Basin

Infantry

Division

Airfield

5 $\frac{x}{x}$ 4 Division boundary between Fifth and Fourth Divisions

xx
4 assault

D+1

Green Beach

Futatsu Rock

CT 27 assault

CT 28 assault

D+2

D+3

Point Hotrocks

xx
5 assault

Mount Suribachi

Tobiishi Point

AREA OF DETAIL

0   500   1,000

YARDS

1 ⚔ 28
3 ⚔ 28
2 ⚔ 28

CT 28's attack, February 19–23

JAMES SINCLAIR

of the individual capacities of its members. They know that their separate skills have been integrated and coordinated by their leaders, who themselves are of the group, to create a new coherent unit to which all are fiercely loyal.

If the group is unique, the first of its type as to equipment or function, the feeling of pride is more intense. If, in addition, the duty performed is dangerous, the intensity of esprit de corps that can develop is almost unbelievable.[19]

At Iwo Jima, the strength and esprit of the 28th Marines would be tested to the breaking point. "Was your training adequate for combat?" inquired a 1995 questionnaire for veterans about the battle from the History Division of the Marine Corps. Pfc. Ted White's response said it all: "Yes. But I am not sure that any training could prepare you for Iwo."[20]

3

THE ASSAULT

dm. William Blandy's Amphibious Support Force, including the entire naval bombardment fleet, arrived off the island before dawn on February 16 and began to rain torrents of high-explosive shells on the Japanese positions. Dust clouds billowed all over the island as thousands of high-explosive shells pummeled targets, obscuring the spotters' views. Still, the first day's bombardment went very well. That night, the top brass briefed more than seventy correspondents on the operation aboard the USS *Cecil*. Admiral Turner spoke first, and with his usual candor: "The defenses are thick. The number of defenders there is considerable and well suited to the size of the island. It is, I believe, as well defended a fixed position . . . as exists in the world today. . . . We expect losses. We expect losses of ships and we expect losses of troops, and we believe they will be considerable." General Smith was about to witness his final Marine attack in forty years in the service. When he rose to brief the reporters, the sixty-two-year-old general had some difficulty controlling his emotions: "It's a tough proposition. That's the reason we [Marines] are here."[1]

The weather was cloudy, with a heavy mist, on the seventeenth, severely limiting visibility and thus the effectiveness of the naval bombardment. The number of targets destroyed was discouragingly low. When twelve LCIs (landing craft, infantry) converted to gunboats came within several hundred yards of the island to take out key targets, Kuribayashi committed his only blunder of the entire campaign: mistaking the small armada for the initial infantry assault, he ordered his heavy artillery to open up on the gunboats, which were firing seven hundred rockets at a clip and highly accurate 40mm gunfire into Suribachi's cliffs and other emplacements covering the shoreline. Despite a heavy smoke screen put up by the Americans during the LCI attack, the Japanese guns inflicted severe punishment on the ships and their crews. One sank; another, squaring off against the cliffs of Suribachi, was shot through with 189 shell holes; the magazines of three of the tough little ships exploded. As a result, 43 sailors were killed, 20 in *LCI 449* alone, and another 153 wounded, many severely. The first casualties of Iwo Jima were sailors, not Marines.

But now, the location of many of the big guns on Suribachi and elsewhere were known to the JASCO spotters, using state-of-the-art equipment for detecting the location of enemy artillery fire. A great many of these weapons were blown to bits on the final day of preassault bombardment, before the first Marines hit the black sands.

While the LCIs were having their David and Goliath duel with the big Japanese guns, about one hundred Underwater Demolition Team swimmers, Navy men we Marines called "half fish, half nuts," dodged enemy shells and made for the shoreline. The good news: no mines or obstructions stood in the way of the landing craft, and only one swimmer failed to return from this mission. The bad news: the water was very deep right up to the shore, which meant our smaller landing craft, especially the light Higgins boats, were likely to broach in heavy surf.

The night of the seventeenth was a tense one aboard Blandy's flagship, as Lt. Col. Donald Weller, the Marines' top naval gunfire officer, pleaded for an extra day of bombardment in light of the fact that, among other things, only three of the twenty blockhouses covering the invasion beaches had been destroyed during the first two days of bombardment. Blandy, fearing worsening weather, declined. Weller and Blandy did agree, though, to focus the final day's bombardment closely on the beach emplacements and pillboxes. The revised plan, an early example of our capacity to adapt to unpleasant circumstances during the battle, worked out well. The big artillery hidden in the north would have to wait until we were ashore, and the intricate tunnel system was untouched, but all except four of the twenty blockhouses covering the landing beach were put out of action, as were dozens of smaller pillboxes.

★

FEBRUARY 19, 1945: a fleet of transports floated ten thousand yards off the eastern beaches of Iwo Jima. Reveille for the U.S. Marines of V Amphibious Corps was at 0300, but only a small percentage of the more than seventy thousand assault troops aboard the fleet of transports ten thousand yards off the eastern beaches of Iwo Jima had managed anything like sleep.

By dawn on February 19, all the troop leaders of CT 28 suspected, along with their commander, Harry Liversedge, that their own lives, and the lives of all the young men with whom they'd trained so vigorously, were about to change forever. But very few men, even the older veterans, could have imagined the ferocity of the greeting the Japanese had in store for the invaders or the intensity of the thirty-six days of combat that followed the initial "hello by fire."

After a final meal of steak and eggs, a great many men attended brief religious services. From the time of its formation, the officers of CT 28 had been encouraged to set a good example for their men by attending church. The Corps knew very well the value of religious belief in binding people together and keeping them functional during traumatic experiences.

Now, at about 0530 aboard *LST 684*, a chaplain with LT 2/28, Navy lieutenant Charles F. Suver, a Jesuit, said Mass. When it was over, young Marines bombarded the chaplain with questions. The talk shifted to the difference between courage and fearlessness. Suver remarked, "A courageous man goes on fulfilling his duty despite the fear gnawing away inside. Many men are fearless, for many different reasons, but fewer are courageous."[2]

As they prepared for the event, CT 28's assault Marines kept their most troubling thoughts to themselves. The combat veterans knew that sharing fears and doubts in times of stress doesn't provide emotional release. Rather, it opens the door for panic attacks. One of CT 28's communicators, Pfc. Jerry Seright, was a veteran of Bougainville. As he waited his turn to move toward the shoreline, he recited a short prayer: "Lord, if you bring me though this ordeal, I'll try to be a better person and serve you always."[3]

Pfc. Robert Snodgrass of I Company, LT 3/28, recalled that up to the point of the invasion itself,

> you're so busy with just minute details, everyday things, doing this, doing that, exercising and listening to the officers' briefings about what you're supposed to do. You're busy cleaning your rifle and putting it back together and organizing the machine guns and looking for spare parts for your weapons so you can save your ass once the thing actually gets going.[4]

The Marines who debouched from their amphibious tractors (LVTs) and Higgins landing craft (LCVPs) that sunny morning carried between 70 and 120 pounds of equipment apiece, depending on their assigned roles. Individual combat gear included a personal weapon, a helmet with a brownish camouflage cover, two small backpacks, a gas mask, and a horseshoe roll of one blanket and one poncho. Men checked their rifles. Grenade pins were bent just enough— so they could be pulled fast without snagging on some piece of equipment. Everyone had tucked away a waterproof packet of precious personal effects—pictures, a small Bible, perhaps a keepsake from a wife or child.

As the Marines pondered their fate from the decks of their transports, they wondered how they would stand up under fire from the punishing array of Japanese weaponry. At 0640, the great guns of Blandy's Amphibious Support Force commenced the preassault bombardment, pummeling the beaches and the main enemy gun emplacements that threatened the landing beaches directly. Rear Adm. Harry Hill's attack force—transports carrying the Marines of all three divisions—had joined Admiral Blandy's Amphibious Support Force offshore only the night before the invasion.

It was not until D-day morning that the men of CT 28 had their first sight of the vast armada—ships as far as the eye could see, many of them belching high-explosive projectiles toward the small island. The preinvasion "softening up" of the target that morning was the largest in the Pacific War to date: seven battleships, including two new, fast battleships sporting sixteen-inch guns that had raced back from Admiral Mitscher's Task Force 58 after its successful raids against enemy aircraft factories in Japan. Joining these vessels were four heavy and three light cruisers, and more than a hundred smaller craft, including destroyers and a variety of gunboats. *Time* magazine correspondent Robert Sherrod wondered how it was possible for anyone on the island to live through such a bombardment, but then he remembered that the defenders could indeed survive such an onslaught—he'd seen them do so at Tarawa and Peleliu.

Even the saltiest members of CT 28 were astonished at the size of the fleet and the sheer magnitude of the bombardment. Guadalcanal seemed a hundred years away, so puny had been the Navy's covering fire and support force for the first landing of Marines against a Japanese-held island.

From the air, a reconnaissance pilot reported that the island looked like a sizzling pork chop. The novelist J. P. Marquand covered the battle as a correspondent, even though he was well into his fifties. Looking out in the early hours at the ugly piece of earth from the deck of one of the flagships, he wrote in his notebook that "its silhouette was like a sea monster with the little dead volcano for the head, and the beach area for the neck, and all the rest of it with its scrubby brown cliffs for the body."[5]

Earlier, at around 0600, the cargo booms of transports had begun to lower landing craft, and cargo netting was cast over the sides of the larger ships. In the amtrac-bearing LSTs, Marines saddled up their gear and descended into the tank decks and into their assigned tractors. There, amid the cacophony of motors and the *clack, clack, clack* of the treads on the ships' decks, the amtracs prepared to take to the sea.

The signal to launch came at 0725. Within half an hour, all the amtracs were seaborne, en route to the line of departure (LOD) about two miles offshore, parallel to the beaches. It would take each wave about thirty minutes to motor from the LOD to the beach.

At 0805, the naval gunfire lifted, and more than seventy attack aircraft from the Navy's fast carrier task force roared in toward the beaches, hitting the eastern and northern slopes of Suribachi and blanketing the landing beach with rockets and bombs. Then twenty-four gull-winged Marine Corsairs followed suit, strafing and dropping napalm. Huge sheets of flame leaped through the smoke and dust wherever a napalm canister ignited.

It was a particularly reassuring sight to the men of Landing Teams 1/28 and 2/28, for they were slated to attack into the thick, 1,300-yard belt of defensive positions covering the mountain that afternoon. By now, all these men were aboard their amtracs and at sea, either formed up behind the line of departure or en route to that line. That most complicated tactical maneuver, moving combat-ready infantrymen and their supporting forces and equipment from sea to shore under the guns of a well-trained enemy, was about to commence.

Combat Team 28 landed in nine waves (the second through the tenth), five minutes apart, on Green Beach. The lead wave on Green Beach carried no assault troops but eleven howitzer- and machine-gun-bearing armored amphibious tractors (LVT[A]-4s). As they made their way toward the shoreline, they sprayed the beach defenses to clear the way for the infantrymen.

The second wave contained the assault platoons of B and C Companies, 1st Battalion. Waves two through five brought in supporting units in addition to Company A, whose initial job would be to swing to the far left and cover the left flank while B and C Companies fought their way across the island's neck to the western coast, some 750 yards away. In covering the flank, they were to position themselves at right angles to the beach, as LT 1/28 punched forward, and lay down suppressive fire on Mount Suribachi and the belt of defenses surrounding its base.

In the sixth wave the crucial 37mm gun platoons came ashore, along with four 75mm-howitzer-bearing half-tracks, heavy weapons useful for attacking blockhouses. Waves seven through nine brought in the entire 2nd Battalion as well as the combat teams' command groups. Colonel Liversedge and his executive officer, Lieutenant Colonel Williams, as well as Fred, who was the tactical control officer for the landing of the entire Team—the seaborne traffic cop, in effect—all arrived in small "free boats," Higgins boats that could land at any time at the behest of the senior officer on board.

Richard Wheeler, a private first class in the 3rd Platoon of E Company, 2nd Battalion, was well aware that the island had suffered intense preinvasion bombardment. On D-day, the preattack bombardment was so relentless it seemed to him that the island itself might sink into the sea. At one juncture, eight thousand shells pummeled the tiny island within thirty minutes. Given this shellacking, Wheeler mused just before hitting the beach that the battle might not be nearly so bitter as had been predicted. He shared this thought with his squad leader and close friend, Sgt. Howard M. Snyder of Huntington Park, California. Snyder had already fought in four campaigns against the Japanese, and he offered Wheeler a sobering dose of Marine candor: "Don't fool yourself. The way the Japs dig in, bombardments just shake them up a little. Maybe I'm crazy, but I'm looking forward to this fight. I think it will beat anything I've seen so far."[6]

Pfc. Ray Jacobs, a radioman in F Company, LT 2/28, who would later join about forty men from Wheeler's E Company in the patrol that raised the first American flag over Mount Suribachi, was on the deck of his LST, awaiting the order to go belowdecks and get into his amtrac:

> We could see the firing, the big guns pounding, and you could see the explosions on the beach and against the mountain. It was exciting; we had this anticipation, and we were wondering what was going to happen. Meanwhile, the fourteen-inch shells from the battleships were just pounding, punishing the beach. It looked like the whole beach area was going up in smoke, as the shells exploded at irregular intervals up and down the landing zones.[7]

At exactly 0830, the first wave of armored tractors crossed the LOD and headed for Green Beach. Although the sea was calm, with only light surf on the shoreline, the tension, the roar of the tractors, and the acrid fumes from the engines combined to make many in the early waves seasick. As Pfc. Floyd O. Holes noted, "My stomach was beginning to act like it had on the Saipan practice landing. If we didn't do something pretty soon, I felt like I would heave my cookies. It didn't help that I had taken a chew of some Spark-Plug chewing tobacco . . . and I needed to spit and probably swallowed more than I should have."[8]

As the landing craft motored for the shore, the drone of the engines drowned out the voices of the assault Marines. Yells, hand signals, and facial expressions were the modes of communication as the crucial moment approached. Men looked at their squad mates with reassuring grins or thrust their thumbs in the air, and some men shouted phrases of encouragement—as much for their own benefit as for that of their fellow Marines. They positioned the cargo they were to toss onto the beach as they passed the high-water mark. Each infantry-bearing tractor carried one box of belted .30-caliber machine-gun ammo, one box of clips for M1 rifles, two boxes of K rations, and six five-gallon cans of water. Carrying these extra supplies in the first waves was a new procedure for us. It proved to be an enlightened one, for it wasn't long before the beach was so fouled up with broached landing craft that additional supplies couldn't be brought in and acute shortages of ammunition and water developed. The stuff thrown off the amtracs proved invaluable later that day.

The men of Combat Team 28 were poised on the final leg of an unforgettable journey—from their homes all over the United States, from the rigors of boot camp at Parris Island and San Diego, to the months of CT 28 training at Camp Pendleton in California and Camp Tarawa. From there, they had boarded transports for the month-long trip to Iwo Jima. Now, they were just a few minutes away from landing on the eastern shore of hell on earth.

The first wave of LVT(A)-4s hit the beach one minute ahead of schedule—at 0859. Within five minutes, many of these vehicles were miring down in the soft, black sand. The first of a long list of Iwo's unpleasant surprises was upon the Marines: even tracked vehicles would have trouble gaining traction on the beaches. Then came unpleasant surprise number two: in most places along the beach, the amtracs couldn't traverse the first of three ten-to-fifteen-foot terraces created by the shifting tides of the Pacific and ran the full length of the landing beaches. The first terrace blocked the fire of the amtracs' 75mm howitzers. Many amtrac coxswains sensed the urgency of the situation. They backed up into the sea and began to fire their weapons into the mountain and along the beach.

Close to the beach, Corporal Carnara Carruth, the commander of an armored amtrac in the first wave, fired a couple of rounds from the howitzer mounted in the turret of the tractor. The second round was a hang fire—it stuck in the muzzle of the gun. As soon as his wave met the beach, Carruth, using the ramrod carried in the lower compartment, was able to remove the hang fire. His amtrac was perhaps the only one of the eleven vehicles supporting CT 28's landing that was able to negotiate the terraces on Green Beach, so he drove up to a point where he could fire on caves on the lower slopes of Mount Suribachi as well as on pillboxes just forward of the mountain. When Japanese artillery and mortars increased the tempo of fire on the beach, an infantry officer nearby told Carruth to move his amtrac either inland or back to sea. It was drawing too much fire to the area.

Carruth maneuvered back through the surf and took a position from which his amtrac could fire directly at the east and northeast slope of Suribachi. A high-velocity Japanese round hit Carruth's turret and jammed it forward. The projectile was probably a 47mm anti-tank round—one of the enemy's best weapons—but fortunately it was only a glancing blow. Carruth and his crew were lucky to escape injury. "The tractor shook like a baby rattle when the round glanced off the turret. For the next several hours, I maneuvered the amtrac around the southern end of the island, firing at any target that might contain Japanese."[9]

The tractor continued to draw fire from Suribachi but somehow escaped. Toward the afternoon, the tractor's engine began to fail. Carruth and his crew climbed aboard an LCVP and put ashore on Green Beach. After a few minutes, they hitched a ride back to their parent LST, which set sail for their camp on Maui, where their armored amtrac battalion would commence training for the assault on Japan. Carruth's short but harrowing battle of Iwo Jima was all over in a few hours. Unlike so many that first day, he lived to tell the story.

The first troop-carrying amtracs touched Iwo's shoreline at 0902. Marines still at sea saw a yellow flare, the signal that the first assault waves were ashore. Wave after wave of amtracs hit the beach at five-minute intervals. On Green Beach, exclusively the province of CT 28, the men of Lt. Col. Jackson B. Butterfield's B and C companies had the distinction of putting their boots into Iwo's volcanic ash first. They landed with both companies abreast, followed shortly thereafter by A Company. Lt. Col. Chandler Johnson's 2nd Battalion companies began to land at around 0935.

As the first assault waves rushed forward, resistance was eerily light—a few desultory rifle shots and an odd mortar round or two landed among the 28th Marines as they scrambled into position. The first thirty minutes ashore were surprising indeed. An occasional shell burst on the beach, and on the neck of the island, according to one historian, "there was a light haze of small-arms fire, almost like a breeze on the prairie."[10]

More and more waves churned ashore. As Cpl. William Byrd of the 2nd Battalion approached the beach in his amtrac at around 0950, he heard

> the deafening sounds of shells overhead and explosions on land as they became louder and louder. I tried to get my mind off of what was going on by remembering the words of Captain Dick Allen, of D Company, an Alabaman. Captain Allen had seen combat before, so he knew what to expect. I couldn't remember his exact words, but his preattack speech reminded me of a football coach talking to his team before a big game. We could tell by the look in his eyes and the way that he talked that he knew that many of us would not return to our loved ones back home.[11]

The biggest problem for the invasion force as a whole in that first hour was not the unseen enemy, but the tumult and confusion caused by hundreds of Marines struggling up the three terraces and trying to organize themselves into squads and platoons. Everywhere, Marines found that their boots were sucked deep into the sand, in some places up to the calf.

At 0919 came a message from Colonel Liversedge to the flagship, the USS *Eldorado*: "Troops ashore and moving to isolate the volcano.

Resistance moderate, but terrain awful."[12] Then, sometime around 0950 hours, with about six thousand Marines crowded along the thirty-five-hundred-yard crescent of beach, the big Japanese guns opened up. First came the thumps of the mortars, then the heavier, deeper report of artillery. Suddenly, utter mayhem reigned over the crowded terraces, as the shrapnel from enemy shells of all calibers ripped into men, equipment, and landing craft.

General Kuribayashi had ordered his heavy-weapons gunners to refrain from firing on the first waves of attackers. He was waiting for the beach to become jam-packed with Marines and equipment before offering up a full response to the invasion. When at last he gave the order to fire, large-caliber Japanese artillery shells began exploding amid thousands of exposed targets. The Marines ashore opened up with machine-gun, mortar, and rifle fire. Hot steel was flying everywhere. Unfortunately, Japanese fire was methodically aimed at visible targets, while the leathernecks were shooting, for the most part, only where they imagined the enemy might be situated.

Machine guns on and around Suribachi incessantly sprayed Green Beach and the isthmus to its front. Unseen enemy riflemen picked off Marines struggling to ascend the terraces and cross the island's neck.

As 1st Lt. Greeley Wells, the 2nd Battalion's adjutant and the man responsible for carrying the battalion flag that ultimately ended up atop Suribachi, observed:

> So we got out [of our boat] and got our feet wet, and sure enough the beach was absolutely packed. I waved at my men to come on and we went up through the groups, I don't know how far but it was a fair distance, fifty feet or something like that. Then we plunked down, we were all loaded [with equipment] and the beach sand was volcanic and very hard to walk in. The artillery fire was getting pretty heavy at this point, there was machine-gun fire, and there was a whole lot of activity that was going on right where we landed. Right next to where I dropped down there was a Marine I didn't know. He was dead, and another guy right next to him had just gotten wounded, so it was obvious to me that we had to get out.

About that time we were all lying together, just hordes of men—the beach was literally covered with men—and suddenly I saw Liversedge and Williams walk up the beach as if they were in the middle of a parade. Williams had his riding crop, which he was slapping on the side of his leg, and both of them were urging us on, saying, "Get up! Get up! Get off the damn beach!"

It was an amazing thing. They walked the length of that dog-gone [Green] beach yelling at the men, and the Marines just did it—they got right up and started to move. Of course it jarred me as well, and I got up, and we got over the high ground. Suddenly we were in the middle of this damn battle and there were casualties like nothing you'd ever seen.[13]

Capt. Joe Cason was determined to pipe the Combat Team ashore. He managed only a few notes. Then the soft black sand and the shelling forced Joe to abandon his prized instrument and dive for cover. Days later, parts of his broken pipes minus the bag were found in the sand and turned over to the intelligence section of the 5th Division. For a couple of days, they were thought to be broken parts from some unknown Japanese infantry weapon!

Pfc. Ray Jacobs of F Company landed at around 0950, just as enemy fire was picking in intensity. As he recalled,

The men, especially the guys carrying flamethrowers and other heavy weapons and radios, ran toward the first terrace. You'd try to go up, but it was slip, slip, slip. But we finally got up there, after a lot of effort, and flopped down on top of the first terrace. I don't think we were there more than one minute when a Marine just below me took a couple of machine-gun rounds right across his legs. So he was out of it at the very beginning. They hauled him back to the beach for evacuation, and I'm pretty sure he lived. I worked my way up to the top of the next terrace, and that's when the Japs opened up with everything they had. I mean everything. The din of all those different-caliber weapons, the blasts of the shells, it was just incredible.[14]

The combat virgins of CT 28 that morning received a crash course in the destructive capabilities of Japanese weapons. An observer looking up and down the landing area from Green Beach late on D-day morning would have seen a mind-numbing array of wounded and dead Marines—amputees, some calling out for corpsmen, others just staring out in shock, and corpses fixed by death in grotesque positions and angles. Pharmacist's Mate 2nd Class Stanley E. Dabrowski, a corpsman in CT 28, landed during the first hour. From a distance, he told an interviewer in the late 1990s, the initial assault looked

> like a beautiful thing and if you had been up in the air it must have been a thrilling sight. But as soon as we got on that beach everything fell apart. It was just mass confusion. The thing I noticed immediately was the tremendous amount of noise, concussion, small-arms fire, explosions of artillery and mortar shells. . . . Units were scattered and casualties began mounting immediately. . . . I lost a very dear friend right there on the beach, Stan Sanders. He was sawed through by machine-gun bullets. It was the most shocking thing you could experience. Here you were talking to the man just a few minutes ago, and now his eyes were glazed over and he was dead. It was a devastating experience. [Enemy fire] resulted in exceedingly severe traumatic wounds and traumatic amputations with extensive blood loss and severe shock. Concussion resulted in a great number of casualties, hearing loss, confusion, and shock. Men had to be evacuated suffering from combat fatigue. Along with agonizing terror, gruesome sights and trauma, it was enough to try anyone's resolve, like going through the gates of Hell.[15]

Nor was the bloodshed limited to the thin crescent of the beachhead where the assault teams were pressing forward. A Higgins boat motored through the surf sometime after the amtracs had deposited the assault units, ferrying perhaps forty Marines. An American flag was attached to one of the gunwales—it was as if the passengers and crew were offering the enemy gunners an invitation to zero in on them. Just as the bow door of the craft plunged into the surf, an artillery round struck directly in the boat, killing all hands.

The Navy coxswains of such boats had to brave fire again and again as they hauled fresh troops, ammunition, or water to the shoreline throughout the first day. They earned the respect of the Marines in a hurry, for they, too, could be destroyed in a fraction of a second. Machinist's Mate 3rd Class Albert D'Amico, coxswain of the Higgins boat *Glamour Gal,* recalled that on the first day, "There was never a dull moment. . . . I saw a boat take a direct hit, thirty-six Marines plus two sailors. You didn't even see a toothpick [left] in the water. But I kept going, and a shell would land here, a shell would land there, all around you, you didn't know where, you just kept going to the beach. You get hit, you got hit, that's all."[16]

Ensign Marvin Veronee neared shore with his spotting team on the left flank of the second wave heading for Green Beach in its own amtrac. His team had orders to stay afloat about three hundred yards offshore, in clear sight of Green Beach, until another spotting team attached to the 28th Marines could coordinate its work with Veronee's team:

> Our task was to locate any enemy artillery, machine gun or mortar emplacements. We had a ringside view of the attack   I don't know when the Japs began their deadly fire, but Pfc. Lattin was the first [member of Veronee's team] to see flashes from a bunker near the shore on the side of Suribachi. I called the *Santa Fe* [the light cruiser responsible for providing naval gunfire to Green Beach]. I continued spotting fire and hit the target with a few salvos. I believe we knocked out the gun emplacement. Even if we did not make direct hits, salvos of six-inch shells would at least prevent the Jap gun crew from continuing fire.[17]

Amid the confusion, noise, and chaos that morning, one thing was clear: no American could find a spot where he would be shielded from flying shards of shrapnel and enemy bullets. In effect, every Marine or sailor on the beach, or just offshore, was a casualty waiting to happen. No set defensive line was especially noticeable, as the Japanese emplacements were so extensive that as soon as one was destroyed, the attacking Marines faced another. One private asked a grizzled sergeant if the landing on Iwo was worse than on Saipan, to which the older Marine replied, "Yeah, I think it is. . . . The shelling on Iwo may have been as on Saipan, but there we were able to get off the beach under cover. The beach was narrow, and there were trees and jungle we could get into. But here everything is just beach and you just can't get off it and there's damn little cover."[18]

While the three-day pasting of the landing beaches had left all too many of the concrete-reinforced blockhouses and pillboxes untouched, the shelling had created hundreds of deep bomb craters willy-nilly about the battlefield. These pits afforded the Marines cover from anything but a direct hit.

But indirect-fire weapons, meaning those that fire on a high angle, usually at targets out of direct sight of the gunners, such as mortars and howitzers, are very effective in reaching these people. This was not lost on the Japanese. Spotters on Suribachi and the other fortified hills would wait patiently until a good number of Marines gathered in a crater before firing high-explosive rounds into their midst. This was why so many Marines who survived the first few days of the battle reported seeing groups of four or five Marines huddled together in death inside a shell crater. A single round in such an enclosed space could take out everybody.

We soon discovered there was almost no room on the battlefield to maneuver around the defenses, for the entire island was covered by enemy fire of one sort or another. In certain isolated areas among the island's many cliffs and ravines the terrain itself prevented maneuver. So we had only one option, and it was not a pleasant one. We had to go through the defenses, using supporting fire to suppress the enemy's resistance. The infantry demolition teams went about the business of destroying the enemy's emplacements methodically, one at a time. Thus, it must be said, that due to the small size of the island, its brilliant defensive system, and the enemy's firm commitment to fight to the death, heavy casualties were inevitable.

In other words, the combination of terrain and defenses made it impossible to alter the basic dynamic of the campaign and to put a fast end to organized resistance. From D-day until we left on March 26, the fighting, no matter where we were or what the next objective was—a ridge, a draw, a hill—had a relentless similarity about it. We would jump off from the line of departure, often with two or three battalions abreast. But quickly the success of the attack would depend on squads zigzagging their way toward single pillboxes or caves. The defenses were so intricate that the advancing infantry would be hit by fire not only from the front, but from the flanks or rear or, all too often, from every direction. Furthermore, the Japanese often reoccupied positions after the original defenders were destroyed.

It was a matter of grinding down one enemy position at a time by teams of riflemen and flamethrower and demolitions men, while other Marines tried to suppress the fire coming from enemy supporting positions.

We knew that Iwo Jima was a prefecture of Tokyo, and thus the first piece of Japanese soil to be attacked by land forces in the Pacific War. We would be seeking to penetrate the inner defensive ring of the enemy's home islands. Because of these stark facts, the officers who did the planning, including myself, expected especially fanatical resistance. We did not anticipate taking many prisoners, and, indeed, CT 28 took a grand total of only 16. The three Marine divisions together took only 216 prisoners during the entire campaign. More than 60 of these turned out to be Korean laborers.

Pfc. Albert Visconti, from Brooklyn, New York, was one of thousands of teenagers with a burning desire to take revenge on the Japanese. He had begged his father to let him join the service at seventeen, but since he was the youngest of four brothers, all servicebound, his father refused to sign the papers. "When I became eighteen, I went down to the conscription board and said, 'I want to join. If I have to go to war I want to go in the Marines. I want to fight with the best.' "[19] He was trained at Quantico on how to call in counterbattery fire—artillery fire against enemy guns—and found himself coming ashore late in the morning, attached to the 3rd Battalion of the 13th Marine Artillery Regiment, a unit that was part of CT 28. Within minutes he was diving into a foxhole dug by a Marine infantryman who had moved inland. He recalled what happened next:

> I jumped in and then this guy jumped in right on top of me. He had his arms wrapped around my stomach, and every time a round landed reasonably close, he would squeeze me like hell, and I remember yelling at him, "If the mortars don't kill me, you're going to!" It turns out he was a friend of mine, an Irishman who was always making fun of me because I was Italian. He would sing me a song, "Ireland must be heaven because there are no Guineas there!" And we would both laugh.
>
> I want to give you the impression of the first dead Marine I ever saw. I can still flash back and visualize him clearly. His rifle was under him and there was a bullet hole right through his helmet. I was going to shake him and say, "Hey, don't stay here; keep going." And I suddenly realized that he's dead and just for a moment all the intense noise on the island ceased, and he and I were surrounded by nothing but utter silence. How do you explain that? I just don't know. The fire was going in all directions, and I said to myself, "This Marine is dead." It was just like he was sleeping there. That's when I realized we were in a real battle.[20]

The initial half of the neck of Iwo Jima was open and relatively flat; the western half afforded more cover and concealment, as it was composed of scrub wood, some broken ground, and large rock formations near the western coast. All 750 yards of the neck were studded with enemy spider holes, small mounds of earth containing pillboxes, and well-placed blockhouses, although the defenses here in the flatlands were not so heavy or numerous as those around the base of the mountain to the Team's left. Naval gunfire on February 18 had concentrated on the beach defenses and some of the largest blockhouses had been shattered. But the defenders were undeterred. The sheer speed of the advance under heavy fire meant that the attacking platoons were disorganized; many would remain so for as much as two days. Marine fire teams and squads were improvised on the spot, under fire, by the veteran sergeants and corporals. In training, the officers and noncoms had pounded home the absolute necessity of knifing across the island's neck at lightning speed, no matter how fierce the resistance, no matter how many casualties incurred.

Once a few leathernecks had secured a foothold on the west coast, they could provide both intelligence and suppressive fire designed to keep the Japanese soldiers' heads down and their guns silent, particularly those weapons on and around Mount Suribachi.

In fact, only ninety minutes had passed after the first wave touched terra firma before a few men from the 1st Platoon of Company B made it to the western shore. These Marines were led by a modest first lieutenant from Pittsburgh, Frank J. Wright. Of the sixty men in the reinforced 1st Platoon, a grand total of four reached the coastline with Wright. As the lieutenant pressed forward, hitting the deck after running at full tilt for thirty or forty yards, he was trailed by Pfc. Lee Zuck of Scranton, Arkansas. Zuck suddenly saw a Marine just in front of him crumple after being shot in the leg from behind. Zuck turned and fired at a single Japanese soldier, who disappeared into a hole. Then, just as he cleared the third terrace, he saw eight Japanese soldiers running in a column about forty yards ahead. He sprayed them with a full magazine of BAR fire, killing or wounding several of them.

Sgt. Harry L. Risher III, Zuck's squad leader, pointed toward a crew-served antiaircraft gun emplacement and told him to open fire on it. Several rounds from the BAR penetrated a box of ammunition, and the emplacement was blown apart by an explosion. Zuck ran toward the gun and sprayed the area. Six more Japanese had fallen. Zuck kept moving in the direction of Wright. Few Marines saw so many Japanese alive or dead on this day as Lee Zuck.[21]

Once Wright and his small band had made it to the west coast of the isthmus, the lieutenant feared that his little cadre would be annihilated. Much to Wright's relief, however, a group of seven Marines from C Company under Lt. Wesley Bates fought their way across the neck. Bates's men had reached Wright's unit thanks to Sgt. Thorborn M. Thorstenson's efforts. The first Japanese pillbox encountered by Bates's platoon halted their advance. Thorstenson took the initiative, pushing toward the enemy emplacement at an angle and tossing grenades as he moved. Then he crawled up to the aperture and threw a shaped charge into the opening, killing eleven Japanese. He was later awarded the Silver Star for his efforts.

Bates's Marines were soon joined by a few more of Wright's men. One of them was Pvt. Ovian W. Von Behren. After dodging and weaving his way across the neck, he eyed a pillbox with its guns facing the western beaches. Crouching low, he affixed a twenty-pound shaped charge onto the back entrance, set the fuse, and ran eastward for about forty yards. When the charge went off, it knocked the Arkansan to the deck, where he lay in semishock, the wind having been knocked out of him by the blast. Then he composed himself and joined Wright's men along the western cliffs.[22]

The rolling barrage of naval gunfire ahead of our attacking troops had been superbly executed by the JASCO units and naval gunners. More-over, we had additional naval gunfire pouring hundreds of high-explosive shells into the northeastern slope and base of Suribachi, as close as two hundred yards from our left flank. This bombardment reduced markedly the flanking fire the Japanese were able to pour into the assault units of both LT 1/28 and 2/28 as they ran from shell hole to shell hole across the neck.

Much credit should also go to the small gunboats, mostly landing craft converted to gun platforms. These were the vessels that had taken such a beating on the seventeenth, but they wouldn't quit. Some of the gunboats drifted in so close that the sailors on board could almost hit the mountain by throwing rocks. There is no doubt that they saved a lot of the assault Marines' lives during the fight to take the mountain.

Pfc. Dick Miller was also in Wright's platoon. He'd fully absorbed the oft-repeated instructions of the trainers back in Tarawa to keep moving. Miller decided when he hit the beach that he would dump everything except what was absolutely essential to do his job. So he abandoned his pack and his blanket roll on the first three terraces. He kept only his canteens, his rifle, his ammunition belt, and his first aid kit. He said, "You know there was no problem in getting whatever you needed because there were so many wounded and dead who left equipment either on the beach or at the battalion aid station. I was able to operate freely throughout the campaign. Carrying so little gear, it was easier for me to move around the battlefield and react quickly to developments. I rarely stayed in one place more than a few minutes and sometimes just a few seconds."[23]

The problem for the infantry and demolitions squads in crossing the isthmus and cutting off Suribachi was that the enemy positions were mind-bogglingly numerous and mutually supporting. The fire teams laying down suppressive fire for the Marines conducting the assault had to make sure that the covering fire not only blanketed the main pillbox under attack, but also those that were supporting it. All too often we didn't know where these were initially, and that's when we could take five or six casualties in a matter of a few seconds. We were most successful when we could provide an envelope of fire around the attacking infantry to keep the mutually supporting defensive positions quiet as we moved west.

As the 1st and 2nd Battalions punched toward the western coast, Lt. Cmdr. John J. McDevitt Jr. and his eleven-man Navy beachmaster party scrambled off their Higgins boat with signal flags, bullhorns, radios, and portable generators. Their job was to remain on Green Beach and orchestrate the landing of supplies in accordance with the needs of the assault troops of CT 28. As the request calls came in over the radios, the beachmasters contacted the appropriate ships for ammo, fuel, and water.

Capt. Phil Roach, commander of C Company, had battled his way more than halfway across the neck of the island when a Japanese bullet broke his leg. His dream of becoming an all-American end at Texas Christian University was shattered as well. But Roach was luckier than his opposite number in B Company, Capt. Dwayne "Bobo" Mears. A popular and energetic commander, Bobo had personally led B Company's attack from the front. He charged several pillboxes and killed a number of Japanese with his .45 pistol. Mears had almost reached the west coast before he was shot in the mouth with a rifle round. When one of his men stopped to help him, Mears waved him off, and as blood poured from his mouth, he signaled to the young man to let him be and keep moving forward.

Another leatherneck in Mears's outfit, Pfc. Dick Young, said, "I was right next to Bobo when he was shot, and a piece of his tongue landed right on the ground near my shoe. I was in the stretcher detail that brought Captain Mears back to the beach and I'll never forget that when we got there, he picked up a stick and wrote 'Good Luck' in the sand just before I headed back across the neck of the island."[24]

Mears died within twenty-four hours of landing on the beach. In any case, he was awarded a posthumous Navy Cross for his inspiring leadership and for the ferocity he demonstrated in his first— and last—firefight on Iwo Jima.

The Japanese had ample antiaircraft weapons in operation. Several struck their mark early in the morning. There were a number of spotter planes flying above the fray, including one carrying Maj. Ray Dollins, spotting for the 5th Division's supporting ships. Over the radio, sailors and Marines heard Dollins singing as he worked:

> Oh, what a beautiful mornin',
> Oh, what a beautiful day,
> I've got a terrible feeling,
> Everything's coming my way!

Dollins's plane was hit by antiaircraft fire and crashed into the sea. He was killed just eight days after his wife had given birth to their first child, a daughter.[25]

Lt. Bill Meisenheimer commanded Mears's second platoon, B Company, in the assault—the unit on the extreme left flank of the entire landing force. He landed literally under the guns of Mount Suribachi. As Meisenheimer's platoon clawed their way up the terraces on Green Beach, he decided it was best for him to take the lead. He told his platoon sergeant, Bob Landman, to bring up the rear. Meisenheimer was a little more than halfway across the neck when suddenly the rolling barrage of naval gunfire temporarily lifted. Then, after what seemed an eternity but was in fact only three or four minutes, enemy weapons of all calibers opened up. Seconds later, Meisenheimer was hit in the right elbow and right hip. He fell into a shell hole.

A few minutes later, one of his squad leaders, a sergeant, fell into the hole with him. Meisenheimer gave the man his map and orders. He waved him on, telling him to lead the remainder of the platoon to the western beach and to stay abreast of Lieutenant Wright insofar as possible. After the sergeant left, two other members of Meisenheimer's platoon jumped into his shell hole with him. Mortars or artillery bracketed their position—one short, one long. The third round, probably a mortar shell, hit squarely in the shell hole. The three Marines were blown sky high. The two latest arrivals were limp and lifeless. Meisenheimer had been peppered with shrapnel from his right ankle to his right shoulder, but he was alive. He later recalled, "I had a front-row seat, on my back, looking up at Mount Suribachi as a flight of Navy dive-bombers dropped napalm and their bomb loads."[26] At this point, he decided to take a chance on contracting blood poisoning by stuffing volcanic ash in his wounds to stop the bleeding. Meisenheimer was virtually immobile.

It was late that evening, probably around 2130 or 2200, when a corporal named Connerly found him. Connerly rounded up two stretcher bearers, and they took Meisenheimer to the beach. Meisenheimer's experience from the time he was wounded until he finally got medical care was typical of the many wounded on D-day. The stretcher bearers put him on a barge loaded with other wounded. The barge then embarked on a wild-goose chase to find a ship that could accept more casualties. It was almost daylight before they finally found a vessel that had room, the 4th Marine Division headquarters ship. When Meisenheimer was lifted aboard, there were no beds available, so he was placed on the deck along with a number of other wounded. He was treated and later transferred to another ship that was headed to Guam.

By the time the assault companies had secured a hold along the western side of the neck, at around 1100 hours, the early reports of casualties in CT 28 were grim indeed. So grim that Colonel Liversedge, recognizing he would have grave difficulties organizing the assault slated for 1545 hours that afternoon, requested that General Rockey release the division's reserve battalion, Landing Team 3/28, immediately. Rockey consented, and Landing Team 3/28 prepared to enter the maw.

★

WHEN FRED HAYNES recalls his first battle as a Marine—something he has been doing almost daily for sixty years—he marks its beginning at about 2200 hours the night before the invasion.

I was in the wardroom of the USS Talladega, *going over plans and contingencies with Bob Williams. We discussed in detail what would happen if the tactical control craft governing the flow of CT 28 men and matériel to the beach were to be sunk or if its tactical control officer (myself!) was hit before landing. I listened intently to Williams, an old combat hand, as Iwo would be my maiden voyage into combat. We talked about a host of other contingencies that could crop up in this sort of operation. Eventually, to relieve the tension, I suppose, we turned to a lighter subject.*

"*What should we do about Tige?*" *I asked Williams. "Should we leave him with the swabbies or take him in with us ashore?*"

"*Tige*" *was short for "Tiger"—a small hybrid terrier with a nervous system made of steel who was smuggled aboard ship by one of Williams's runners, a corporal named Yates. Williams made a command decision: Tige would come in with the assault waves. That tiny, terrible terrier thrived on Iwo Jima. Although his master, Corporal Yates, was shot in the leg and evacuated, Tige served with his brother Marines for the entire campaign, then embarked with the regiment for Hawaii when we had finished the battle. On reaching Camp Tarawa, where the Team underwent refitting and training, Tige was awarded a Pacific Area Campaign Ribbon with Battle Star, which he proudly wore on his collar. Later, he was given the Presidential Unit Citation as a full-fledged member of the 5th Marine Division.*

After retiring for a few hours' sleep, I rose, choked down some steak and eggs, the traditional preassault fare, and at about 0700, clambered over the side onto a landing craft. My mind was racing with a peculiar mixture of anticipation and anxiety, coupled, I must confess, with a sense of relief that the big day had finally come.

As I clambered down the nets into the three-foot swells, I looked up, and the beautiful blue sky I expected to see was completely obscured by Colonel Liversedge's gigantic field shoes! I was soon ferried to the tactical control craft, PC 463, which marked the line of departure, about four thousand yards off the beach. From that vantage point, I had an unobstructed view of the island. As tactical control officer, I joined the CO of this small craft in making certain the assault waves were properly organized and crossed the line of departure according to the schedule.

I myself hit the beach at around 0950, but not before the control vessel almost sank after an amtrac rammed its hull on the port side. The craft began to take on water rapidly, and the fast-thinking Navy skipper had all of us go to the starboard side as a counterbalance. Then he quickly sent his crew belowdecks, where they plugged up the gash in the hull with, among other things, their bunk mattresses. I learned

later that the little ship made it all the way back to Pearl Harbor for re-
pairs.

After all CT 28's assault waves had been dispatched, I boarded a "free
boat" LCVP and went ashore. Within a couple of minutes, I was laying
low on the beach as I described in the preface, along with Joe Bush.
Shortly thereafter, the machine-gun rounds came stitching along, and
then, as you remember, a severed Marine calf landed just a few yards
from us. The next hour or so is a bit of a blur. I remember getting very,
very busy, too busy to be worried about all the bedlam around me, or
about getting killed myself.

After a while, and still under very heavy artillery and mortar fire, I
hooked up with Colonel Liversedge and Maj. Ty Cobb, our communi-
cations officer. We found a blockhouse that had taken a direct hit from
our naval gunfire. Around that blockhouse I saw my first dead Japan-
ese—eight or ten men. It didn't smell very good in there. Their uni-
forms were gray, so they were probably part of the naval force on the
island rather than Imperial Army troops. A number of these people had
died of concussion—they looked almost peaceful, but there were also
intestines and arms and legs scattered around. In any case, this was
where we set up shop to begin the afternoon assault on Suribachi.

By that point, just after noon, the 3rd Battalion was fording the shal-
lows, clambering onto the beach. It had been a morning of scary
surprises. The afternoon brought more of the same.

4

THE ASSAULT, PART II

he afternoon of the first day of the assault was marked by the murderous cacophony of combat—men yelling and moving, the steady report of weapons of all types and calibers. The 5th Division engineers' bulldozers struggled to pull vehicles through the deep sand to counter the increasing congestion on the beach. An abortive assault on Suribachi's defenders was also in the offing—this after LT 3/28 found its way ashore under an intense bombardment. Unexpectedly, Charlie Shepard's Landing Team 3/28 was battered mercilessly in moving from ship to shore, more so than either battalion in the morning assault. The unit took heavy casualties in the water, as relentless Japanese mortar and artillery fire wreaked havoc with the landing craft and amtracs. The 3rd Battalion landed between 1200 and 1305, but it was immediately raked by fire and remained mired in the black sand of the steep terraces for several hours.

John Lyttle, a squad leader in H Company, remembered his harrowing ride into the beachhead:

The Lieutenant and I had the best view of everything. We were within two hundred yards of the beach when I looked to my right and saw a weasel, a small amphibious tractor loaded with ammunition. It was trying its best to keep up with us. It had very little freeboard, and it looked like the two men driving it were sitting in the water. It actually looked quite comical, like the Little Engine That Could. I was looking at the driver and gave him a thumb's up. He smiled and then took a direct hit and disappeared. I looked at the Lieutenant, he leaned over and threw up, and then I followed suit. This always haunted me because I'm sure that I was the last thing that fellow ever looked at on earth.[1]

The Team's scheme of maneuver for the assault, it will be recalled, required the 1st Battalion's B and C Companies to cut across the neck with the greatest possible speed so that the 2nd Battalion could follow in trace, then pivot to the left (south), and focus on Suribachi's defenses. According to the original plan, both LT 1/28 and LT 2/28 were to begin the attack against the defensive ring protecting Suribachi at 1545. However, 1/28 had taken heavy casualties; many of its platoons were temporarily disorganized and scattered about the battlefield. Colonel Liversedge decided to use LT 3/28 in the attack, allowing 1/28 to regroup.

By about 1630—an hour later than planned—the 2nd Battalion had reached the prescribed line of departure for the attack, but the 3rd had taken too many casualties crossing the beach to do anything more than dig in and mop up bypassed Japanese positions. Many of these had been reoccupied by enemy troops wending stealthily through the elaborate trench-and-tunnel network.

In any event, 2/28's attack lacked sufficient infantry and fire support. Late in the afternoon, as dusk settled, Iwo remained awash in fire. Marine correspondent Sgt. Alvin Josephy recalled the initial assault toward the mountain. Suribachi, he wrote,

> spouted death from hundreds of openings. . . . The Japanese had erected every conceivable obstacle along the approaches to

the volcano base, from tank ditches to barbed wire. These had to be stormed by frontal assault. One of our boys perched atop a pillbox and leaped down on the back of a running Jap and killed him with his knife. Another lost his rifle and wrested a samurai sword from a charging Jap officer and cut his head off.[2]

In our initial assault on D-day, several of 2/28's platoons gained 150 yards, but the attack was underpowered. We needed more than two companies of one battalion to make any real headway. We did not yet have all the artillery of the 3rd Battalion, 13th Marines ashore, although several guns of the 3rd and 4th Battalions were blasting away at suspected positions on Suribachi. But the fire direction center was not set up until the end of the day. Liversedge soon realized that attacking the defensive ring around Mount Suribachi without armor and coordinated heavy fire support would be futile. We needed tanks and more big guns for both suppressive and destructive fire against those emplacements.

Most of all, we needed a few "Zippo" flame tanks to take out enemy soldiers who manned the mutually supporting pillboxes, blockhouses, and caves. Many of these emplacements had survived the naval and air bombardment and remained almost impossible to detect until our men were right on top of them—and drawing their fire.

Beach congestion and the narrow mine-cleared routes of advance slowed the tanks in coming to the aid of CT 28 in the afternoon.

As the tanks finally approached CT 28's line of departure single file, Japanese fire knocked out three of the Shermans. As the afternoon waned and the landing teams struggled to get themselves in line for the assault, congestion on the beach exploded into bedlam, as though some demonic giant had scooped up military equipment and amphibious craft, along with hundreds of Marines, and thrown them onto the beach. The dead and the dying, in addition to a ghastly assortment of body parts, bobbed in the red-stained surf. Several charred and broken corpses sprawled not far inland. Some Marines had stepped on anti-tank mines and had been blown to pieces.

Battalion aid stations sprang up along the narrow lodgment. Of all the horrible sights on Green Beach, none was more gruesome than injured leathernecks lying on stretchers taking fresh wounds from artillery and mortar shrapnel. The Japanese were zeroing in on these helpless souls, many of whom were already in shock. A surgeon working with the 4th Division had suffered a nervous breakdown within hours of the invasion from the intense pressure of tending to so many men missing limbs and parts of skulls, and suffering from sucking chest wounds.

Marine Sgt. T. Grady Gallant was attached to the 4th Division, just a few hundred yards to the right of the 28th's position. Along with a fellow Marine, Gallant hunkered down near an aid station that came under Japanese fire.

> The shells beat against the beach. Gravel pattered over the silent, strangely motionless bodies of wounded who lay on their backs facing the sky. As the shells burst, as they crashed and shrieked, one of the wounded rose from his stretcher. He rose slowly. . . . His head was bare and his arms were straight and rigid at his side. He sat upright and tilted his chin upward, tilted it high. Then he opened his mouth as wide as he could. His eyes were staring and fixed upon the sky, his forehead deeply furrowed and his eyebrows lifted, pulling at his eyelids, almost. He sat this way—taut and stiff and straining every muscle of his body . . . and screamed . . . and screamed . . . and screamed.[3]

A Japanese shell finally ended this Marine's misery. Sergeant Gallant and his buddy were relieved that his agony was over.

A great mystery of the combat on D-day was that, despite such ghoulish sights and sounds, men continued to go about their business, intensely focused on pushing forward. The extreme danger and shock of brutal combat derailed only a very few that first day. (There were only ninety-nine Marines evacuated for combat fatigue on D-day out of a total force of about thirty thousand, according to official records.) A Marine private first class, a stranger from another unit, called out in fatherly fashion to Richard Wheeler and his 3rd Platoon mates from E Company. "You'd better start digging in. You've got to keep busy or you'll go nuts!"[1]

About one thing I am convinced: for most of the Marines on Iwo Jima that first day, the need to get on with the attack, to do their part of the work, was a more powerful force than the fear of death. Intensive training and excellent leadership by squad, platoon, and company commanders were very much responsible for this fact. It's also true that Marine Corps training, in general, has a way of making you more afraid of failing to do your job than dying. I'm not the first Marine to have said this. It's widely recognized, and one of the mysterious products of Marine Corps indoctrination. So by midafternoon, men all along the beach were adapting, finding ways to put together fire teams, taking care of the wounded and dead, who were everywhere in plain sight. In general, we were sorting ourselves out and getting on with the business at hand. Somehow, amid the mayhem, little pockets of order and purpose emerged.

Cpl. Wayne Bellamy agreed with Fred. "There's a great deal of fear as you approach the beginning of a battle, great stress. Everyone has fear; I don't care what anyone says. But if you have the training and indoctrination we had, you will go ahead and do your job regardless of fear. You have an idea of what has to be done, and you just automatically go ahead and do it. It seems, too, at Iwo anyway, there were always guys at the critical moments, officers, noncoms, even some Marines who had never been in combat before but who took to the work like they'd been doing it all their lives."[5]

The command post was up and operating, and runners were out with the various battalions, and all the while the Japanese were raining down every caliber shell in their inventory. Calls from units for ammo, or water, or fuel for the flamethrowers flowed in frantically. Our men couldn't seem to get enough of those flame tanks. We had a logistical control officer for the Combat Team on a patrol craft at the line of departure, and he would call in to the beach whatever was most urgently needed. The systems we had developed over the past year were working well, despite the rigors of combat.

Hand-printed messages on small yellow pads flowed rapidly to and from the division CP as well as between CT 28 units. One of these, marked "urgent," was given to messenger Jim Scotella to be delivered to one of the assault battalions. Scotella had just finished running messages to 2/28, so he handed the message to Bob Lankford to deliver it. Lankford took the message and left the safety of the shell hole where the message center was located. A few yards later, he was hit twice, probably by machine-gun fire, and was immediately evacuated. Scotella ended up delivering the message himself. He returned to the center unscathed and survived the battle.

New Yorker correspondent John Lardner spied one Marine on the beach that afternoon who refused to be deterred from his work, despite the swirling chaos and destruction. We do not know his full name or rank or whether he was attached to Combat Team 28. No matter which unit he was from, his performance offers us a clear window onto the resolve of the entire landing force:

> We went up to a boat whose ramp was slapping the waves a few feet out from the shoreline and whose coxswain was trying to hold her to shore by keeping her engine running. There we encountered a Marine named Connell, who for the next half hour gave the most spectacular demonstration of energy I have ever seen. Though he moved with great speed and fervor, there seemed to be no fear in him. He had been helping moor and unload supply boats all afternoon. He was stripped down to his green Marine shorts and he spent as much time in the water as out of it, his lank, blond hair plastered to his skull. . . . His problem at the moment was to make this boat fast, so that the ammunition aboard her could be unloaded. . . . It was quickly obvious that the crew of the boat, though they remained calm, were of no help to Connell whatever and considered the odds against succeeding at this time overwhelming and the situation irremediable. Connell shouted orders or suggestions at them,

but they simply stared at him and then stared up and down the beach at the shell bursts. Connell got hold of a rope, made it fast to the boat, then darted up the beach to tie the other end to a tractor. . . . Connell persuaded the [tractor] driver to start his engine and try to pull the boat in. The rope broke. Connell tied it again and it broke again. He swam out to get another rope, but by the time he returned to the beach the driver and the tractor had disappeared. Swimming furiously, he then approached [us] at the stern of the boat and called out the courteous suggestion that we get ashore. "This is going to take a long time, and you fellows will do better somewhere else!" He never once showed the slightest sign of temper or desperation. He appeared to regard the wild scene and his own mighty efforts and constant frustrations as wholly rational and what was to be expected.[6]

The 3rd Battalion of the 13th Marines had been scheduled to land in the fourteenth assault wave. But because of the rapidity of the advance across the neck of the island, most of their personnel were ashore early, by 1100 hours. But their weapons, 105mm howitzers, weren't able to land until around 1400. These were brought ashore in DUKWs driven by black U.S. Army soldiers in segregated units who earned the admiration of the Marines in a hurry. The DUKWs were partially swamped by the high surf and the weight of the cannons. They managed to get ashore, and then to unload the precious 105s in the soft sand under fire.

Capt. George Dike, commander of I Battery's four howitzers, realized that the guns should be deployed near the southern end of Green Beach, not the northern end, as called for in the original landing plan. "It was at the south end, near Suribachi, that the guns and their crews were protected from small-arms fire and the flat-trajectory heavy weapons that appeared to be firing on the 28th Marines from the north, quite a way inland. I told Lt. Col. Henry T. Waller, the battalion commander, that we couldn't put the guns up on the neck and fire into Suribachi given all the enemy fire and the nature of the terrain there."[7]

Dike spotted a DUKW coming in with Sgt. Joe L. Pipes's 105mm gun, *Glamour Gal,* of G Battery. Dike found an armored bulldozer to haul the DUKW through the soft sand near the southern end of Green Beach. Working at a rapid pace, Pipes and his crew readied the gun. Under the direction of Dike, the crew fired on a large Japanese artillery piece on a carriage halfway up the mountain's face. It was shooting at intervals directly onto the landing beaches and was protected by steel doors. The gun would fire a few rounds and then slide back inside the mountain.

Pipes's first round was high; the second low. The third round found the mark, destroying the enemy weapon. "One of the reasons we won the battle, in my opinion," said Dike, "was that we had more men like Joe Pipes than the Japanese. It was a privilege to see him and his crew in action."[8]

CT 28's supporting artillery had made the first of many contributions to the conquest of Mount Suribachi. It was just about 1440 hours. Pipes's cannon was almost certainly the first Marine artillery piece to fire on Iwo Jima's soil. And by 1745, despite all the confusion and enemy fire, 3/13's fire direction center was fully operational.

Meanwhile, the Marines of Capt. Severance's E Company, 2nd Battalion—Richard Wheeler's unit—were tasked with mopping up "captured" ground in the scrub brush along the western half of the island's narrow neck. It was grim, tricky work, undertaken by leathernecks who might at any moment be blown to bits as they attacked Japanese blockhouses and pillboxes to their front, flanks, and rear.

As Keith Wells's E Company platoon moved warily forward around dusk, the lieutenant examined a wrecked Japanese aircraft and nearly stepped on a large land mine. Minutes later, as fire swept over his position, Wells leaped into a pit, and his knee landed in the intestines of a dead Japanese. His pants stank so much from the fouled intestines that he cut part of them off right in the midst of the fight. That dead Japanese soldier was one of the few seen by the leathernecks during D-day. "The Japanese were very astute," remembers Pfc. Anthony Visconti, a member of the 3rd Battalion, 13th Marines. "They were very good fighters; they always dragged their dead away; all we saw was dead Marines. It was very demoralizing. They put their dead in caves, heaped up on top of each other. When you see the enemy dead in combat, you know you're doing something. Toward the end of the battle we got into the caves and you've never smelled anything like it. There were hundreds of decaying corpses."[9]

As Wells and his men approached Landing Team 1/28's lines, they happened on a large mound with closed black concrete doors. Wells thought it a threat and wanted to blow it up with satchel charges before moving forward, but an officer from the 1st Battalion told him not to waste the charge because the mound had been silent all day and wasn't likely to cause any trouble now. Wells didn't challenge that assessment, but as he and the platoon eccentric, Pfc. Donald Ruhl, investigated some brush to the front of the mound, the concrete door on its right flank opened, and a large fieldpiece fired shells along the 2nd Battalion's perimeter. Quickly, a squad began a coordinated assault on the mound, and Wells and Ruhl joined in. A thermite grenade was tossed into an aperture. Smoke poured out of the emplacement, and three Japanese soldiers staggered out, running for their lives. Wells let go an entire clip from his Thompson submachine gun, and Ruhl emptied his eight-shot Garand rifle. All three Japanese fell. One tried to rise and flee. Don Ruhl rushed forward and killed him with his bayonet.[10]

★

AMONG THE FOUR combat teams that hit the beach on D-day, all fought with tenacity, but CT 28 was the only one to reach its first-day objective, which was to isolate Mount Suribachi from the force defending the body of the island to the north and commence the attack against the garrison protecting the volcano. By the end of the first day, it was apparent that the planning staff in Hawaii that had projected a timetable of ten to fourteen days for reducing the entire island was far too optimistic. The depth and resilience of the Japanese defense was shocking.

None of the American senior officers ashore or at sea doubted, at the end of that harrowing first day, that the Marines would ultimately prevail. Yet it was becoming apparent that, as tough as the fighting had been in the jungles of the Solomons or on the islands of Tarawa and Peleliu, Iwo Jima was going to be the Marines' worst fight yet. One Marine correspondent later summed up this realization:

> At Tarawa, Saipan, and Tinian, I saw Marines killed and wounded in a shocking manner, but not like the ghastliness that hung over the Iwo beachhead. Nothing any of us had ever known could compare with the utter anguish, frustration, and constant inner battle to maintain some semblance of sanity, clarity of mind, and power of speech. Everybody tells me they felt as I did. As long as you could speak, you believed you had a slim chance to live. None of us would concede that death would have been a merciful coup de grace. Everybody was seized with an insensate lust to live.[11]

Carl von Clausewitz has described the key obstacles standing in the way of a combatant as types of "friction." Friction manifested itself in a staggering array of forms on Iwo Jima for the Marines. The Japanese were masters of the terrain. The wheeled vehicles of the leathernecks were immediately mired in the soft, black sand that comprised the beach's terraces. Once the Marines had advanced inland a few hundred yards, enemy fire besieged them from every direction, including the rear, because they had bypassed so many Japanese positions in the race across the island's neck. Marines also had to cope with the psychological strain of knowing that they were under the eyes and guns of thousands of Japanese warriors who had been conditioned to choose death over surrender.

And yet for all the friction and for all the casualties among the 30,000 Marines who pushed ashore that day—550 Americans killed or died of wounds, almost 1,800 wounded in the first twenty-four hours—Fred had a positive outlook:

CT 28 had been mauled, and the initial attack late in the afternoon had fallen short, but the unit as a whole had performed very well during its first day of combat, all things considered. We were across the neck and in good position to begin a strong attack early on D plus one. Most of our artillery was up and firing, which was little short of miraculous when one considers that the beach was under continuous fire throughout the day. We were sorting ourselves out, unit by unit, and buttoning up for a much-anticipated counterattack that first night. The year of intensive training had paid off. Panic had not ensued.

In CT 28's zone at least, it seemed a kind of collective "muscle memory" factor was at work. In other words, the Team's assault units had been programmed through endless repetition in training exercises to dash forward in small groups while other Marines laid down suppressive fire, supporting their movement.

Attacking the enemy on Iwo Jima was not a job for the fainthearted. Nor was it a job for the average World War II American infantry unit. Something more was required. The men of Combat Team 28 who scrambled up the terraces on Green Beach were certainly not supermen. But they had been superbly trained for the ordeal of D-day. And they had met that challenge head-on. What happened on D-day confirmed what I had come to believe about CT 28 as a whole: we were blessed with a small cadre of Marines who were not only very brave men themselves but also understood the art of leading men who might otherwise hang back out of the line of fire. Bobo Mears was such a man. So was Phil Roach. Frank Wright was this sort of Marine. His Navy Cross citation tells the story:

> Landing under intense hostile fire, First Lieutenant Wright led his platoon in a daring frontal attack against heavily armed and fanatically defended Japanese blockhouses, pillboxes and gun emplacements: Armed with only a carbine in the face of intense . . . mortar, machine-gun and artillery fire, he attacked and destroyed the occupants of an enemy pillbox that was holding up the advance of his platoon and then, rallying his troops, was one of the first men to reach the opposite side of the Island. Advancing seven hundred yards in one hour and thirty minutes, he severed the Island and isolated the Japanese forces on Mount

Suribachi. His aggressive fighting spirit, high courage and un-wavering devotion to duty were in keeping with the highest tra-ditions of the United States Naval Service.

Frank Wright had a kindred spirit in Cpl. Tony Stein of A Com-pany, a twenty-four-year-old toolmaker from Dayton, Ohio. Stein couldn't get enough of the Japanese that first day. He was by now in his fourth Pacific campaign. On D-day, Stein, with the able assis-tance of his fire team mates, a demolitions man and rifleman, knocked out one pillbox after another. Stein frequently ran out of ammunition because of his rapidly firing weapon—a custom-made light machine gun—and his zest for dispensing with the enemy. In-stead of waiting for ammunition to be brought up to the front line, he'd dash off to the beach without shoes or a helmet to replenish his supply, often carrying a wounded comrade to the aid station en route. He was awarded the Medal of Honor for his actions on D-day—posthumously.

Most of the steadfast men who fought against Suribachi's guns were dedicated sea soldiers who believed in their comrades, in their leaders, and in themselves. Take, for example, Sgt. Mike Strank, the only one of the six flag raisers in Joe Rosenthal's photo to have joined the Corps before the war—the only "regular" Marine. The recruiting officers apparently hadn't noticed that Mike Strank, a strong six-footer who worked in the Pennsylvania coal mines, was actually a citizen of Czechoslovakia.

Strank was a born leader, someone everyone in his platoon ad-mired, mostly because he always looked after his Marines' welfare, just as he had looked after the welfare of his two brothers back in the coal mining community of Franklin Borough, Pennsylvania. When Mike was twelve, he'd saved the life of his eleven-year-old brother, John. The two boys were digging for coal in a local mine, and John's shovel hit a live wire. The electric current froze the boy to his tool. Mike Strank barreled into him, knocking John to the ground hard—but also to safety. Like Harry Liversedge, Mike had been a Marine

Raider. The motto of the Raiders, adapted from the Chinese Communist guerrillas in the 1930s by Evans Carlson, was "Gung Ho!" meaning, "Work together." Mike had liked the tough life in the Raiders, and he took "Gung Ho!" as gospel. "He was the finest man I ever knew," said one platoon member who survived the battle.[12]

Combat Team 28, as the fight went on, seemed blessed with more than its share of men of Strank's caliber—daring men who led from the front and looked after their men. A few of these Marines, such as Richard Wheeler's squad leader, Howard Snyder, approached combat on Iwo Jima with a calm confidence that steadied the nerves of those who were apprehensive or just plain scared. Snyder was, in Wheeler's words, "quite casual about his security." After a couple of firefights during the first afternoon, Snyder "hadn't only remained cool but had maintained a bold curiosity about the action around us. . . . His zest for combat was obviously stronger than his concern for his safety."[13]

Snyder was cut from the same cloth as his charismatic battalion commander, Lt. Col. Chandler Johnson, who paraded around under fire standing upright wearing a utility cap and with a .45 pistol in his belt, chomping on a cigar butt and exhorting his men to keep moving, keep attacking. Chaney Johnson, it might be pointed out, seemed as impervious to the emotion of fear as the two Marines that led the Team, Liversedge and Williams.

Both Williams and Liversedge moved around Green Beach that first day as if they were invulnerable to the effects of flying steel. In fact, as I think back on it, neither man ever showed the slightest hint of apprehension during the battle, and I worked closely with them both every day of the fight.

Marine combat correspondent Francis W. Cockrel also remembered seeing Harry the Horse on D-day:

But you saw only a few [Marines] at a time, in near by holes, or when they were up and moving. A little above me to the right, however, one was sitting on a sort of hummock, inspecting Suribachi with the reflective look of a gentleman farmer wondering whether he would have this field planted to corn or spring wheat next year. That was Colonel Harry Liversedge, commanding officer of the 28th Marines. . . . I think several factors contributed to my not having a bad D Day. One was that when I saw Colonel Liversedge sitting there so coolly, I did not know he was noted for being unconcerned under fire, so I thought that things couldn't be very bad. I guess the sight of him helped a lot of other guys too.[14]

It was the presence of such men that goes a long way toward accounting for what the Team accomplished on February 19, 1945, and during the battle that followed. As Richard Wheeler put it,

It's true that a combat team must be composed mainly of cautious men; wholesale heedlessness under fire would certainly bring the team to disaster. But there is also a need for an audacious minority. It's this minority that sets the pace for an attack. If everyone were to dig in deeply and move only when it was really necessary—which is all that duty requires—the team's effort would lack vigor. There must be a scattering of men who neglect their safety and act with a daring initiative. Most of the tough feats that win the medals are performed by men like this. Though they are called damned fools by many of their more cautious comrades, they are nonetheless greatly admired. They do much for morale, since they seem entirely unafraid; and their cool aggressiveness sets a standard that the cautious, not willing to be too far outdone, follow to the best of their ability. And that's how objectives are taken and battles are won.[15]

★

BY DUSK, LIVERSEDGE had halted offensive operations for the day. The beach at gloaming was a very congested place, and figuring (correctly) that the Japanese would be laying down artillery fire from the north onto the beach, the colonel called into his command post the regimental communications officer, Maj. Ty Cobb, and Capt. Jack Downer, who as headquarters commandant was responsible for organizing the *defensive perimeter around the entire headquarters group. "Let's move this CP inland," said Liversedge. "I don't want to have to run the morning attack from here. This beach is worse than a traffic jam after a Yankees game. And it's a hell of a lot bloodier!"*

Downer and a small group of riflemen settled on a spot about 350 yards north of the sheer face of Mount Suribachi and roughly halfway between the eastern and western beaches. Nearby was the skeleton of a wrecked Japanese Betty bomber. The airplane was an excellent potential reference point for enemy forward artillery observers, so Downer called over a demolitions team and had it blown up.

Cobb and Downer quickly brought up the advance party and laid out the CP. Then the backbreaking work of digging in and filling sandbags began. It was 1800—half an hour of daylight remained, during which the rest of the CP personnel moved up to the new CP area. Inexplicably, enemy fire came to an almost complete halt as the latter group of more than one hundred Marines walked to the west. Not a single casualty was incurred. The most likely explanation is that the Japanese gunners had received an order to lift their fire on the beaches and focus their attention on the incoming landing craft trying to get to the shoreline one more time before nightfall.

The eerie silence during the move was soon broken by the steady pop of star shells from destroyers, the staccato of small-arms fire, and the sound of incoming mortar rounds. Coleman lanterns were used for light in the headquarters dugouts, and the chilly night air of the western Pacific was tempered by the warmth of the volcanic soil.

Everyone in the landing force had been told repeatedly that the first night would be a critical test. It was essential that the Marines in the ragged front line, which totaled about one thousand yards for CT 28, hold their ground if counterattacked. And a strong counterattack, the intelligence officers predicted, was likely, requiring extreme vigilance. The Japanese were superb night soldiers, capable of inflicting great damage through terrifying banzai charges or, more furtively, by infiltrating with small groups of saboteurs and blowing up ammo and supply dumps. All Marines on Iwo Jima were well versed in stories of earlier Pacific battlefields, where Marines were sometimes found dead at dawn, their throats having been slit as they dozed off in the night. All along the line that first night, the apprehension was very high.

Much to the surprise of VAC's intelligence section, General Kuribayashi dismissed the dramatic banzai charge in favor of the "slow squeeze" approach. As the night wore on, sporadic Japanese mortar and artillery fire grew steadily in volume. Kuribayashi was trying to destroy as much of the supply stocks on the beach and kill as many leathernecks as possible while risking very few of his own men.

At about 2200 near the CT 28 command post, the sounds of combat were shattered by the ear-splitting whoosh of an approaching spigot mortar projectile, hurtling in from the north. I said to Maj. Oscar Peatross, "Sounds like a Cotton Belt freight train at midnight on a north Texas prairie!" Nerves were a bit near the surface. Throughout the night, jittery lookouts all along the front line let go with rifle or machine-gun fire. This would set off yet more bursts in the vicinity, aimed at phantom Japanese infiltrators lurking amid the shrubs, rocks, and small trees along the line, illuminated by the spooky yellow light from the star shells.

For the men of 1/28, the big event of the first night came early, about 2300, when a barge full of Japanese soldiers attempted to land on the western beach. Marine riflemen picked off thirty-nine Japanese as they waded toward the shoreline. The Japanese stepped up their artillery fire soon afterward. Shells rained down with such intensity that the landing beaches were temporarily closed to all boat traffic.

Throughout the night, Iwo buzzed with activity. There were two or three Marines to each foxhole. At least one had to be alert and on guard, while the others tried—and usually failed—to catch a couple of hours' sleep. Meanwhile, coxswains worked to bring in supplies in Higgins boats and DUKWs throughout the night.

Across the crescent of land that constituted the lodgment, the bark of weapons mixed with the sounds of runners, litter bearers, and the wounded. Through the night, Liversedge worked with Peatross, Capt. Art Neubert, the Team's intelligence officer, and me on the plan of attack against "Hot Rocks" for the next morning. Liversedge opted to maintain steady suppressive fire on all enemy emplacements that could be identified on the cliffs and the base of the ugly mountain—that meant naval gunfire and air strikes as well as fire from our own artillery and our weapons company's 75mm half-tracks, 37mm guns, and heavy machine guns. The 2nd Battalion would advance on the left flank, the 3rd on the right, and the 1st Battalion would be in reserve initially, though we knew that ultimately it would require all three battalions in assault to take the mountain. Once we had succeeded in breaking through the protective belt, the assault battalions of CT 28 would encircle the mountain from both directions, linking up on Tobiishi Point at the southern tip of the island. Then, reconnaissance patrols would be deployed to determine the best way of reaching the crest.

The command team crammed into the "3" dugout ("3" is the Marine term for the operations section of a headquarters group). Joe Cason opined that canned sardines and smoked oysters enjoyed more wiggle room. Division had earlier informed Liversedge that before his assault, he could count on at least fifteen aircraft to soften up the north face and base of Suribachi. Red smoke was used to mark the front lines to ensure that the pilots didn't release their bombs too close to the Marines on the ground.

After further details were worked out, my clerk and runner, Cpl. Leonard Bulkowski, and I prepared the attack order on the standard, yellow message pad and sent it to the message center for distribution.

Later, alone in the dugout, Peatross and I discussed the day's events. Peatross said he had never seen anything remotely like the combat of the day.

I then settled down in Peatross's dugout with another rifleman/runner, Cpl. Eldon Myrick. Myrick tried for a little shut-eye. I had the first watch, giving me just a bit of time to reflect on the first day. I remember thinking how Lady Luck had smiled on me on my first day in combat, after more than two years in the Corps. I saw many shocking things on D-day. Yet, I also learned something very important that I couldn't possibly have known from my many months of training other Marines and participating in live-fire exercises. I could stand the sights, sounds, and stress of heavy combat and remain relatively unflappable. In short, I could function during combat. That knowledge brought more than a little relief, for it looked like we were going to face a great deal of fighting in the days ahead.

Light eased onto the battlefield at 0549, February 20, with sunrise at 0707. And in a little more than an hour, Combat Team 28 would commence its first full-bore attack on Hot Rocks.

Amid the confusion and violence of the first day, initial casualty reports soon proved to be woefully inaccurate. For example, the headquarters staff of the 1st Battalion calculated that 600 of its 900-plus men were casualties. In fact, the majority of these men were only missing from their units; they had fought with men of the 27th Regiment to the right of CT 28 or with Marines of other CT 28 units. In the rifle companies of the 1st Battalion, the losses were actually as follows:

A Company: 9 killed; 2 mortally wounded; 36 wounded and evacuated.

B Company: 15 killed; 6 mortally wounded; 44 wounded and evacuated.

C Company: 6 killed; 3 mortally wounded; 29 wounded and evacuated.

The 1st Battalion incurred very few casualties on that first night, so these numbers were for the most part a result of the fighting on D-day, February 19, between 0900 and 1800.

Even granting the harrowing first day of combat, none of the Marines of Combat Team 28 could possibly have guessed how much fighting and dying lay ahead; nor could they sense the profound effect this campaign would have in shaping their future lives and values. Many of the old salts, however, were beginning to suspect that they were in the midst of one of the most ferocious ground battles in the history of American arms.

When the 28th Marines left the island thirty-five days later, more than half their number were dead or wounded. For decades to come, the survivors would be haunted by memories of war at its most savage. Yet the battle also gave them an enduring sense of obligation and responsibility. When they thought about their comrades who did not leave the island alive, a sense of wistful regret would flood in. They would think often about their absent friends, and imagine what their lives might have been like, the families they might have raised, and the good works they would have done for their communities and for their country.

Many of the veterans of CT 28 have gone on to live more than sixty years after the guns on Iwo fell silent. What did it all mean? Dick Bishop, a tall, avuncular Washington, D.C., attorney in his mid-eighties who commanded a battery of the 13th Marines supporting CT 28, spoke for hundreds of the Team's survivors when he said, "I learned from my days on Iwo Jima that life was a precious thing, something to be treasured. After Iwo, I realized that I had to do something useful with my life. I owed that to the many guys I knew who were killed on that godforsaken island."[16]

5

THE FIGHT FOR "HOT ROCKS"

D awn on February 20 brought welcome relief to the 28th Marines. Throughout the night, limited Japanese infiltration attempts had drawn Marine small-arms fire, and a few grenades were tossed forward of the lines, often at phantoms rather than infiltrators, yet the much-anticipated banzai attack failed to materialize. Robert Leader, a former art student from Boston in Dick Wheeler's platoon, felt grateful to be alive. His squad had been forced to spend the night on a rocky outcropping near the west coast. There was no "digging in" for Leader and his mates—the earth proved resistant to picks and entrenching tools. His squad felt vulnerable with no cover to shield them from mortar and artillery rounds. Leader opted to play dead most of the night, hoping for the best amid spooky shadows and the eerie light of the star shells.

It was cold on the morning of D plus one. A light rain fell as the men of CT 28 prepared to reenter the fray. The scene on the beachhead was graphically described by veteran war correspondent Robert Sherrod:

The first night on Iwo Jima can only be described as a nightmare in hell. About the beach in the morning lay the dead. They died with the greatest possible violence. Nowhere in the Pacific have I seen such badly mangled bodies. Many were cut squarely in half. Legs and arms lay 50 feet away from any body. All through the bitter night, the Japs rained heavy mortars and rockets and artillery on the entire area between the beach and the airfield. Twice they hit casualty stations on the beach. Many men who had been only wounded were killed.[1]

The assault commenced on schedule at 0830, following a dawn attack by carrier-based Corsairs. Robert Leader was one of many Marines there who found the aerial attack on the mountain defenders "heartening. Like angry wasps, our planes swarmed over the volcano with the ripple of rockets and the roar of napalm." When one plane flew directly over Leader, he "felt a searing pain" in his back.[2] Putting down his rifle, he clawed at his back, discovering two spent cartridges that had slipped down his shirt collar. There would be no Purple Heart. At least, not yet.

Almost immediately, the Team's infantrymen bogged down under sustained Japanese fire. The Marines weren't going anywhere fast without tank support to suppress the torrential fire from the mountain.

Liversedge and Williams had been apprehensive about the tanks even during the planning stages. Once the initial waves on D-day hit the beach, we all worried whether the Shermans would be able to support the attack on Suribachi, given the broken terrain, the loose sand, and the fact that they were prime targets.

There was immense pressure on Colonel Liversedge to complete the reduction of Suribachi fast, for both strategic and psychological reasons. The success of the entire operation depended on silencing its guns and denying the Japanese the best observation post on the island. Otherwise, the Marines from the other combat teams, already heavily engaged in the main assault across the airfields and up through the center of the island, would be taking devastating fire from their rear as well as their front. Not a happy picture. The observation post on Suribachi could call in artillery fire from the big Japanese guns hidden in the hills and ridgelines north of the Motoyama plateau. These guns were well protected by the terrain from destruction by our naval gunfire.

In fact, most of the vehicles and men of Company C, 5th Tank Battalion—CT 28's tank unit—had completed the journey from sea to shore on D-day. But those that survived Japanese fire that first day could not reach the line of departure for the initial assault on the morning of February 20 for lack of fuel and ammo. The tank crews scurried around the beach looking for parts from disabled Shermans scattered about the beachhead.

On at least three occasions that morning, just as the crews attempted to form up for the attack, Japanese mortars found their mark, firing directly into the tanks' assembly area, forcing the steel behemoths to disperse, seeking cover. Finally, at 1100 hours, eight Sherman tanks arrived on the scene to offer firepower to the infantry attack. Yard by yard, the Team's assault made slow but steady progress.

Earlier, as the infantry of CT 28 was sorting itself out in preparation for the attack, the 105mm howitzers of the 3rd Battalion, 13th Marines pumped a steady flow of rounds into the face of the mountain. Pfc. Don Traub worked in the artillery fire-direction center, receiving information on Japanese troop movements and positions from the forward observers and converting the data into windage and elevation coordinates for the unit's guns. Early on the second day, Traub was

> lying in a hole next to three amphibious tractors full of ammunition. One of them took a direct hit from an enemy gun near Suribachi, and it blew up in a tremendous explosion, sucking me out of my hole and dropping me on my head and neck. After the barrage ended, I recovered somewhat, crawled around in the open, and saw that the entire contour of the land around me

had been rearranged and pocked with shell holes strewn with mangled bodies, body parts, and countless wounded.[3]

A pattern of movement soon emerged in the attack on the mountain: tanks and infantry would target a single pillbox or blockhouse while a flamethrower team slithered its way up to one of the apertures. After a few blasts of liquid napalm, a squad of infantrymen would charge forward and toss grenades into the enemy position. Then demolition teams blew up the emplacement to ensure it wouldn't be reoccupied. Simultaneously, other riflemen and machine gunners laid down hundreds of rounds on mutually supporting enemy positions in the vicinity.

Each yard yielded additional Marine casualties. By midday the line had crept forward only seventy-five yards. But by 1700, thanks to the tanks and to the split-second timing of the assault squads, both the 2nd and 3rd Battalions had moved about two hundred yards closer to the mountain's base and blown the entrances to many caves in the process. Lieutenant Colonel Butterfield's men in 1/28 experienced repeated "cutting in" attacks—the English translation of the Japanese term for lightning-fast strikes by small units of enemy soldiers attempting to infiltrate the Marine lines. These very often resulted in short, savage, hand-to-hand melees. The 1st Battalion counted 75 enemy corpses inside its perimeter before nightfall. The cost in blood for the 28th Marines as a whole for the day's fighting was 29 men killed and 133 wounded.

Cpl. William Byrd of the 2nd Battalion recalled that the wind picked up on the second afternoon, making him tremble with cold. His M1 rifle jammed, its receiver clogged with loose volcanic ash. He grabbed a carbine, but it, too, was jammed. He found yet another carbine. Much to his relief, this one fired.

Like several hundred other enlisted Marines that day, Byrd spent considerable time running back to the beach to obtain more ammunition. "On one of my trips to get ammunition, I found the body of my best friend, Walter Kaufman. Half his head was gone. I wasn't prepared for that. It knocked everything out of me. After the war was over, I went to St. Louis to see his family. His Mom cried when she saw me. It would have been so nice if Walter could have been there with us."[4]

We got word at the end of the day that the rebel nonconformist in our recon platoon, Cpl. Louis Boone, who had broken into the officers' liquor supply back at Camp Tarawa, was found dead. He was alone, near a demolished pillbox. With respect to Boone's actions on Iwo Jima, it could be said that any sensible person stayed close to his foxhole until it was absolutely necessary to push forward. But not Boone. He moved about constantly, with no fear of the large Japanese presence. Land mines and pillboxes were his specialty. He would attach a thirty-foot rope to a mine and drag it out of the way of his fellow Marines. If it did not explode after the first few feet, he hauled it to his private dump. He played a key role in the destruction of at least six pillboxes.

When Colonel Liversedge returned to Camp Tarawa, he scrubbed the court-martial and awarded Boone the Navy Cross posthumously. His loss so early in the battle was a great blow to the many men in the unit who had known, tolerated, and loved him. He'd always been in trouble away from battle, but Louis Boone, the Alabama country boy, proved himself a very able Marine in combat. I often think about him with affection and respect.

During this second day of battle, the shore party Marines on the beach continued to take a vicious pasting from enemy mortars and artillery. The beaches had opened for general traffic at 0600, but at 0930 they had to be closed due to heavy incoming fire, a massive amount of beach wreckage, and four-foot swells. Underwater Demolitions Teams blew up some of the unsalvageable landing craft, and CT 28's shore party men spent as much time diving for cover as they did handling cargo.

During one mortar attack, a group of shore party Marines scrambled into a large shell hole. Among them was Pvt. Robert Allen, who

later went into frontline combat with Landing Team 1/28 as a replacement. Allen recalled that "one man reached down and picked
up an object protruding from the sand. The sight of a detached hand
destroyed the last of his fragile sanity. Dropping the gruesome article, he leapt from his refuge. Screaming, he began to tear the cloth-
ing from his body, and he disappeared down the beach."[5]

The mountain itself imposed a powerful psychological burden on
the Marines, not unlike that faced by the American and Allied sol
diers who had to seize Monte Cassino, the medieval monastery that
blocked the Allied attack up the boot of Italy earlier in the European
theater of the war. "On this day," wrote 5th Marine Division historian
Howard M. Conner,

> and increasingly as the days went by, Suribachi seemed to take
> on a life of its own, to be watching these men, looming over
> them, pressing down upon them. When they moved, they moved
> in its shadow, under its eye. To be sure, there were hundreds of
> [Japanese] eyes looking at them from the mountain, but these
> were the eyes of a known enemy, an enemy whose intent was
> perfectly clear. In the end, it is probable that the mountain rep-
> resented to these Marines a thing more evil than the Japanese.[6]

In terms of yardage, the gains of February 20 were not large. Yet
after two days of fighting, the Japanese garrison in and around Suribachi had been dealt a serious blow. After considering the intense
pressure of the attack and his mounting casualties, Col. Kanehiko
Atsuchi, the fifty-seven-year-old officer in command of the Suribachi
defense, contacted General Kuribayashi, importuning the general to
permit his remaining garrison to conduct a massive banzai charge.
Kuribayashi demurred. Atsuchi's garrison must hold fast to his basic
plan, which specified that "even if the enemy does capture our positions, we will defend Suribachi Yama to the utmost, and even though
all positions fall into enemy hands and organized resistance becomes
difficult, we will continue fighting fiercely to the last man and inflict
heavy casualties on the enemy."[7]

Late in the day, engineers found the buried cable connecting the Suribachi sector with Kuribayashi's command post and the Japanese forces in the four other defense sectors north of the mountain. There is no evidence of communication between the two officers after February 20.

Capt. Leslie W. Babbin of Lynn, Massachusetts, opened up the division's post office on Iwo Jima on this day. Forty-three years old, the father of five, he had received the Purple Heart while fighting in the trenches of France in World War I. Babbin had somehow managed to ferry his post office gear ashore on D-day, thanks to a handful of sailors who helped to carry it on a stretcher from the beach.

Early in the morning of February 20, Babbin was spotted digging in and setting up shop. The first mail call wasn't until the twenty-fourth. But many CT 28 survivors, even long after the battle, have mentioned that early mail delivery, including newspaper stories recounting the Marines' courage and resolve, was a huge morale factor.

★

THE DEATH OF every Marine in Combat Team 28 was felt keenly not only by his buddies on the island, but by his family members and the citizens of his hometown. Take, for instance, the case of one of the most popular noncoms in the 3rd Battalion, Sgt. Joe Riley Crow, a high-spirited Marine with dark hair, a broad smile, and the carriage of an athlete. Sergeant Crow was one of the battle-tested veterans who joined the Combat Team soon after its formation in late 1944. Earlier in the war, he had fought as a Paramarine under Bob Williams at Vella Lavella. He had also seen grueling combat on Bougainville.

Back home at Ennis High School in Ennis, Texas, where he was popular with the girls, Joe Riley Crow had starred as a quarterback in the first season (1941) that his school had joined the "big leagues" by beating Waco High, a much larger school. Pfc. Harry Lloyd served in G Company with Joe. He remembered that, back at Pendleton, there had been a regimental track meet, and Crow won just about every event. "We also had a football team, and Joe played halfback. Nobody could catch him. They played tackle with no equipment, and boy, it was fun to watch."[8]

On Iwo, Joe Riley Crow led a demolitions squad from G Company. Crow's squad was in the process of attacking three mutually reinforcing pillboxes on the second day of battle when he was killed. His citation for the Silver Star tells the story:

> For conspicuous gallantry and intrepidity as Demolition Squad Leader, serving Company G, 3rd Battalion, 28th Marines, 5th Marine Division in action against enemy forces. . . . Leading his squad through intense automatic fire from the concealed enemy in a relentless assault on three mutually-supporting Japanese pillboxes, Sgt. Crow succeeded in reaching his objectives despite [incurring] two casualties and, skillfully maneuvering his men to destroy two of the hostile emplacements, annihilated the third before he fell, mortally wounded His expert leadership and relentless fighting spirit in the accomplishment of his daring mission contributed materially to a two-hundred-yard advance on Mount Suribachi by his company and reflect the highest credit upon Sgt. Crow and the United States Naval Service. He gallantly gave his life in the service of his country.

Sergeant Crow had just set off a satchel charge when a Japanese machine gunner struck him down. Crow's squad mate and friend, Cpl. Merrill "Bud" Crippen, was only ten feet away when he saw his friend fall to the earth with shocking violence. Crippen counted six bullet wounds, two in the arm and four rounds stitched across Crow's chest.

Only twenty years old, Joe Riley Crow had been on Iwo Jima since around 1300 on D-day. He'd survived his third campaign of World War II for less than twenty-four hours. A few days later the Crow family received an official telegram bearing the eagle, globe, and anchor emblem of the Marines along with the sad news.

The story of Joe's earlier life in Ennis and his friendship with three other young men from the town who, like Joe, joined the Marines, reveals a great deal about the spiritual and moral forces that sustained the 28th Marines. All four Ennis men were football players. Three of them—Joe, James W. "Airedale" Goodwin, and William T. "Dooney" Pierce—were close boyhood friends and teammates on Ennis High's fine 1941 gridiron squad. Goodwin was known as the quiet man with a strong streak of determination, and Pierce, according to one of Ennis's local historians, served as a kind of "balance wheel" between the other two boys and "had an air of mischief about him."9

The fourth Ennis man in the story, Jack Lummus, was several years older than the three boyhood friends, but all three, as football players, would certainly have known him. A superb Ennis High School athlete, a standout on both the gridiron and on the diamond in the mid-1930s, Jack had gone on to star in football at Baylor University and played minor-league baseball until he was recruited by the New York Giants in 1941 to play end. After attending Marine officer candidate school at Quantico, Virginia, Jack was assigned to the 27th Marines, elements of which fell under the operational control of the 28th Marines at several junctures during the Battle of Iwo Jima.

The other three Ennis men joined the Marines together and left by train, again together, for the recruit depot in San Diego. As luck would have it, all three, like Lummus, were assigned to the newly formed 5th Marine Division.

On March 8, 1st Lt. Jack Lummus set off a mine while leading his platoon in an assault on a strongly fortified enemy position. Lummus's demise came in the wake of a gallant one-man charge into one of the last defensive positions between his company and the island's northern coast. Lummus had personally destroyed two enemy emplacements just before he stepped on the mine, mangling both legs. His men were so incensed at the sight of their fallen leader that they rose in a spontaneous charge, gaining three hundred yards and overrunning a series of critical enemy emplacements in the 27th's area of operations.

The official Marine Corps history of operations in World War II notes that Lummus's "devotion to duty and personal sacrifice had supplied the impetus for the wild charge. A mixture of love and compassion for their leader, mixed with anger and frustration, had supplied the spark . . . which set off a reaction that was for all practical purposes the American equivalent of the traditional enemy banzai charge."[10]

Jack Lummus received the Medal of Honor posthumously. Before he died, he told the surgeon working on what was left of his legs, "Doc, the New York Giants lost a mighty good end today."[11]

Airedale Goodwin, in the 26th Regiment, was shot in the abdomen a few hundred yards from where Lummus fell. He died aboard a hospital ship on March 9. Four days later, Sgt. William Pierce was killed by a Japanese sniper just after he had assumed command of a heavy-weapons platoon.

Today, all four men are buried near one another in Myrtle Cemetery in Ennis. As the battle wore on there were hundreds of small towns like Ennis, beset by the loss of one, two, or more young men who had fought and died together on Iwo Jima.

★

ON FEBRUARY 20—the day of Crow's death—Pfc. Robert Snodgrass of I Company, 3rd Battalion, the former Raider, saw his last day of combat. Luckily, Snodgrass lived to tell the tale:

> I received five machine-gun slugs up my backside that severed a lot of nerves. I've still got a lot of shrapnel in there today. Well, the only thing I can remember about getting shot is that my legs went into muscle spasms, and it reminded me of my high school days when I'd hunt rabbits, and I'd shoot one, and he lay there on the ground and kicked. After I got shot, they put a bunch of seriously wounded guys on a Higgins boat. We were all on stretchers, of course, and we headed out to a hospital ship. The Japanese lobbed a shell into the boat just after we left the island, so the corpsmen had to come out into the water and rescue those of us who hadn't been killed.[12]

The night of February 20 passed in relative peace. Liversedge, Williams, and the rest of the Team, however, remained convinced they'd soon face an all-out night banzai attack.

By dawn on February 21 the weather worsened: six-foot surf pounded away on the welter of broken and blasted equipment littering the landing beach, and the wind came out of the northeast at nineteen knots. The jump-off for the assault was at 0825, preceded by the usual bombardment. This would be the last day of air support in the attack on the mountain. Henceforth, Marine infantrymen would be too close to the enemy's thick belt of emplacements to risk the use of air support. As it was, the Corsair fighters strafed as close as one hundred yards to the front of the attacking Marines, focusing particularly on areas that were inaccessible to tanks.

On the first two days of the fight, sightings of Japanese corpses were rare, and their very absence chipped away at morale. Where were these phantoms who fought so fiercely before giving up ground? They had, of course, been quickly pulled back into the mountain's elaborate tunnel-and-chamber network by their comrades. But by midafternoon on the third day of the campaign, this was changing. Robert Leader of E Company recalled:

> We were now encountering increasing numbers of dead Japanese and swarms of great green flies. We figured the Japs were no longer able to reclaim their dead. . . . The men of the 312th Independent Infantry Battalion [who defended the approaches to Suribachi] looked like first-class troops. From the scattered memorabilia that festooned the battlefield dead, we concluded that these were veterans with service in China and Southeast Asia. Japanese dead were a problem for us. Booby-trapping was endemic and some of the dead were feigning. It became necessary to shoot their dead to be sure they were. I found this coup de grace repulsive.[13]

The assault again commenced slowly. On the right flank, the 1st Battalion was assigned a one-company front. A Company led the charge along the western side of Suribachi, with Companies B and C in trace. Under cover of naval gunfire off the west coast, A Company reached the base of Suribachi by noon. The 37mm gun platoon supporting Company A played a critical role, knocking out more than half a dozen pillboxes. The ground here was too uneven for tank support. The 37mm guns proved invaluable throughout the battle in attacking positions the tanks couldn't reach.

Pvt. Ovian Von Behren, the BAR man from Company B who had been among the first to cross the isthmus of the island on D-day, once again distinguished himself at a crucial moment, earning the Silver Star for his efforts:

> Observing that his platoon was pinned down by heavy enemy machine-gun and small-arms fire, Pvt. Von Behren leaped from his covered position and, signaling a flamethrower tank, coolly guided it ahead of the platoon, directing its fire until two enemy pillboxes had been destroyed, thereby enabling his platoon to advance and seize its objective.

Landing Team 3/28, in the center of the attack, was stopped cold until 1100. Then Sherman tanks joined the half-tracks, laying down sufficient fire to spark the infantry assault. A vicious counterattack halted the advance at 1145, but the Japanese were rapidly turned back. By 1400, the 3rd Battalion's leading assault units were approaching the foot of the mountain. Pfc. Bernard Link of I Company recalled the events leading to his serious injuries:

> On the morning of D plus 2, as we exchanged fire with the Japanese in the bunker, I wondered how in the world they could out dance all of those bullets that kept ricocheting around inside the bunker. . . . Of course, the extensive trench network that supplied fresh replacements for casualties in the bunkers was unknown to me at that time. Directly ahead was a destroyed antiaircraft gun emplacement with a mound of dirt in front of a small entrance. I dashed for it. From that position, the bunker was only about thirty yards away. Just as I stuck my head out from behind the mound to pick out my next move, two fellow Marines flopped in behind me. Since I didn't see them coming, I instinctively pulled my head back to see who it was. In that instant, a stream of machine gun

bullets piled into the wall of the gun emplacement where my head had been just a split second before. One of the Marines said, "That almost tore your f–cking head off!"

Every Marine was a target on the island, but those of us who carried Browning Automatic Rifles were singled out. The bipod on the end of the BAR was an attention getter. As I jumped out from behind the mound and headed for the bunker, firing as I went, a Japanese soldier came out from behind the bunker and threw a hand grenade at me. Fortunately, I did not catch the full impact of the explosion. The biggest piece slammed into my face and embedded itself in my jawbone. The blood seemed to pour out, and I thought my jaw was broken. As I tried to stop the bleeding, I noticed that the Japanese soldier just stood there, admiring his work, I guess. That was a fatal mistake because our bazooka man took advantage of the moment and laid a round right in his gut. That was not only conclusive, but also messy.[14]

On the left flank of the regimental attack, the reserve company of the 2nd Battalion had to enter the fray in a hurry. Yet by 1400, elements of the battalion were also near the mountain's base, and Company F, with the sea on its left, pushed rapidly toward Tobiishi Point, at the southern tip of the island.

On the drive toward the mountain, a combat correspondent glimpsed a rare sight: three Marines were surprised by a group of Japanese at the mouth of a cave as the leathernecks approached.

There was no room to use rifles. One Marine made a flying tackle at the nearest Jap and, when felled, twisted the Jap's neck and broke it. Another plunged feet first on a Japanese lieutenant, catching him in the groin. The third Marine leapt Tarzan-like from atop the cave, his jungle knife flashing. The Jap he landed on was stabbed in the heart before they hit the ground. There were no rules, no quarter, no surrender.[15]

In the 2nd Battalion's zone of attack, E Company's 3rd Platoon—Keith Wells's unit—engaged in a classic Marine frontal assault late that morning. The unit swept forward, jumping from shell hole to shell hole. Small-arms fire greeted them, followed soon by a mortar barrage. Several men in the platoon fell within two minutes. A former Raider, Pfc. Chick Robeson, understood that the fire was the worst he had seen up to that point. "The Jap mortars seemed to be playing checkers and using us as their squares. I still can't understand how any of us got through it."[16]

Five other 3rd Platoon Marines, including the future author Richard Wheeler and his hard-charging sergeant, Howard Snyder, leaped into a large crater carved out by a five-hundred-pound bomb. An instant later a Japanese shell landed too close for comfort, and off the Marines charged toward the menacing bunker.

The platoon's assault raged on. Sgt. Hank Hansen, known as "the Count" for his refined manners and debonair attitude, along with Pfc. Donald Ruhl, jumped atop a pillbox and unleashed a torrent of fire on a group of enemy soldiers running crouched down in a trench. Suddenly a Japanese grenade fell right in their midst. Without hesitation, Ruhl jumped on the explosive, smothering it with his body. It was the ultimate selfless act; as his squad mates recognized, Don Ruhl clearly had the option of jumping clear of the blast and saving his own life. His sergeant had no such option. During his three days on Iwo Jima, Ruhl had rescued a wounded Marine about forty yards in front of his unit's lines, spent one night manning a Japanese machine-gun pit, and saved the life of his sergeant. He was awarded the Medal of Honor posthumously.

Although the 3rd Platoon had already taken substantial losses, including Richard Wheeler, who'd been seriously wounded, the assault pressed on. A Marine carrying a .30-caliber machine gun set up his weapon in the platoon's zone and laid a stream of rounds into the entrenched Japanese. He was shot and killed within minutes. Several other leathernecks dashed for the machine gun, but they, in turn, were wounded or killed. Ultimately the gun itself was damaged beyond repair.

The main obstacle now was a bunker, from which flowed a current of Japanese hand grenades. The forward movement of the unit had been brought to a halt. Then, burly Chuck Lindberg and his assault squad moved up on orders from Wells. Lt. Col. Chandler Johnson was seen at this time, looking over the action with binoculars from a high ground two hundred yards away. Sadly, Johnson wasn't the only interested observer. A Japanese mortarman dropped a shell right into the crater where Wells and four other Marines were lying. Wells recalled, "It went right off at my feet. . . . My clothes were nearly all blown off me from the waist down and I was full of shrapnel."[17]

At this time Marine tanks joined the fight in earnest, and the ground assault gained momentum. Corporal Lindberg and another flamethrower man, California native Pvt. Robert D. Goode, now charged into the Japanese emplacements and trench system, firing short bursts of flame, covered by riflemen. The smell of burning enemy flesh wafted into the air.

Wells finally relinquished command to Sgt. Ernest "Boots" Thomas, a lean, tough Floridian who had shown great coolness under fire. Thomas accompanied the tanks, picking up the telephones attached to their rear and directing the gunners' fire where it was most needed. And it was twenty-year-old Boots Thomas who found the soft spot in the Japanese defenses through which his own platoon and others from the 2nd Battalion followed to the base of Mount Suribachi.

Both Thomas and Wells were awarded the Navy Cross for their leadership this day. Unfortunately, Boots didn't live long enough to read his own citation. Remarkably, seventeen Purple Hearts were also awarded to members of the 3rd Platoon of E Company for their actions on the morning of February 21. The flamethrower-toting corporal, Chuck Lindberg, earned a Silver Star for continuously exposing himself to enemy fire while blasting out pillboxes and other enemy fighting positions.

Heroism of a different sort was on display that day near the eastern base of Suribachi where two wounded Marines lay stranded. A corpsman had kept them alive by crawling up to them periodically and treating them under fire. One of the men was breathing through a glass tube in his throat. Finally in late afternoon a group of Marines led by Staff Sergeant Charles Harris manned a raft, landed under cover of rocks on the shoreline, and evacuated both Marines before the enemy realized what had happened.

The fighting on the third day of the battle cost the 28th Marines 34 killed and 153 wounded. The 1st Battalion had gained 1,000 yards of ground, the 2nd about 650 yards, and the 3rd 500 yards. The Combat Team had reduced virtually all of the emplacements that constituted the protective belt around the mountain.

The Marines were now close enough to the slopes of Suribachi to hear muffled Japanese voices. Gasoline was poured into the crevices in the mountain's base and set afire. Although Colonel Atsuchi himself was dying from a severe shrapnel wound, what was left of the Suribachi garrison had plenty of fight in them. Before he died, Atsuchi ordered his men to send a small squad through the American lines to report on the Suribachi situation to General Kuribayashi.

At dusk, the great American fleet surrounding Iwo had to fend off a fifty-plane kamikaze attack that flew in from Haha Jima, one of the other islands in the Bonins. It proved to be the sole kamikaze mission of the entire campaign, but it was a costly one for the Navy. The planes sank the carrier *Bismarck Sea* and severely damaged another, the *Saratoga*. During the night, cold rain along with two infiltration attempts robbed the CT 28 Marines of precious sleep.

On the night of February 21, Platoon Sergeant Gene Bull of H Company, 3rd Battalion, a hard-charging, regular Marine with an abiding love for his men and the Marine Corps, realized suddenly that it was his twenty-fifth birthday. His thoughts were interrupted when his platoon, the 2nd of H Company, had to withdraw from the fairly solid dirt road at the foot of Suribachi's western side. Bull recalled that

the terrain to the north of the road was a mass of small gullies running in several directions, and there was no easy way to make a stand there. Most of the area was covered with small trees and some undergrowth. . . . It was just then, while I was prone on the dirt road trying to see where the enemy was shooting from, when someone called to me. Several men of the platoon were warning me to watch out for my legs. When I turned to look, bullets were kicking up the dirt just below and between my knees. Which way should I turn? I picked the right way. We moved back amid the gullies, and I encouraged everybody to take cover quickly. It was then that Pfc. Willard G. Sparks held out his BAR to me, saying, "You need this more than I do, Sgt. Bull," and he dropped dead. . . . Even with the danger of the situation, and at a time like that, it was very hard to keep one's composure. I was so very fond of all those people.[18]

The rain continued on the fourth day of the fight. Among the artifacts of combat recovered after the fight for Suribachi was a poignant letter home written by Shozo Matsumura, dated February 22. It hinted at the level of resolve among the dwindling Suribachi garrison. "Dear Mother and Family," the young soldier concluded, "I shall repay as well as I can all my obligations to you by suffering here, and I shall acquit myself well. Please, all of you, take good care of yourselves and do [your] utmost until victory comes. The battle is on. . . . I leave this, expecting to die."[19] So far as is known, Matsumura may still be entombed in Suribachi.

★

FOR COMBAT TEAM 28, February 22 began badly. Before the morning jump-off, a mortar shell hit squarely near Colonel Liversedge's CP, killing the regimental surgeon, Daniel J. McCarthy. Fred and Colonel Liversedge were standing a few feet from McCarthy when he fell to the ground instantly with a small piece of shrapnel lodged in his heart.

So often on Iwo, whether you lived or died was a matter of inches. Here McCarthy was, right next to Colonel Liversedge and me at 0800, business as usual, when a mortar round went off, and a small fragment of shrapnel killed him instantly. Neither the colonel nor I suffered even so much as a scratch. It was just plain luck. There is no way to explain who was hit and who wasn't in those early days. Lethal Japanese fire could come from anywhere at any time.

Near Suribachi, Colonel Johnson's 2nd Battalion had eliminated all fixed enemy defenses in its zone of action. Elements of the battalion pressed forward on the rocky eastern shoreline at the base of the mountain, along a ledge about fifty feet above the surf. The regiment's intelligence section reckoned that the enemy garrison had been whittled down to about six hundred from about sixteen hundred enemy soldiers.

The 3rd Battalion cleared out the remaining positions covering the northern base of the mountain early in the day. It continued forward along the western shoreline against light resistance, and by 1100 hours was only four hundred yards from the advance elements of 2/28, approaching from the east.

Yet the mood of the Team was hardly jubilant. The weather had continued to worsen. Mud was everywhere, including inside weapons. A great many M1 rifles were jamming. Shepard's 3rd Battalion sealed shut nineteen caves, but the battalion's after action report for the day claimed that morale had ebbed because of the cold, wet weather and the sheer number of enemy positions to be reduced. Indeed, "it seemed almost impossible at times to clean the Japs out," said the report.[20] In fact, the after action report was unduly pessimistic. The 28th Marines had completely disrupted the enemy defense around Suribachi, and the Japanese inside the mountain were already contemplating escape to the north or suicide.

There were, however, two very bold individuals in I Company who believed the Japanese garrison on Suribachi had thrown in the towel, and they wanted to confirm their suspicions. Fred interviewed one of them, Gerald St. Aubin, and tells their story, which does not appear in any of the official Marine histories of the battle:

By 1100 on February 22, I Company had reached the base of Suribachi. Most of the afternoon was spent mopping up, i.e., blowing caves and bulldozing pillboxes, spider traps, and trenches. In the early evening, while digging in for the night, Sgt. Bob Whitehead, 3rd Platoon, said to a couple of his squad members, "Hey, guys. I think I can climb that beast (Suribachi)!" Pfc. Cliff Tozer and Cpl. Gerry St. Aubin told him he was nuts. Whitehead asked if anyone would go with him. Silence. Finally, St. Aubin said, "Okay, I'll go."

The two men, with their rifles slung, climbed the northwest face. St. Aubin told me they made it to the top, despite the slippery conditions from the daylong rain. They communicated by touch and muted whispers. They neither saw nor heard any Japanese. The two Marines returned after about an hour and three-quarters. Nothing was said to anyone up the chain of command.

The 2nd Battalion's commander, Lieutenant Colonel Johnson, had wanted to send a patrol up Hot Rocks on February 22, but Liversedge told him, "No. Send a patrol up early tomorrow." Charlie Shepard, leading the 3rd Battalion, surely was aware of this, and if he knew of Whitehead and St. Aubin's daring climb, he wisely kept it to himself.

During the night of the twenty-second, about one hundred Japanese from Suribachi were killed as they tried to cross through the American lines near both coasts to join their brothers in the north. Sergeant Bull's 2nd Platoon, H Company, had an eventful night:

> We were subject to constant and exhausting harassment by the Japanese . . . for hours they were running all over the place. During a particularly rough period multiple tracers were ripping through the air just inches above our heads. Those bullets were coming from a machine gun beyond the left of our line. I later learned that [it was an American] gun and a Jap had gotten control over it for a while, and he did some damage. I picked up some more shrapnel that night and got part of my two front teeth broken off in the process. I felt someone had punched me in the mouth and I was tasting blood. . . . I finally worked [one tooth] free, and spit it in my hand, then I put the tooth into my

pocket, for the tooth fairy, I guess. . . . As it became lighter toward morning, I began to dread learning what had happened to the men of the platoon during the night. I had become convinced that they all must have been hit at least once. Daylight finally arrived, and by then, we were very low on ammunition and very, very tired. That morning, the light of day was exceptionally welcome, even in that hell hole.[21]

Bull was relieved to find out that morning that his platoon was intact—no one had been seriously wounded or killed in the melee. They would all live to see the twenty-third of February—a day no survivor of the battle has ever forgotten. CT 28 had essentially surrounded the mountain's base, and the level of enemy resistance had diminished markedly. Word spread quickly: there was nowhere to go but up to Suribachi's crest.

★

BEFORE DAWN ON February 23, Lt. Col. Chandler Johnson met with his company commanders to brief them. The first thing he wanted was a small reconnaissance patrol to push toward the summit. That job was assigned to F Company under Capt. Art Naylor, a popular officer who was fond of using football metaphors in conversations with his officers and noncoms.

It fell to Sgt. Sherman Watson, a highly experienced NCO in Naylor's 3rd Platoon, to select the personnel for the first officially sanctioned patrol up Suribachi. He chose three men: Cpl. George Mercer of Iowa, Pfc. Ted White from Kansas City, Missouri, and a Crow Indian from Montana, Pfc. Louis Charlo. Slowly, warily, the patrol made its way up the slopes, stopping periodically to listen for sounds of the enemy. They passed cave openings and tangles of war detritus. Within a half hour, they arrived at the crest of the mountain, happily surprised by the absence of small-arms fire. After peering into and around the crater for a few minutes, they began a rapid descent, sliding, running, and falling down the hill back to the comparative safety of the base. Reaching there without incident, they reported to Naylor that the Japanese must be dug in at the top, as there were a number of weapons emplacements there. Naylor conveyed this information to Johnson, who promptly called Capt. Dave Severance of E Company, ordering him to send a platoon to Johnson's CP.

Severance told his executive officer, 1st Lt. Harold Schrier, to march the 3rd Platoon over to Johnson, along with a few reinforcements from other elements of E Company. Schrier, a career Marine who had joined the Corps in 1936, was a former Raider who had fought at Guadalcanal and Bougainville.

When 3rd Platoon, E Company arrived at the CP, Johnson asked the battalion adjutant, 1st Lt. Greeley Wells, for the American flag he had carried in his map case since Camp Tarawa days. According to Lou Lowery, the Marine combat photographer who was attached to the patrol to film the first flag raising on Japanese soil, Johnson turned to Schrier and offered these words: "If you're able to get up the mountain, I want you to take this flag. . . . If you can't make it all the way up, turn around and come back down. Don't try to go overboard."[22]

Then, he handed Schrier the battalion flag. Most of the men who had survived the heart-thumping charge on February 21 were in the patrol, including Sgt. Henry Hansen and Sgt. Howard Snyder, who were close to the front of a long column of about forty men. The patrol included flamethrower men Chuck Lindberg, Pvt. Robert Goode, Boots Thomas, and Robert Leader.

Bringing up the rear were two teams of stretcher bearers along with corpsman John Bradley, who would later receive the Navy Cross. Along with the E Company patrol was at least one F Company man—a Marine whose identity has long been a subject of controversy, but who, after years of careful photographic detective work, has been authoritatively identified as Pfc. Ray Jacobs of San Francisco. Art Naylor of F Company had been told that the E Company patrol would pass through his lines and that a radio operator was needed to ensure close communication between the ascending patrol and the battalion CP. Ray Jacobs was that radio operator.

The patrol wended its way up the mountain, cautiously staying off obvious trails for fear of Japanese mines or booby-trapped grenades.

I can still see that patrol in my mind's eye, making its way up the north face of the mountain. Our 75mm guns were firing rounds on both flanks of the patrol. Liversedge and Williams were watching the patrol through field glasses and monitoring the covering fire. We were all getting pretty excited. We had to adjust the fire very carefully, as the patrol was moving in serpentine fashion upward, toward the crest. They stayed clear of established paths, fearing booby traps. One stray 75mm round would have made a real mess of things, yet we had to keep firing, for we didn't know then what we now know—that the Japanese would not fire a single round at the patrol until it got to the top and had finished putting up the first flag.

There was a feeling of immense accomplishment when that first little flag waved in the breeze. Accomplishment, and yes, no small measure of relief that that dragon's head was no longer breathing fire down on us. Mount Suribachi was now the property of Combat Team 28!

Dave Severance watched with great anxiety as his Marines climbed ever higher. He told author James Bradley, son of John Bradley, the corpsman who helped raise both flags on Suribachi, "I thought I was sending them to their deaths. I thought the Japanese were simply waiting for a larger force [than the initial Watson-led patrol]."[23]

As the men ascended the steep slopes, they encountered several Japanese corpses. It took about a half hour to reach the crest, at which point about half the Marines circled the rim of the crater atop Suribachi, rifles and BARs at the ready, and then, one at a time, the remaining Marines crawled over the rim. There they found a broken water cistern, as well as a fully loaded Japanese machine gun. But there were no Japanese in sight. Two of the first men over the top were Leo Rozek and Robert Leader. After Leader relieved himself at the edge of the crater, Sergeant Hansen ordered the two young Marines to find a piece of pipe from the cistern to use as a flagpole. Once they procured a suitable pipe about twenty feet in length, a number of Marines attached the flag to the pole.

The first flag was raised on the northern edge of the crest of Mount Suribachi at 1020 hours. Thanks to Lou Lowery, we have a series of excellent photos showing this event in detail. Among the Marines on the site when the first flag was planted were Sgt. Boots Thomas; Lt. Harold Schrier; Cpl. Chuck Lindberg; Corpsman John Bradley; Pfcs. Ray Jacobs, Phil Ward, and Jim Michaels; and Sgt. Hank Hansen (see photo insert).

A sustained wave of elation swept over the Marines below. Ray Jacobs remembered the scene:

> Just moments after the flag was raised we heard a roar from down below. Marines on the ground, still engaged in combat, raised a spontaneous yell, when they saw the flag. Screaming and cheering was so loud and prolonged that we could hear it quite clearly on top of Suribachi. The boats on the beach and the ships at sea joined in blowing horns and whistles. The celebration went on for many minutes. It was a highly emotional, strongly patriotic moment for us all.[24]

The Japanese inside the mountain's defensive system had chosen to remain silent while the Marines worked to put up the flag. And then, just a few minutes later, they attacked. Ray Jacobs recalled the event:

> I noticed motion below and to my left. Looking over I saw a Japanese soldier dressed in a brown field uniform running out from behind a mound of earth on a low part of the crater rim. He slapped the grenade on his helmet and made a quick throw. He then disappeared back behind the mound. The grenade fell short of our group [and] fortunately no one was injured. Then, the Japanese, apparently enraged by the sight of our colors, hit us with rifle fire and a barrage of grenades. We responded with flamethrowers, grenades, BARs and rifles. I remember seeing individual fire teams running toward the caves firing as they ran.

We burned and blasted the caves on both sides of the crater rim, and soon it was over.[25]

By Japanese reckoning, the mountain fortress was meant to hold out for at least ten days. It had taken the Marines four days to seize it. The fall of Suribachi, as we know from a few Japanese survivors, was dispiriting in the extreme for the entire enemy garrison on the island. Regrettably, we have no record of General Kuribayashi's reaction to the fall of the mountain.

Dave Severance, the commander of E Company, is an indispensable authority on the sequence of events that comprised both flag raisings on February 23. Colonel Severance summarized what happened in a letter to Fred, explaining what unfolded immediately after the raising of the first flag and how a second flag raising—far and away the more celebrated of the two events in the popular imagination—occurred:

> Soon after the first flag was raised, Colonel Johnson heard that secretary of the Navy James Forrestal [who, together with Lt. Gen. H. M. Smith, had just landed on the beach] had expressed a desire to have the small flag. Colonel Johnson sent 2nd Lt. Albert Tuttle to the beach area to find another flag. He planned to use it to replace the original flag, thus saving the first flag as a battalion memento. Lieutenant Tuttle had stated that the colonel, almost as an afterthought, said, "See if you can get a larger flag." Tuttle obtained a large ceremonial flag from *LST-779.*
>
> At about that time I received an order to provide a detail to string telephone wire to the Suribachi patrol and sent Sgt. Michael Strank, Cpl. Harlon Block, Pfc. Ira Hayes, and Pfc. Franklin Sousley to the battalion CP. A Company E runner, Pfc. Rene Gagnon, was at the CP obtaining radio batteries for Schrier's patrol, and he joined Sergeant Strank's detail for the ascent. As they were about to depart, Colonel Johnson handed Gagnon the ceremonial flag [that Tuttle had procured], and told Strank to have Lieutenant Schrier replace the small flag and save it for the colonel.
>
> Climbing the volcano at about the same time as Strank but at some distance away were Associated Press photographer Joe

Rosenthal and two Marine photographers, Sgt. Bill Genaust and Pfc. Bob Campbell. About halfway up the volcano, the photographers met Lou Lowery coming down to look for another camera. Lowery told the group that he had already photographed the flag being raised, but there was a terrific view to be seen if they continued to the top. As the photographers reached the summit they saw a group of Marines attaching a large flag to a pipe and were told that the small flag was to be replaced and kept as a souvenir. Rosenthal and Genaust backed away from the flagpole site and prepared to film the large flag being raised. Campbell moved into another position where he could capture the movement of both flags. Genaust started filming with his movie camera using color film as the Marines prepared to raise the second flag. Rosenthal was caught by surprise when the large flag started up and was lucky to snap one exposure, which was to become the famous photograph.[26]

The six men in the iconic photo were all from Dave Severance's E Company. They were ultimately identified as follows (from left to right in the photo): Pfc. Ira Hayes, a Pima Indian from Sacaton, Arizona; Pfc. Franklin R. Sousley, from Flemingsburg, Kentucky; Sgt. Michael Strank of Conemaugh, Pennsylvania, who had been born on the Marine Corps' birthday (November 10) in 1919; Pharmacist's Mate John H. Bradley of Appleton, Wisconsin; Pfc. Rene Gagnon, from Manchester, New Hampshire; and, at the base of the flagpole, Cpl. Harlon H. Block of Weslaco, Texas. In an extraordinary coincidence, the six Americans who raised the second flag on Suribachi hailed from a wide range of geographical regions in the United States—just one more fact that fueled long-standing public suspicions that the second flag raising had been staged by a Marine Corps known for its remarkable public relations acumen.[27] When an AP editor asked Rosenthal a few days later if the shot had been posed, the modest photographer answered in the affirmative. Unfortunately, Rosenthal was not referring to his flag-raising photograph at all, but to a shot of a group of about twenty-five jubilant CT 28 Marines lifting their weapons under the flag, their mission accomplished. Thus was born the misconception that the five Marines and one Navy corpsman raising the second flag had been posed.

It took all of 1/400ths of a second for Joe Rosenthal's shutter to open and close. He'd set the aperture between f/8 and f/11. Rosenthal himself often said that luck played a crucial role in the shooting of the most famous still photograph of World War II. He had piled up some stones to stand on, as he was too low on the slope to see what was happening. Lieutenant Schrier then walked into Rosenthal's line of vision. Just as Schrier moved away, Rosenthal swung his camera around and held it until he guessed the moment was right. Later, amid inflammatory accusations, Rosenthal freely admitted that he hadn't been around for the first flag raising, but he flatly denied his famous shot was a phony. "I did not select the spot nor select the men, and I gave no signal as to when their action would take place. It wouldn't have been any disgrace at all to figure out a composition like that. But it just happened. Good luck was with me, that's all."[28]

After the battle, back in Hawaii, Fred was charged with sorting out who exactly had been in the Rosenthal picture and ensuring that the surviving flag raisers made it back to the mainland where they would lead the seventh war bond drive. Thus, he has a unique perspective on the confusion surrounding the famous picture.

The Rosenthal shot had not in any sense been posed. On that question, there can be no dispute. It happened because Chaney Johnson told his Marines to replace the small flag with a bigger one. He wanted the smaller flag for his battalion and was afraid someone like General Smith or General Rockey might want it as a memento. Because the image is so powerful and evocative—because it struck such a deep chord of emotion with the people back home—it is often forgotten that both flag raisings were essentially business as usual for the men involved, and for those who commanded them. It was not orchestrated in advance for effect by division headquarters, or anyone else for that matter. It just flowed out of what had happened earlier. The

28th Regimental Combat Team had defeated the mountain fortress's defenders and had seized the high ground.

The Rosenthal picture guaranteed a place in history for the 28th Marines and, of course, for the six men who had together raised the second American flag over sovereign Japanese territory. Yet the second flag raising, it must be pointed out, was a nonevent for the American sailors, soldiers, and Marines on and around Iwo Jima. Rather, it had been the drama of the small patrol's ascent and the first flag raising that had set off a riot of celebration both ashore and afloat.

It was the first flag raising—not the second—that prompted Secretary of the Navy Forrestal's oft-quoted statement to General Smith, "Holland, the raising of that flag on Suribachi means a Marine Corps for the next 500 years."[29] The two men had just set foot on the beach at that fateful moment.

The Rosenthal image became an instant cultural icon. Even today, the photo of these six Americans working together on top of Mount Suribachi remains a prominent national symbol of resolve and courage in times of the utmost adversity. Moreover, the image captured the collective effort and the characteristics that have come to define the Marine Corps: teamwork, discipline, resolve, professionalism, esprit, and valor.

As such, we have come to think of this image—and by extension the battle—as the connective tissue between the Marine Corps and the American people. The bond between the Marines and the American public, already strong at the time of Iwo Jima, has been made a good deal stronger as a result of the photograph.

The photo's symbolic resonance was felt by just about everyone who saw it, and almost everyone did, for it appeared in newspapers across the entire country within forty-eight hours after it was taken. It appeared on the front page of the *New York Times* on February 25. The *Los Angeles Times* ran the image across three columns the same day. A few days later, it was featured on the cover of *Life* magazine. It has not disappeared from public view since that day in February 1945.

The immediate reaction to the image was all the more significant because the American people had grown weary of war and discouraged by the extraordinary lengths to which the Japanese appeared willing to draw out an unwinnable conflict. Morale in America had flagged. The more candid and aggressive Navy policy toward press releases meant the American people knew far more about Iwo Jima as the battle unfolded than they had known about earlier engagements in either the Pacific or Europe. Reports of early Iwo Jima casualty figures had cast a pall over the nation's spirit. In fact, they ignited a firestorm of editorials across the country castigating the Marine Corps' leadership for incurring such heavy losses, and calling for Gen. Douglas MacArthur of the Army to assume control of the entire Pacific theater on the grounds that the Marines were incapable of achieving victory at an acceptable cost.

In reaction to one particularly strident editorial by William Randolph Hearst's *San Francisco Examiner*, about seventy-five off-duty Marines stormed the editorial offices of the newspaper. The incensed Marines demanded that the paper's editor, William Wren, contact his boss, Hearst, immediately so the Marines could weigh in with a response. Wren obliged, but Hearst refused the call. This potentially explosive incident was defused when the shore patrol arrived, and the editorial page editor agreed to give the Marine side of the story the next day. He never followed through on that agreement.

But the rival newspaper in San Francisco, the *Chronicle,* rose to the challenge, taking the Hearst paper to task for slurring the good name of the Corps, whose island assaults, the *Chronicle*'s editorial pointed out, were destined to produce higher casualty rates by their very nature than MacArthur's battles, which were waged on much larger land-masses. At the time, the *Chronicle* was owned by four sisters, one of whom was Mrs. Phyllis de Young Tucker. Her only son, 1st Lt. Nion R. Tucker Jr., a platoon commander in the 1st Battalion, 28th Marines, had been killed in action on Iwo Jima on D-day.

When President Roosevelt saw the Rosenthal image, he immediately recognized its symbolic value for the war effort. He ordered that the raisers of the second flag be shipped back to the United States for public relations duties on the home front. The only three flag raisers who survived the battle—Gagnon, Hayes, and Bradley—returned to tour the nation in support of the seventh war bond drive, which brought in $26 billion—far in excess of any previous war bond drive.

Within a few weeks of the event, the image adorned posters, calendars, and billboards. A three-cent stamp bearing the image was issued, and an unidentified writer for *Life* was surely correct when he wrote that the photo "arrived on the home front at the right psychological moment to symbolize the nation's emotional response to great deeds of war."[30] Yet, as Lou Lowery was later to say, it was "a darn shame that the men who actually were on the first patrol never received the credit they deserved."[31] The first flag raisers for many years were indeed shunted aside in formal commemorations of the battle—including the November 1954 dedication of the Marine Corps Memorial in Arlington National Cemetery.

Bitterness still lingers in the community of Iwo survivors and their families over the way the first flag raisers were treated. Yet it was Chuck Lindberg, the last of the first flag raisers to die (in 2007), who offered the most generous and relevant comment about the whole controversy at a reunion in the late 1990s. His words invoke the true spirit of the Marine Corps about the famous event: "I have always felt it was a mistake to identify the Marines that raised the flag on Iwo Jima. Every man that went ashore at Iwo, and every man at sea, raised that flag—every one of us. We carried it up there, and we had our hands on the pole, but all of you here raised it, and most of all, the men who didn't come back—they all raised it."[32]

Ironically, the inspirational photograph had another unintended effect: it obscured the horrific and sustained fighting the Marines endured for a full month *after* the mountain fell into American hands. As the 3rd Battalion after action report put it:

> The part of the operation conducted in the northern end of the island was much harder [than the campaign for Suribachi]. The terrain features were difficult and the enemy was "dug in" better. The defense he had was better concealed and harder to knock out due to there being piles of stone and small holes cut down into the stone, all being well concealed. Then in addition the ground was undermined with many caves and tunnels. These could not be bypassed but had to be left under guard and blown shut with demolitions, which, due to the number of men available for this work, slowed the operation. . . . The fighting in the northern end was very discouraging. Troops were so close to the enemy positions that supporting weapons, even 60mm mortars, could not be used with safety. Yet the enemy was so well concealed that he could not be seen. The fire received was close and extremely accurate.[33]

Though the mountain belonged to the 28th Marines, there was still plenty of work to do around the base of Suribachi. For the remainder of February 23 and 24, elements of all three infantry battalions of CT 28 engaged in dangerous mopping-up operations.

Late that day Gen. Harry Schmidt, commander of VAC, came ashore to set up his command post near the first airfield. He joined Gen. Clifton Cates, commander of the 4th Division, and General Rockey at the 5th Division CP to discuss the basic plan for the battle ahead. It would fall to the two regimental combat teams of the 3rd Division under Gen. Graves Erskine to drive up the middle of the Motoyama plateau, the island's high ground. In gradually clearing the central high ground of defiladed enemy artillery and rocket positions, the 3rd Division Marines would reduce the pressure on the 4th and 5th Division troops on the right and left flanks, respectively, as they attacked across the ravines and ridgelines that radiated outward from the plateau.

On the night of February 23, Cpl. Wayne Bellamy, an A Company mortarman, was startled to see about fifty Japanese running stealthily right by his foxhole, near his company. Corporal Bellamy recalled that the enemy soldiers were not in attack mode but were simply trying to steal through the 28th Regiment's lines to join the main forces in the north:

> I know I killed or wounded quite a few of them with my carbine, because they were sky-lining themselves right up above me. I was firing at them from no more than seventy-five to one hundred feet away, like shooting ducks crossing in a line in front of you. I heard a lot of moaning out there, but I was pretty much out of ammo, so I wasn't about to go out there and check them out. But some guys in B Company nearby who'd managed to appropriate some .45-caliber Thompson submachine guns heard them, too, I guess. Because, around dawn, they came out and put them out of their misery. They weren't about to take any prisoners.[34]

The following day, C Company of the 5th Engineer Battalion blew up cave after cave on the slopes and base of Suribachi, in addition to clearing land mines from the newly captured area. They sealed off two hundred caves in the zone, some of which had entrances on three levels. Now that the enemy's fire in the area was reduced to the odd mortar or artillery shell, the business of building roads commenced as well. Work had already begun on forming the 5th Marine Division cemetery, which was located on the flat plain just north of the mountain.

In the fighting on invasion day, the 28th Marines had taken 385 casualties. Over the next four days of fighting, another 519 men fell, including 115 killed in battle. The casualties were, of course, heavy, but they might very well have been far worse had it not been for the inspired leadership of Colonel Liversedge and his officers and noncoms. And there was almost certainly one more important factor that kept casualties lower than they might otherwise have been. John McLean, the Japanese language officer, believed that CT 28 was the beneficiary of a major tactical intelligence coup. Late on the second day of battle, a runner from one of the rifle companies brought to the Team's CP a large Japanese map. It appeared to be a master map of the defenses in the entire Suribachi sector.

McLean and his fellow language officer attached to CT 28, Lt. Richard White, had been trained to translate Japanese military maps. They rapidly pored over the map's critical information, revealing the precise location of scores of Japanese blockhouses, pillboxes, and other defensive positions. The 5th Division Intelligence Journal recorded the following message at 0230, on February 21: "Phone call R-3 13th requesting location of mortar positions Suribachi. Told him location mortar positions on latest situation map and referred him to 28th, which has captured map showing defensive installations of Suribachi."[35] In plain English, this meant that the 5th Division intelligence section was able to provide the 13th Marines, its artillery regiment, with the exact coordinates of Japanese mortars around Suribachi. As Maj. John Erskine, head of the 5th Division language section, noted in a report, as a result of the map captured by the 28th Marines, "Naval gunfire was called down on pin-pointed targets and a noticeable decrease in the volume of enemy fire was observed."[36]

At 0630 on February 25, Combat Team 28 was ordered into corps reserve for a well-deserved rest. The Team still had plenty of mopping up to do in the Suribachi area of operations, but it would not return to the front line until the first of March, when CT 28 would begin its next great challenge of the campaign: the struggle to break through the western anchor of the main belt of Japanese defenses, Hill 362A and Nishi Ridge.

6

THE ENEMY

We had heard," wrote Iwo Jima veteran Ensign Toshihiko Ohno, "that the American Marines were the best fighters in the world and had hoped that we might have a chance to encounter them."[1] Ensign Ohno's wish came true, as he often encountered American Marines on Iwo, narrowly escaping death on several occasions. Ohno hid with several wounded comrades in a series of caves and tunnels as the American force battled its way inexorably up the island toward Kitano Point. He was one of about two thousand Japanese who evaded capture or death during the Marines' campaign, only to be killed or to surrender to the Army's garrison force after the Marines had sailed back to Hawaii to train for the invasion of Japan.

More than two weeks into the battle, Ensign Ohno, commanding the crews of two 25mm antiaircraft guns, found himself in the northern sector of the island, near a large sulfur field. Because the sulfur vapors were both hot and malodorous, Ohno felt sure the Americans would close in on his position via the road adjacent to the field. He and his men planted twenty mines alongside the road and waited. Ohno described what happened next:

> The Americans were being blown 50 feet in the air by mines and there was no movement of tanks. The Japanese soldiers sat quietly in their foxholes and watched. Despite everything, the Americans continued to advance. The Japanese Army on Iwo Jima evaded the American attacks by moving from foxholes to the previously prepared . . . tunnel-shelters. The U.S. Marines attacked these shelters with flamethrowers, hand grenades and dynamite. The Japanese counterattacked by hiding in the entrances to these underground shelters and striking by night. But once you were found it was gruesome. The Americans would burn any survivors with flamethrowers as if they were chickens being fried.[2]

Hundreds of Japanese hiding too far back in their underground bunkers and tunnels to be incinerated were entombed when Marine engineers blew up cave complexes and sealed their entrances. Large numbers of enemy soldiers also committed mass suicide when further resistance became impossible. Such was the fate of about 150 soldiers who defended Suribachi. They killed themselves with pistols and hand grenades deep inside the upper regions of the mountain's bunker complex shortly after we had raised the flag on the mountain. It was shocking to find so many bloody corpses huddled together. The stench inside the mountain was horrific, and more than one combat-hardened Marine vomited.

At least a couple of thousand other Japanese suffered the same fate as we began to corral them into an ever-shrinking area in the northwest, near Kitano Point. All of which confirms an often-overlooked truth about Iwo Jima: as bad as conditions on the island were for us, they were in many ways more hellish for the Japanese. As Maj. Yoshitaka Horie was later to write in an official report, General Kuribayashi instructed the garrison on Iwo Jima to think of their final defensive positions as their grave. As the battle moved toward its conclusion, the conditions these men fought under became increasingly desperate.

Combat Team 28 survivors have made their peace with their erst-while foes. With few exceptions, they speak today of the island's defenders with respect and even begrudging admiration. "They were tough little bastards," said former Raider and CT 28 machine gunner Bob Mueller. "The Japanese soldiers were tenacious as hell. They showed few signs of fear." Mueller then smiled wryly, uttering a conclusion shared by many of his comrades. "Yup, they were damned good. A little nuts, maybe, but good soldiers. However, we were a lot better."[3]

Interestingly, only one of the CT 28 survivors we interviewed while researching this book spoke about the enemy with the visceral hatred that was so common among American soldiers and Marines in the Pacific during the war. "At these reunions," said this Marine, a member of the weapons company, "you always hear a lot of talk about forgiveness and reconciliation and making peace. I think it's a lot of bull. It's been sixty years since I killed my last Japanese soldier, and I will tell you right now I still hate the whole lot of them. If I had an M1 rifle today, I'd be more than happy to go out and shoot a few more."[4]

It is universally agreed by historians that the level of hatred and revulsion on both sides for "the other" in the Pacific War far exceeded that of the Americans and Germans in the European theater. There were plenty of battlefield atrocities in Europe but nothing on the scale of what happened in the Pacific. More than sixty years of peace—and the natural mellowing that comes with age—has softened the views of CT 28 survivors. The survivors we interviewed for this book admitted that the Japanese were extraordinarily tough and resolute soldiers. But even today, they fail to comprehend either the motivations or behavior of their adversaries. Indeed, the ethos and behavior of the Imperial Japanese forces on Iwo Jima remain shrouded in mystery and cliché sixty years after the battle. Few historians writing in English about the Pacific War have made a serious attempt to analyze the Japanese soldier's mindset at the time of the battle, or during the war in general.

What was the worldview of Ensign Ohno and his twenty-two thousand comrades who had sworn to defend the island until they were shot, buried, or burned alive? How are they to be understood? Only by attempting to answer these questions can we fathom the extreme pressures—psychological, physical, and moral—that the battle placed on all its participants, particularly those in the assault battalions. By coming to grips with the enemy's training, experience, and outlook we can recapture the hellish zeitgeist of CT 28's fight on Iwo Jima.

★

ALL THE JAPANESE units on Iwo Jima, whether the elite 145th Infantry Regiment, the Special Naval Landing Force—Japanese marines—or the 26th Tank Regiment, under the command of the urbane equestrian playboy Lt. Col. Takeichi Nishi, who had won a gold medal in the 1932 Olympics, fought with mind-boggling ferocity until annihilated.

The Japanese on Iwo were exceptionally resilient, capable of hard fighting even after enduring sustained air and artillery bombardments. They stood their ground against repeated infantry assaults for days on end under horrific living conditions. Their caves, tunnels, and underground barracks were filled with stinking, stifling air. The temperature underground often reached 120 degrees. The wounded, the dying, and the dead inhabited underground lairs where soldiers and sailors slept, prayed, and tried with minimal medical supplies to keep their wounded and dying comfortable. During the last two weeks of the campaign, the Japanese soldier on Iwo Jima was lucky to get a single hard biscuit and a cup of water that reeked of sulfur. Nonetheless, with only a handful of exceptions, they fought with great resolve.

Throughout the battle, wrote a Marine correspondent attached to the 28th Marines,

> the Japs were hard to kill. Cube shaped concrete blockhouses had to be blasted again and again before the men inside were

silenced. Often the stunned and wounded Japs continued to struggle among the ruins, still trying to fire back. A Marine assaulting a pillbox found a seriously wounded Jap trying to get a heavy machine gun into action; he emptied his clip at him, but the Jap kept reaching. Finally out of ammunition, the Marine used his knife to kill him.[5]

While early in the war Marines and Japanese alike held stereotypically racist and grossly misleading images of each other, by the time of the battle for Iwo Jima, a more realistic and complex view of the "other" had emerged. The Marines' widely held belief that the Japanese infantryman "owned" the night, for instance, was firmly grounded in truth. For all their aggressive fighting spirit, the Marines conducted little training in night offensive operations for Iwo or any other battle in the Pacific. Not so the Japanese.

British general William Slim, who fought the Japanese in Burma, attributed the Japanese soldier's superior night performance to the plethora of rural recruits who had been raised far from the lights of the big cities and were used to getting around under the stars. But far more important than the high percentage of rural soldiers in the Japanese army was the intensive training all recruits underwent in night-fighting techniques. Night operations were, of course, very much in keeping with the Japanese penchant for hand-to-hand fighting where they could use the knife, the sword, and the bayonet. Even at the beginning of the war, the Japanese favored stealth and surprise attacks over direct, well-coordinated assaults under cover of supporting artillery.

The Japanese soldier spent hundreds of hours learning how to crawl silently while carrying his weapon. He was a master at using terrain to limit enemy fields of fire. The night ambush and the raid were the forte of the Japanese fighting man; no army in the world was so proficient in the art of camouflage. The Japanese soldier was taught to wrap the metal blade of his bayonet and the hobnails of his boots in cloth to avoid glints of light and dampen sound before moving from his lair. He was far better than American and British troops at disguising his silhouette at night.

Assault leaders would sometimes drench themselves in a strong scent so their men could follow them in all but complete darkness. The soldier was taught to fall to the ground frequently when moving toward an objective, and then to scan the horizon for suspicious movement. No wonder Japanese raiders and suicide commando squads were so effective in blowing up ammo dumps and inflicting casualties at night, all of which had a psychological effect on Americans out of proportion to the damage they caused.

The Japanese on Iwo, particularly in the first two weeks of the campaign, deftly infiltrated Marine lines with "cutting-in attacks," fierce, small-unit penetrations with bayonets fixed, designed not only to kill any Marines caught off guard but to destroy command posts and supply dumps with satchel charges.

Another favored night tactic of the Japanese infantryman was to jump into Marine foxholes, attempt to stab one man, and then flee back toward their own lines in an instant. The objective was to provoke the startled leathernecks to kill or wound one another in the confusion. Indeed, the night was a nerve-wracking time for Marines manning defense perimeters, for frontline units on Iwo were often protected only with a few strands of concertina wire—and were only twenty or thirty yards from Japanese lines.

As the battle wore on, Marine infantrymen became increasingly proficient at detecting infiltrators and dispensing with them before they could inflict serious damage. One Marine who participated in fighting off an enemy nighttime raiding party recalled seeing about a dozen enemy soldiers running into a ravine where a naval star shell illuminated them against the night sky: "They looked like little devils running through the gates of Hell. All they needed were pitchforks."[6]

The Japanese soldier did not quit even after "organized resistance"—meaning coordinated units fighting to a plan—had ceased.

Even after the entire Marine force departed, the Army's 147th Regiment, which garrisoned the island, killed more than one thousand Japanese. Most of these poor souls were half starved, sticklike figures who did more scrounging than fighting, prowling American garbage dumps at night and taking the odd rifle shot when opportunity presented itself. Only a handful of these men are alive today. It is extremely rare for them to talk with anyone about their experiences, even their own families.

One of the very few who has spoken to an American journalist in the last several years is navy sublieutenant Saturo Omagari. Omagari held out for two full months after the Marines departed, hiding out in caves filled with corpses and the excrement and filth of his dying comrades. Like Ohno, he narrowly escaped being incinerated by Americans who discovered him with a group of live Japanese in a cave. He barely evaded capture that day. Near the end of May, an American soldier found him prostrate, outside a cave. He was then on the verge of death, suffering from dehydration, exhaustion, and dysentery.

Omagari had been scrambling around furtively with ad hoc groups of survivors since the second week of March, when he linked up with a few men from Baron Nishi's 26th Tank Regiment, all of whose tanks had been destroyed by that point. On March 9, Omagari joined three or four Japanese in cutting open the corpses of his countrymen and, after stuffing their own uniforms full of the corpses' intestines, played dead, hoping to destroy an American tank or two before dying themselves. He recounted his harrowing experiences in an interview with journalist David McNeill:

> I didn't feel fear any more, but I could sense the dead. Their wide-open eyes became thousands of sharp arrows, piercing my skin, flesh and bones. I tried hard to remain calm, clenching my teeth to avoid nausea. . . . Lying among the bodies I waited for the enemy tanks to appear. We attacked the tanks, but it was without avail. . . . As the weeks passed, we no longer fought in an organized way. . . . We moved in groups of

three or four with soldiers we met randomly. [Japanese] guards stood in front of bunkers and shelters, trying to prevent friendly forces from entering. We had to negotiate for water. Surviving in those shelters became more serious than fighting [against the Americans]. . . . We became obsessed with water. . . . Soldiers became extremely careful not to let water in their canteens make a sound when they walked around the shelters. When they heard that sound, some soldiers tackled the owner of the canteen, and it sometimes developed into murderous fights. No one cared about the injured. If they groaned with pain, they were told to shut up or strangled.[7]

Those Japanese who surrendered often did so only when the option of committing suicide had been closed off by circumstances. We treated our few prisoners very well, in fact, but they typically begged us to kill them. To surrender was both a formal breach of Imperial Army regulations—the no-surrender policy, known in Japanese as sinjinkun, *was at the core of the Army's Field Service Code—and, culturally speaking, an act of great shame. And the shame extended beyond the soldier to his family and ancestors.*

The lion's share of Japanese soldiers and sailors who became POWs on Iwo were captured just moments after fierce engagements, when they were too shocked by fire to continue to resist or were too badly injured to kill themselves.

Sinjinkun was widely followed because the Japanese perceived it as almost a holy sacrament, a religious act. Interestingly, many of the Japanese soldiers who were captured, after going through a period of intense shame, cooperated freely with their captors because, in effect, the only way they could bear to go on living was to cease to think of themselves as Japanese at all. They had become men without a country.

Sinjinkun achieved such an iron grip over the Japanese military in large part because the officer corps represented it not as a departure from old values but as their reaffirmation. "Even if this representation was not entirely accurate," writes historian Ulrich Straus, "the concept's success was assured because it fit into the fabric of a highly nationalistic society at the time. *Sinjinkun* demanded unlimited service to the state and a romanticized and moral notion of death."[8] Straus has pointed out that even contemporary Japanese have difficulties understanding *sinjinkun's* role in the war effort. It joins horrific treatment of Allied POWs and conquered civilians as a part of "an entire bundle of shameful war-related issues many Japanese institutions and individuals still prefer to leave shrouded in silence. . . . It is an extremely difficult matter to address since it involved routinely reckless expenditure of lives in an ultimately losing cause. In particular, veterans and their families are understandably loath to voice criticisms that could be interpreted to take away from the supreme sacrifice made by their fallen kin."[9]

Many Japanese whom Strauss consulted in trying to understand the no-surrender policy invoked the word *bigaku*, which is written using a combination of the Chinese characters for beauty, learning, and study and still "evokes in the minds of many Japanese the thought that those who died were exemplary in their 'purity' and models of 'manliness.'"[10] This only intensified the Marines' effort to get the job on Iwo done, and fast, stoking the impression that the enemy lurking under the ground was a fanatical automaton—a subhuman creature who could not be beaten by traditional military means.

Brave as he was, the Japanese soldier had a well-earned reputation among the 28th Marines on Iwo—and indeed throughout the Pacific— as a devious trickster who often behaved savagely and without pity in dealing with wounded, helpless Marines. The Japanese on Iwo tortured and desecrated several members of CT 28, leaving their mutilated bodies for their comrades to find. One Marine lieutenant in the 28th Marines was recovered after being listed as missing for several days. As best our medical people could tell, his torso had been used as an ashtray while he was still living. Another Marine was found with the unmistakable signs of torture. Many of his fingers were broken, and his head was bashed in with an entrenching tool or rifle butt.

Green Beach, circa 1200 hours, February 19, 1945. Capt. Fred Haynes's face is visible about halfway up the first terrace. (*USMC photograph by Lou Lowery*)

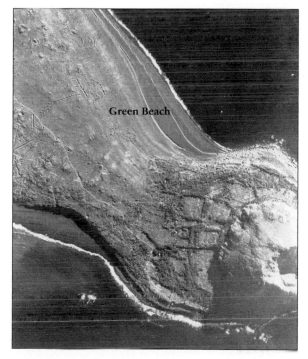

Vertical aerial photo of Mount Suribachi, Green Beach, and the narrow neck of Iwo Jima. (*Army Air Force photograph*)

Green Beach

ABOVE LEFT: Colonel Harry B. Liversedge (left), CO of CT 28, and Lt. Col. Robert H. Williams, his executive officer, going over maps. *(Haynes collection)*

ABOVE RIGHT: Louis Boone, later killed in action, holding Roscoe as a cub. *(Coster collection)*

RIGHT: Captains Haynes (left) and Aaron Gove Wilkins. This photograph was taken at Camp Pendleton, when Haynes was the operations officer of CT 28 and Wilkins was his assistant. *(Haynes collection)*

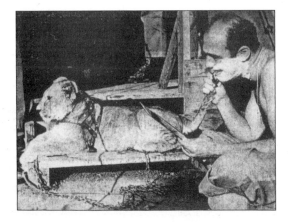

Sgt. Manfredi uses Roscoe's tail as a shaving brush. When the Team returned to Tarawa after Iwo Jima, Roscoe welcomed the sergeant back from war by licking his bald head! *(Coster collection)*

Three of CT 28's staff: Capt. Haynes; Maj. Ty Cobb, communications officer; Maj. Oscar Peatross, operations officer. Cacti in the background had been imported for planting on the Parker Ranch. *(Haynes collection)*

LEFT: Map of known enemy defenses on Iwo Jima as of January 1945. *(Haynes collection)*

BELOW: Marine-laden LCVPs—Higgins boats— head for Green Beach. *(USMC photograph)*

Burdened with heavy packs and equipment, Marine communicators dash for cover during the drive across the neck of Iwo Jima. (*USMC photograph*)

ABOVE: The soft black sands swallow this jeep as Marines hurriedly salvage the wheels. (*USMC photograph*)

RIGHT: Within hours, smashed equipment hindered the landing of vital supplies, as well as the evacuation of casualties. (*USMC photograph*)

The 5th Engineers clearing mines. (Note: White face cream was for protection from burning fuel the Marines thought the Japanese might use as part of their beach defenses.) (*USMC photograph*)

ABOVE: The price of the assault. Dead Marines share the black sands of Green Beach with foundering jeeps and smashed landing craft. (*USMC photograph*)

RIGHT: A CT 28 rifleman takes cover as engineers blow up a large blockhouse in front of Suribachi. (*USMC photograph*)

Japanese dead—the result of a night attack against CT 28 near Suribachi. (*USMC photograph*)

RIGHT: CT 28 Weapons Company provides covering fire with a 37mm antitank gun. The Navy managed to land seven of these guns on Green Beach within the first hour of the assault. One was destroyed as it approached the beach. (*USMC photograph*)

CT 28 Marines wielding flame-throwers attack a position near Suribachi. (*USMC photograph*)

"Butch," a Doberman pinscher war dog, guards his partner, Pfc. Rez Hester. Teams like this helped CT 28 destroy the enemy in caves and bypassed pillboxes. (*USMC photograph*)

Lt. Col. Johnson issues orders during the final assault on Suribachi. Left to right: Lt. Greeley Wells, who carried the first flag ashore; Lt. Schrier, about to lead a patrol to the summit; Col. Johnson; and Maj. Tom Pearce, XO of 2/28, who later became CO when Johnson was killed (*USMC photograph*)

BELOW: The iconic photo of the second flag raising. All the men are from E Company. Left to right: Ira Hayes, Franklin Sousley, Mike Strank, John Bradley, Rene Gagnon, and Harlon Block. Block, Strank, and Sousley were killed in action. (*AP photograph*)

ABOVE RIGHT: The first flag is raised, much to the jubilation of Marines and sailors below. The men, left to right: The Marine on the far left has never been identified. Just to his right, kneeling, barely visible, and talking on the radio to Lt. Col. Johnson, is Harold Schrier, patrol leader; Ray Jacobs is the radioman; Hank Hansen, with cap, holds the flagpole; Boots Thomas is seated at the base; John Bradley has both hands on the pole, his helmet is just above Thomas's; Jim Michaels stands guard with carbine in the foreground; Phil Ward is seated behind Michaels. Chuck Lindberg is standing directly behind Michaels. (*USMC photograph by Lou Lowery*)

LEFT: About 2 p.m., February 23, the first flag is lowered as the larger flag is planted. (*USMC photograph*)

RIGHT: On board the flagship *Eldorado*, Lt. Gen. Holland M. Smith congratulates Sgt. Ernest L. "Boots" Thomas, one of the raisers of the first flag. Thomas was killed later in the battle. (*USMC photograph*)

ABOVE: A Japanese gun at the base of Suribachi destroyed by naval bombardment. A CT 28 Marine stands watch. Positions like this were frequently connected by tunnels to other defenses on and around Suribachi. (*USMC photograph*)

The master defensive strategist and commander of all Japanese forces on Iwo Jima, Lt. Gen. Tadamichi Kuribayashi. (*Dept. of Defense photograph*)

LEFT: Schematic drawing of Hill 362A, prepared by Navy Seabees. The north face is in the foreground. The drawing shows gun emplacements and the tunnel system (dotted lines). (*U.S. Navy diagram*)

ABOVE: The cross marking the grave of Gove Wilkins, Fred's close friend, in the 5th Division Cemetery. (*Haynes collection*)

Capt. Fred Haynes takes a smoke break during his darkest day on Iwo Jima, March 2. (*Haynes collection*)

The bodies of three Marines killed during an assault on a Japanese gun emplacement. An enemy round struck one of the Marine's flamethrower, killing all three instantly. *(USMC photograph)*

RIGHT: A squad leader takes cover as rocket fire is laid on Nishi Ridge, March 3. *(USMC photograph)*

BELOW: A Sherman tank blasts enemy positions on Nishi Ridge. *(USMC photograph)*

A coastal defense gun casemate as it appears today on Nishi Ridge. (*Haynes collection*)

ABOVE: Marines gather around *Dinah Might*, the first B-29 to make an emergency landing on Iwo Jima. (*USMC photograph*)

LEFT: Mopping up enemy positions in the badlands of northern Iwo Jima. (*USMC photograph*)

ABOVE: Marines dig in amid the sandstone outcroppings that often hid Japanese snipers. (*USMC photograph*)

BELOW: Two sketches of Marines helping the wounded by Pfc. John Lyttle, drawn on Iwo Jima. (*Courtesy Lyttle collection*)

Blasting an enemy cave in Bloody Gorge. (*USMC photograph*)

Tank dozers were indispensable in cutting roads for gun and flame tanks in Bloody Gorge. (*USMC photograph*)

ABOVE: A flamethower-bearing Marine clears out a cave in the gorge under cover of riflemen. (*USMC photograph*)

LEFT: John Henry Harrison, artilleryman, who became an infantry replacement, with the sword and pistol he took from a Japanese officer who attempted to attack Harrison in the gorge. (*USMC photograph*)

Interrogation of Japanese POW Matsushita. Left to right: Lt. John Lloyd, language officer; Capt. Arthur Neubert, CT 28 intelligence officer; Lt. John McLean, language officer; the POW; Lt. Rich White, language officer. The Marine in background is unidentified. Humane treatment yields valuable information. *(Coster collection)*

LEFT: Capt. "Candy" Johnson (after the war) and his helmet. The bullet miraculously missed his scalp. Sgt. Taizo Sakai, Kuribayashi's chief code clerk, surrendered to Johnson at about the time the bullet struck. *(Johnson collection)*

Wes Plummer mans a .30 caliber heavy machine gun against Suribachi. *(USMC photograph)*

ABOVE: The last banzai. Predawn, March 26. About three hundred Japanese attacked Army Air Force and Marine units near Airfield No. 2. 1st Lt. Martin of the Pioneers, who served with CT 28, was killed leading the counterattack. He was given a Medal of Honor posthumously. (*USMC photograph*)

ABOVE LEFT: Late afternoon, March 25. Having cleared the last pocket in the gorge, Brig. Gen. Leo Hermle gathered the leaders of 3/28 for a victory photo op. Left to right: Capt. Bob Spangler, 3/28 operations officer; Capt. Misty Rice, CO, I Co.; Maj. Tolson Smoak, CO, 3/28; Gen. Hermle; Col. Harry Liversedge, CO, CT 28; Lt. Fiorenzo Lopardo, CO, H Co.; Maj. Oscar Peatross, operations officer, CT 28; 1st Lt. Parker Stortz, XO, G Company. (*USMC photograph*)

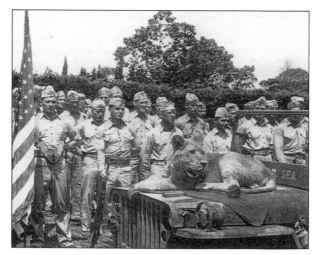

RIGHT: CT 28 parade at Camp Tarawa. Note: Roscoe on hood of jeep. His howls could drown out the band! (*USMC photograph*)

The Japanese on Iwo Jima seemed to relish shooting severely wounded Marines who lay on open ground and posed them no threat; they killed as many medical corpsmen as possible, knowing of their capacity to give aid to the wounded. At one point in the battle, three Japanese attempted to surrender to an H Company infantry squad. When the Marines stood up to take the surrender, the enemy soldier in the middle went down on all fours and became a human machine-gun tripod—a Nambu light machine gun had been strapped to his back, and one of his comrades fired off half a belt of ammunition, wounding several of the Marines before he was killed, along with his two comrades. Booby-trapped corpses, both Marine and Japanese, were found everywhere on the island, but especially in caves, where a good number of Marine souvenir hunters were killed or wounded.

Of course, these infractions of the rules of war seem almost mild when compared with atrocities the Japanese committed in China and the Philippines, where there was a large civilian population. In China, the Japanese conducted biological warfare experiments on civilians with horrific results; in Hong Kong, Japanese servicemen bayoneted hospital patients, raped nurses on top of corpses, and raped nuns in the streets in an orgy of depravity. A Japanese soldier on Guadalcanal reported dispassionately in his diary that "two [American] prisoners were dissected while still alive by M. O. Yamaji and their livers taken out. For the first time I saw the internal organs of a human being. It was very informative."[11]

Some historians have pointed out that being a prison guard was considered the worst duty in the army, and many guards were former petty criminals or low-grade mental defectives. These men, in turn, were supervised by bitter, passed-over officers, more interested in whoring and drinking than in soldiering. Hence the abominable record of the Japanese in treating POWs. There is a shard of truth in this notion, yet there are more compelling reasons for what historians Meirion and Susie Harries call "the number and hideous variety of the crimes [that defy] even the most twisted imagination: murder on a scale amounting to genocide; rapes beyond counting; vivisection; cannibalism; torture; American prisoners taken in the Philippines were allowed to drown in excrement in the 'hell' ships taking them back to Japan for use as forced labor."[12]

Atrocities were also committed in large numbers by well-trained, frontline units. In fact, training in the Imperial Japanese Army was suffused with a strong measure of brutality. Troops were encouraged to inflict pain and humiliation on prisoners and civilians of the "inferior" races.

Japanese military training instilled absolute adherence to orders given by all superiors, even if those orders were unequivocally immoral and did nothing whatsoever to forward a given mission's success. There was no recognized moral authority beyond the orders themselves. Soldiers were taught to believe that all orders were in effect issued directly by the emperor through his officers. Thus, many Japanese soldiers felt that atrocities were institutionally sanctioned. With very few exceptions, Japanese servicemen did what they were told, no matter how hideous or inhumane.

Why? Again, Meirion and Susie Harries offer trenchant insight. Military conditioning reinforced a basic underpinning of Japanese society: "The Japanese [culture] did of course distinguish between 'right' and 'wrong' along the same lines as Western cultures; but the distinction could be overridden according to the demands of a particular situation. 'Right' tended to be what was deemed right by the group in a particular situation. In this context, individual conscience was a meaningless concept."[13]

As the war dragged on and defeat followed defeat, enormous psychological pressures allowed even the most reluctant, morally sensitive soldiers to commit acts of the utmost savagery and cruelty. In Japan, the war was presented in a variety of media—all controlled by the militarist clique in Tokyo—as a great moral crusade against decadent and imperialistic Western powers bent on world domination. "The roots of Japan's self-destructive conflict with the West go far back into the country's past," writes the British military historian John Keegan,

> and centre above all on its ruling caste's fear that "Western-isation" . . . would disrupt the careful social structure on which the country's internal order rested. At the beginning of the seventeenth century, therefore, they closed their coasts to the outside world and succeeded in keeping them shut until the appearance of Western seamen who commanded a new technology, the steamship, in the middle of the nineteenth century forced them to reconsider their . . . decision. In one of the most radical changes of national policy recorded in history, the Japanese then accepted that, if Japan were to remain Japanese, it must join the modern world, but on terms which guaranteed that the processes of modernisation were retained in Japanese hands. The technology of the Western world would be bought; but the Japanese would not sell themselves or their society to the West in the course of acquiring it.[14]

The Japanese saw themselves as a divinely inspired people, the purest race on earth. The war was thus sanctioned as an exercise in worldly purification, and the killing of prisoners only ushered the purification process along. John Dower, an American historian of Japanese and American cultural attitudes toward "the other" in the Pacific War, frames the issue in this way:

> The Japanese were indoctrinated to see the conflict in Asia and the Pacific as an act which could purify the self, the nation, Asia, and ultimately the whole world. All Japanese were to participate in this process, not merely those on the battlefield; but the purest accomplishments, of course, entailed the greatest sacrifices, culminating in the supreme sacrifice of life itself. For the Japanese during World War Two, that is, the "sacrifices" of war were portrayed as truly sacerdotal.[15]

In the new world order, the Japanese nation would be venerated for putting the races in their proper place. In all forms of Japanese media, the Americans were depicted as degenerate materialists and exploitative beasts. A favorite caricature portrayed Americans as devils who could never be trusted; thus, they must be destroyed.

In the wake of the defeat on Saipan and the beginning of the bombing of Japanese cities in massive raids by B-29 bombers in late 1944, the Japanese government could no longer hide the fact that the war was going terribly wrong, and in desperation, the level of propaganda skyrocketed. A major aim of the war cabinet in Tokyo became inciting greater hatred toward the Americans among the populace. By January 1945, Dower points out, the cabinet "adopted a further policy of informing the people of Japan that there were only two choices before them: to be victorious, or perish."[16]

An article in a popular Japanese magazine, entitled "Naming the Western Barbarians," was accompanied by a drawing of an ogre with a necklace of skulls removing a smiling mask of FDR. The article read in part: "It has gradually become clear that the American enemy, driven by its ambition to conquer the world, is coming to attack us, and as the breath and body odor of the beast approach, it may be of some use if we draw the demon's features here. . . . Since the barbaric tribe of Americans are devils in human skin who come from the West, we should call them *Saibanki*, or Western Barbarian Demons [a pun on *Saipanki*, demons from Saipan]."[17]

The U.S. Marines, according to Japanese propagandists, were infected with a particularly virulent strain of decadence. They had to kill their own parents to prove they were tough enough to join the Corps. In addition, Marines had raped and pillaged throughout Asia and the Pacific.

Now, it must be said, American propagandists on the home front were no slouches in producing grotesque caricatures of the Japanese people and their soldiers as slant-eyed monkeys and rodents who must be exterminated. Such propaganda clearly intensified the hatred of the combatants toward each other in their life-and-death struggles on Saipan, Iwo, and Okinawa, among other battles.

One of the finest memoirs to come out of the Pacific War is *With the Old Breed: At Peleliu and Okinawa* by Marine corporal E. B. Sledge, a classic of war literature for its haunting and candid observations of frontline combat against the Japanese. Sledge was appalled by the sheer cruelty and violence of combat, and he wrote of it with intense honesty and feeling. "The War," he writes, "resulted in savage, ferocious fighting with no holds barred. This was not the dispassionate killing seen on other fronts or in other wars. This was a brutish, primitive hatred, as characteristic of the horror in the war in the Pacific as the palm trees and the islands."[18]

Sledge tells of Marine POWs being found bound and shot in the back of the head. One Marine in Sledge's own unit, the 5th Marine Regiment, used his K-bar knife to pull gold teeth from a wounded Japanese; when the enemy soldier tried to resist, the Marine cut his throat. Sledge admits that both sides defiled the corpses of their enemy. He himself stumbled upon a Marine whose head had been placed on his lap, with his penis stuck inside his mouth. According to Sledge, the collection of Japanese skulls by Marines became so popular on Okinawa that the practice had to be officially forbidden.

Japanese behavior in combat across the breadth of the Pacific often seemed bizarre beyond measure. "There he was," reported Cpl. Donald S. Griffin, a veteran of the fighting on Guam, about an enemy officer, "jumping up and down, cutting this way and that. Maybe he was exhorting his men, but it's my guess he was going through some sort of ritualistic dance. Or maybe he was trying to impress us with his bravery by doing a dance while exposed to the enemy."[19]

A group of shirtless Japanese emerged from a large gun emplacement on Guam and paraded single file directly in front of a Marine firing line and continued to do so in plain sight until they were all shot and killed. On Saipan, the Japanese attempted an assault on Marine positions using children as shields. And they forced other children to run through cane fields on that island to draw American fire.

It was apparent to a growing body of Japanese officers by late 1944 that Japan could not win the war and that further fighting would only result in useless destruction and, ultimately, national disaster. Why then, did the Japanese continue to wage a futile war? A partial answer lies deep in the history of Japan itself. The small clans of peoples from the Asian mainland who migrated around the first century A.D. to the home islands of Japan were warrior tribes; Korean writings from as early as the fourth century attest to the toughness and ferocity of the Japanese fighting man. From the twelfth century through the middle of the eighteenth century, Japan was controlled by a succession of powerful military families. The heads of these successive dynasties, called shoguns, are widely celebrated even today in popular literature and film.

By the mid-1500s, this agrarian island country had been divided into about 260 fiefdoms, each ruled by a single shogun with his own army of samurai—a dedicated class of warrior poets with an ethic of absolute loyalty, discipline, supreme battlefield courage, and unhesitating sacrifice. It was the samurai class that had ousted the Mongol invaders in the thirteenth century, and they played a pivotal role in the development and transmission of Japanese spirituality and national identity in the following centuries.

The formidable army that fought the Americans with such ferocity on Guadalcanal, Tarawa, and Iwo Jima had been built at breakneck speed after the Meiji Restoration of 1868 along Western, and more particularly Prussian, lines, but it drew its strength from Japan's feudal past and from the samurai ethic known to the world as Bushido, or the "way of the warrior." As Meirion and Susie Harries write in their history of the Imperial Army,

> In many ways the soldiers of the sun were in the twentieth century but not of it. . . . In the West feudal attitudes toward honor, death, and the meaning of the soldier's life had vanished centuries before. But the men who created the Imperial Army had themselves been raised in the feudal tradition. They knew that the repeating rifle had made the sword obsolete and so they built an army based on the rifle unit—but they did not abandon their own heritage, the ethos that made the samurai so formida-

ble. America's enemy in the Pacific was an uneasy blend of ancient thought and modern methods, a matrix of unresolved tensions fueling the extremes of heroism and barbarity.[20]

"Uneasy blend" indeed. The great modern tragedy of Japanese history—and a key to understanding the World War II Japanese soldier's behavior—was that the honorable tradition of Bushido was co-opted and corrupted by a coterie of military extremists in the late 1920s and 1930s who mistook their own deluded dreams of Japanese hegemony over Asia and the Pacific for the divine will of history.

Extremist senior officers in both the army and navy quickly gained ascendancy over the moderates in Japanese political life and began to deftly exploit the entrenched cultural traits of deference to authority, respect for hierarchy and, even more tellingly, the abiding penchant for sublimating the desires of the individual to those of the group. By eliminating all voices of political dissent from foreign policy and manipulating a weak emperor into believing they were acting in the national interest, the Japanese high command was able to marry its own ambitions of world conquest with the emperor's will. In so doing, they gained the unquestioning loyalty and spiritual support of the Japanese people, especially the ordinary soldiers and sailors who had to fight their war.

The extremists depended upon the "way of the samurai" to fuse the military together, to motivate and to guide their men to victory. But the militarists' version of Bushido was a far cry from the honorable tradition that prevailed for many centuries before the Meiji Restoration. It was in fact a watered-down, carefully selective version of its feudal forebear, lacking its subtlety and humanity, and heavily imbued with xenophobia.

The traditional samurai, writes John Keegan,

were not mere thugs. . . . They were certainly fierce and talented warriors. . . . "Style" was central to the samurai way of life—style in clothes, armour, weapons, skill-at-arms and behaviour on the

battlefield. . . . The Japanese were a literate people and the liter-
ary culture of the samurai was highly developed. . . . The samurai . . . wished to be known both as swordsmen and poets.
Buddhism in its Zen form, that adopted by the samurai, encouraged a meditative and poetic outlook on the universe. The greatest warriors of feudal Japan were therefore also men of the mind,
the spirit and the cultivated senses.[21]

The Japanese soldiers who manned Iwo's pillboxes were utterly ig-
norant (with few exceptions) of feudal Bushido's cultivation of the
mind, its insistence on compassion and humanity in dealing with an
honorable adversary. Instead, the Japanese army's World War II–era
ethos emphasized the audacious use of force and submission to higher
authority, whether or not the orders issuing from that authority were
morally tenable.

The mid-twentieth century form of Bushido, write Meirion and
Susie Harries, "generated a range of mental attitudes that bordered
on psychopathy: a view of death as sublime and beautiful, the fall of
a cherry blossom; surrender as the ultimate dishonor, a belief whose
corollary was total contempt for the captive; reverence for the sword,
inherited directly from the samurai, which gave beheading as a punishment a special mystical significance."[22]

The Japanese fighting man in World War II was heavily indoctri-
nated to believe that he was the direct descendant of the samurai
who had repelled Kublai Khan from Japanese shores in the thirteenth century. He conceived of his army as utterly invincible, especially against the corrupt and decadent Western soldier, who
depended more on material goods and modern weapons than on what
really mattered according to contemporary Japanese military doctrine: fighting spirit.

It was the extreme focus on fighting spirit that compelled the
Imperial Japanese Army to train and to drill almost exclusively on
the tactics of the offense. Since the cult of the sword had long been
at the very center of samurai tradition, the Japanese officer in World
War II mastered this ancient weapon, and the banzai charge re-

mained a viable option to Japanese troops—even a preferred one. Indeed, there was little variance from unit to unit: Japanese training officers and commanders in the field alike stressed that the army's main weapon was "fighting spirit." "The Japanese tended to regard 'spirit' as their main strength, with almost mystical potency—an amulet, whose loss would be fatal."[23]

Moreover, the concept of "fighting spirit" played an irrational role in the highest echelon of the Japanese military in response to repeated defeat. As the Japanese historian Saburo Ienaga has argued, the top admirals and generals in Tokyo, in their arrogance and blindness, refused to lay the blame for defeat after defeat where it belonged—at their own feet. They relied on the myth of "superior fighting spirit" like a crutch, as if it were compensation for inadequate supplies, poorly armored tanks, insufficient artillery, and inept strategic leadership. In the wake of each battlefield loss, the senior leadership criticized the ordinary soldiers who fought and died for their lack of aggression in combat. They refused to look at the real problem: their own ineptitude and arrogance. As Professor Ienaga writes,

> A striking feature of the doctrine [contained in the Infantry Manual of the Imperial Japanese Army issued to World War II Japanese enlisted soldiers] is its excessive emphasis on "spirit." The literature is full of phrases about "the attack spirit," "confidence in certain victory," . . . and "sacrifice one's life to the country, absolute obedience to superiors." Primary emphasis on esprit de corps and morale . . . continued despite fundamental changes in the nature of warfare. Enormous advances in weaponry meant that victory was no longer necessarily determined by the battlefield bravery of soldiers. The military went into the Pacific War still clinging to the concept of fighting spirit as decisive in battle. The result was wanton waste of Japanese lives, particularly in combat with Allied forces whose doctrine was based on scientific rationality.[24]

By the time of the battle of Iwo Jima, only the most gullible Japanese officers could have believed that continuing to fight would lead anywhere but to national disaster. Only the incurably optimistic could have believed that the garrison on Iwo Jima would be resupplied or reinforced by air or sea after the American naval cordon around the island was established. It was common knowledge that the offensive arm of the navy—air power—had been destroyed, as had most of Japan's military and civilian transport shipping. And yet, bizarrely, despite the enormous psychological pressures these facts must have placed on the garrison on Iwo, the Japanese on the island, from General Kuribayashi on down, fought the Americans with every ounce of energy and purpose at their disposal. It was their fate to die. The vast majority accepted that fate stoically.

For all but a very few Japanese on Iwo Jima, the impending defeat of their nation offered them no option but to battle to the death. Alvin M. Josephy Jr., a Marine combat correspondent on Iwo Jima, wrote a revealing story about his experience with a small group of POWs on Guam who had been seized by the U.S. Army and Marines in the summer of 1944. He asked one of them, an officer named Nito, if he had it to do all over again, would he have opted to commit suicide rather than surrender. Nito's reply: "If you give me a knife, I will kill myself now. I will kill you, too. Then we can go to paradise together as friends." Josephy asked this small cadre of prisoners why they believed in hara-kiri. Nito "whispered with reverence, it is *bushido*." When asked to explain what "Bushido" actually meant, Nito, a well-educated officer, said in clear English:

> Please. I could argue with you all night trying to convince you that Christianity is all superstition and untrue and there was no such person as Jesus Christ. I might even force you to say you believed me. But in your heart you would not be swayed. You have been born to it and raised and educated to it. In the same way you can argue with me all night that bushido is wrong, that hara-kiri is senseless. But you cannot convince me. It is my faith and my spirit. I am Japanese. I was born and brought up Japanese. I cannot change.[25]

Virtually all Japanese who fought on Iwo Jima felt similarly. The poignant drama of Iwo Jima emerges, we think, from the tragic effect of this blindness—this detachment from reality and retreat into a vague metaphysical fatalism where the Japanese soldier imagined himself fulfilling God's plan and Japan's glory in killing as many Americans as possible before dying himself.

Thus, the Japanese soldier facing off against Combat Team 28 was in many ways a victim of forces far outside his control, so strongly had he internalized the precepts of obedience to his superiors and the grotesque, dumbed-down version of Bushido. "The Japanese Army's absolute obedience to orders," wrote one Japanese veteran of the Pacific War, "is grounded . . . upon a psychology of submission to those who have power [i.e., his officers and their ultimate superiors on the Imperial General Staff]. As soldiers, we were unable to hold the conviction . . . that you must not surrender to power when it fails to live up to your own idea of what is right."[26]

★

ONE OF THE ironies of the fighting on Iwo Jima is that in certain important ways, the Marines and the Japanese approached war along similar lines. Like the Japanese, the Corps had always emphasized "fighting spirit." It was called "esprit de corps," eloquently defined by the 28th Marines's executive officer, Lt. Col. Robert Williams, earlier. Marines were a breed apart, even within the armed forces. They were taught, and still are, in the power of belief—in their officers, their brother Marines, and their rigorous training—to get the mission accomplished no matter what the odds. The Marines, like the Japanese, had their own warrior code. As one World War II Marine officer put it,

> To the Marine, the Corps is his religion, his reason for being. He cannot be committed up to a point. For him, involvement is total. He savors the traditions of his Corps and doubts not the veracity of them. He believes implicitly that he must live up to those epics of physical and moral courage established by those

who preceded him. He believes his Corps is truly unique—that it is the most elite military organization ever devised, and he, as an integral part of that organization, must never bring disgrace or dishonor upon it.[27]

Like the Japanese, the Marines were primarily trained as shock troops. Underscoring their doctrine was a strong faith in the vital importance of fighting spirit. Most, but not all Japanese army units were trained under Spartan conditions, as we were. But there were telling differences between the adversaries on Iwo Jima. One was that the Marine Corps was not led by fanatical military or political leaders who consistently failed to provide their units with the tools of war. Much was asked of us as fighting men, but stupendous supporting logistical efforts were undertaken to make sure we had what was needed to win at Iwo Jima.

Marine esprit was buttressed by informed and open leadership—a leadership also ready to admit to errors and mistakes, and willing to correct them. And it was strengthened further by informed popular support at home. Yes, we Americans put out our share of hate propaganda against the Japanese, but the American public had a realistic understanding of what was happening to their men and women at war. The Japanese people had no such understanding, until it was too late, at which point they, like their army, retreated into a wistful fatalism— and prepared to die to the last man and woman in the expected invasion of the home islands.

While Lieutenant General Kuribayashi obviously deviated from the normal offensive doctrine in adopting a strategic defense, his order to each defender to kill ten Marines before submitting to death himself was in keeping with the bizarre fatalism that was at the heart of the Japanese war effort.

It was only the threat of the destruction of their civilization in the form of the atom bomb that finally broke Japan's commitment to fighting the Americans to the last man. The 28th Marines were in training on Hawaii for the invasion of the Japanese island of Kyushu when Tru-

man dropped the bombs on Hiroshima and Nagasaki. The invasion of Japan proper, if it had actually happened, would have been a bloodbath for Americans and Japanese alike too hideous to contemplate. When the Japanese finally surrendered in August, I think I can speak for every man in the regiment when I say that we were euphoric, as if a death sentence had been lifted.

For sixty years, Americans have been debating the decision to drop the bomb. Some historians believe the Japanese were on the verge of surrender and that cordoning off Japan from the sea, cutting off her shipping, would have done the trick eventually. They are entitled to their opinion, but I think they have grievously underestimated the horrific momentum that was driving the governments, the people, and the armies involved in the Pacific War. That momentum cannot be recaptured sixty years later through careful study of documents and books, but in our view, it played a pivotal role in the decision making on both sides.

I am quite sure we will be debating the decision to drop the bomb for another sixty years, and probably longer than that, which is fine and good. Still, I don't know a single survivor of Iwo Jima, and certainly no one in Combat Team 28, who does not believe Truman made the correct decision in using the bomb. It simply had to be done. It was the only responsible decision to make, given the realities—emotional and moral as well as strategic—that prevailed at the time. One of the most prominent of those realities was the savagery of the Battle of Iwo Jima. Another key factor was the casualty projections for the invasion of the home islands, which varied a bit over time, but in every case were exceedingly, frighteningly high.

It's a little known but very significant fact that Col. Paul Tibbets, who dropped the first bomb on Hiroshima, rendezvoused directly above the island of Iwo Jima with two other B-29s that were to accompany him on his world-changing flight. One of these escort Superforts carried scientific measuring equipment; the other photographic specialists. On Iwo Jima's main airfield, a bomb transfer pit was dug as a contingency measure in the event that Tibbets's plane had to make an emergency landing *en route. If that had happened, the B-29 taking off for Hiroshima would have taken off from Iwo Jima.*

Of course, that didn't happen. But what did happen suggests to both James and to me that Iwo Jima stands at the crossroads between the timeless combat waged by strong men on foot with rifles on the one hand, and the ambiguities of warfare in the atomic age on the other.

7

BREAKING THROUGH THE MAIN BELT:
THE BATTLE FOR HILL 362A
AND NISHI RIDGE

---

n retrospect, the survivors of CT 28 would look at the five days between the fall of Suribachi and their entry into the terrible fighting in the north as a welcome period of rest and refitting. This was the only time in the campaign when the Team's assault units were not fully engaged in protracted combat against entrenched enemy positions. Many of the leathernecks in CT 28 allowed themselves the luxury of thinking the worst of their fight on Iwo was already part of history. After all, they had raised the flag on Mount Suribachi following four days of bitter fighting. The Battle of Gettysburg had been a three-day engagement, as had the first true Marine amphibious assault of World War II: the battle for Tarawa.

By the time of the flag raising, many Marines in the assault units had seen more close combat than the average professional soldier or Marine sees in a decade of service or longer. More than one enlisted man in CT 28 hoped that the rest of the battle would be carried to its conclusion by the seven other teams already on the line in the north.

Pfc. Eugene Hubbard of the 2nd Battalion, for example, recalled fifty years after the battle that "we figured when Mount Suribachi was done, then we were all done. We were in for one hell of a surprise!"[1]

CT 28 spent the days between February 25 and March 1 licking wounds, replenishing depleted frontline units with men from the replacement drafts, and in mopping-up operations. "Mopping up" is something of a misleading term, for several CT 28 units were engaged in lethal duty: each day, men were lost to mines or sniper fire, and there were fierce encounters with small groups of enemy fighters around Suribachi.

Rations, drinking water, and ammunition were readily available to the leathernecks at this point. The shore party Marines, engineers, and Seabees had forged some order on the beach, but bodies of Marines and Japanese still littered the area. Thousands of fat green flies buzzed around the corpses.

From atop Mount Suribachi, men from the 28th Marines gazed down upon virtually the entire island. Everywhere there were signs of battle. As Harold Keller of E Company watched the 4th Marine Division attack the elite Japanese 145th Infantry Regiment that protected Airfield No. 2, he couldn't help but feel the pain of his brother Marines. He later said, "The Japs had all the cover, and our men got clobbered."[2]

The fighting on the 4th Division's right flank was even worse. Whole squads were wiped out within minutes of jumping off in attack. The men were attacking through a cluster of ugly terrain features—a bowl-shaped depression in the earth called the Amphitheater, the heavily fortified Hill 382, and a gnarled outcropping of rock called Turkey Knob. Collectively, these features formed the Meatgrinder, a word that still sends shudders through the 4th Division's survivors.

The mopping-up phase for CT 28 proved a veritable picnic compared to what followed: the assault into the jaws of the main defensive belt, anchored by the highest points of terrain on the western flank of the attack, Hill 362A, and Nishi Ridge. Breaking through these defenses proved more costly and more difficult than taking Suribachi.

On February 24, the day after the flag raisings on Mount Suribachi, CT 28 became VAC's reserve unit. Colonel Liversedge sent me as liaison officer to the VAC command post. I reported to Col. Edward Craig, who was the operations officer for VAC. He told me to stand by where he could get in touch if he needed to transmit anything to Colonel Liversedge. While I was in the CP, I purloined a can of pork and beans C rations and then searched for a place to spend the night.

I found a spot where a large fuel drum had been cut in half and the ends knocked out. It was in a foxhole about three feet deep. No blanket or poncho was necessary, as the earth was very warm. I dug a small hole for my can of pork and beans, hoping that it would be warmed by the soil's volcanic heat. At about midnight, a Japanese 47mm antitank gun opened up from the north. The gunners were firing indiscriminately, knowing that the southern end of the island was crowded with Marines. The rounds shot directly over me with a soul-jarring whoosh! Most of the rounds landed around the 5th Division intelligence section, which was between me and Mount Suribachi. Map boards and a jeep were pretty badly torn up; but, fortunately, no one was hurt.

The next morning started out well because the pork and beans were nicely warmed. I enjoyed a breakfast the likes of which did not occur very often on Iwo. That day, I spent some time with Colonel Craig. He showed me some of the aerial photographs of the area where we were fighting, as well as where the 4th Division was attacking. We discussed the problem of terrain "compartments"—the military term for areas bounded by two ridgelines. Iwo Jima was chock-full of such compartments of all shapes and sizes. Most were formed by ridgelines running more or less east to west from the Motoyama plateau, the center of the island.

In our zone, the compartments, for the most part, lay at right angles to the direction of our attack. Colonel Craig thought that this was the most treacherous terrain he had seen in the Pacific, because the enemy had strongly fortified the major ridgelines with large-caliber weapons in concrete, steel-reinforced emplacements and caves. In addition, there were hundreds of well-camouflaged spider holes and machine-gun nests trained on the approaches to these ridgeline defenses.

Hill 362A, the highest point on the western flank of the defensive belt, and Nishi Ridge, three hundred yards to the northwest, formed the southern and northern boundaries of the deadliest of the many compartments we faced in the battle.

After I returned to the CT 28 command post, Colonel Williams, Major Peatross, and I made our way to the top of Suribachi. We carefully inspected the terrain to the north over which we would have to fight. The view from Suribachi was good, although we were at that point unable to glean how incredibly difficult the terrain would be to traverse, given the depth and soundness of the Japanese defensive system in the zone.

We understood that the attack north by the 26th and 27th Marines from February 25 to 27 had been very productive until they came up against the southern approaches to Hill 362A. The Japanese could see the entire western half of the island from atop 362A. They also retained ample artillery and mortars well north of this compartment. This meant the defenders could call in and observe artillery and mortar fire wherever we attempted to attack. We had no idea of the extent to which the Japanese defenses on the south side of 362A were connected by tunnels to fighting positions in the sheer eighty-foot-high cliff that formed the northern face of the hill.

The fight to take the hill, Nishi Ridge, and the three hundred yards between the two, cost the 28th Marine Regiment alone (not counting the specialized units attached to the 28th Marines as part of the Combat Team) an average of 236 casualties per day in three days of fighting.

The ridgeline that Hill 362A crowned radiated from the Motoyama plateau to the cliffs along the west coast. The southern slope of 362A was studded with guns, including antiaircraft weapons used by the Japanese as direct-fire infantry weapons. There were also mutually reinforcing pillboxes and many spider holes for individual riflemen.

Directly below 362A's north side was an ingeniously fortified ravine with steep walls, running parallel to the north face of the hill. The ravine was cut with an antitank ditch that ran perpendicular to the north face of the hill. Covering this draw was a large gun emplacement on the east end and a considerable number of caves and spider holes (see the drawing in the photo insert). North of the ravine, about 250 yards ahead, stood Nishi Ridge.

Inside Hill 362A, the Japanese had enlarged natural caves and prepared many interconnected firing positions on the sheer north face. The hill itself contained four separate tunnel systems. One of these stretched a thousand yards long and had seven entrances. Other tunnels connected the caves on the north face to ammunition and supply chambers inside the hill. Nishi Ridge also contained an elaborate defensive network. Japanese infantrymen embedded in and around the ridge's approaches could easily switch firing positions once they were about to be overrun by advancing leathernecks.

Thus, Marines attempting to strike across the ravine between 362A and Nishi would find themselves under torrents of machine-gun, rifle, and mortar fire from every direction. As a defensive system, the entire complex was an inspired piece of work. CT 28's only substantial "cover" during the assault itself would be whatever suppressive fire could be brought to bear by supporting weapons.

The presence of so much Japanese weaponry in so confined a space meant that ground reconnaissance beyond the front line was impossible. The only way to locate enemy strong points was to move forward, draw fire, and then destroy the unmasked enemy positions.

★

THE BATTLE FOR 362A commenced on February 27, when Col. Thomas A. Wornham's leathernecks, Combat Team 27, made its first assault against the guns on the southern slope. The objective for the day was to gain the crest of 362A. The bombardment of the southern slope of 362A was so powerful and sustained that it seemed the entire hill might collapse and fall below the ridgeline. Smoke and dust from the high-explosive shells billowed out, engulfing the entire southern slope in haze.

Combat Team 27 struggled mightily to take the rolling terrain in two days of brutal fighting, with three battalions fighting abreast, but Wornham's Marines were stuck on the southern slope. The Japanese held the crest, but the 27th's repeated attacks and the massive artillery and naval gunfire barrages had succeeded in knocking out many of the pillboxes and other heavy fortifications. Perhaps eight hundred Japanese remained firmly embedded inside the hill complex. Colonel Liversedge received orders that night to relieve the 27th Marines early the next morning and continue the attack at 0830 hours. On March 1 at 0630 CT 28 moved through Wornham's team under cover of a thunderous bombardment and began their attack on 362A.

Not long before the 28th's attack commenced, Lieutenant Colonel Johnson spotted a badly limping Keith Wells from the 3rd Platoon of E Company and chewed him out for returning to the fray too soon. He ordered Wells to the rear for medical attention. Once again, Sgt. Boots Thomas, the quiet Floridian who had earned the Navy Cross on the twenty-first, was put in charge of the platoon for the attack on 362A. Thomas had seen the action from atop Suribachi, and he had formed a good idea of what lay ahead. A Marine overheard Thomas say to a friend, "My twenty-first birthday is coming up March 10, but I'll never see it."[3] Sadly, Boots was right.

The preassault bombardment for March 1 was extended from thirty to forty-five minutes. Two battleships and a cruiser pumped several hundred large-caliber shells into the terrain around, and on, the hill. Into the clouds of dust and smoke the 28th Marines jumped off with three battalions abreast: the 1st on the right, the 2nd in the center, and the 3rd on the left.

Within three hours, the assault companies reached the crest of the hill and the ridgeline. There they were greeted with crushing defensive fire from Nishi Ridge, as well as from the enemy positions in the ravine below the hill. The drive north was stopped dead in its tracks.

There was no choice but to attempt to attack around the hill and into the ravine. The 2nd Battalion assaulted around the left side of the hill, and the 1st—including Capt. Gove Wilkins's A Company— swept in from the right flank down into the ravine. This attack quickly stalled. Scores of Marines were killed or wounded in minutes.

I was on a reconnaissance to check on routes of approach to the area at around noon the day before our attack on 362A. While I was walking back to the Combat Team command post, I happened to meet Captain Wilkins as he was moving north. He said to me, "I hope we don't go into the line on the right flank!" Gove sensed that the eastern side of our zone of action would be the most difficult. He was right. I didn't have the heart to tell him that the plan of attack called for his A Company to lead the attack on that flank.

Early in the afternoon of 1 March Wilkins's Company A moved into the ravine in front of the northern face of 362A. His mission was to neutralize the maze of cave positions on the hill's vertical northern face. His company was pinned down by mortar and machine-gun fire. Wilkins, in an attempt to break the deadlock in which his Marines found themselves, ran to the front to assess the situation and was mortally wounded. Wilkins was my best friend in the Marine Corps at that time, and when I heard of his death, I was devastated.

One of the things to remember about CT 28's experience is that hundreds of us saw our closest friends, men we had trained with for a year, killed or severely wounded. Many Marines saw their buddies blown to smithereens before their eyes. That shocking experience makes an indelible impression on your psyche. It changes you. Forever.

Gove Wilkins was later awarded the Silver Star for leading from the front on the last day of his life. The citation reads in part:

> With his company pinned down by devastating hostile fire emanating from a series of heavily fortified emplacements . . . deeply entrenched in rock-studded cliffs, Captain Wilkins fearlessly exposed himself to the shattering barrage to maintain contact among his assault platoons and . . . skillfully located strong points and personally directed powerful gunfire against the enemy, inspiring his men to hold fast. . . . Realizing the necessity for close observation, he dauntlessly penetrated Japanese-infested territory alone under a concentrated barrage of mortar and small-arms fire to single out designated targets and then, returning to the skirmish line, promptly directed his machine-gun and mortar section in delivering an assault to gain the objective. . . . Constantly in the forefront of action, he again led a daring strike against a fiercely resisting enemy . . . and was fatally struck down by a sudden hostile shell burst. Inspired by Captain Wilkins' heroism, indomitable spirit and aggressive determination, his company pushed relentlessly forward to silence a number of enemy positions.

Lieutenant Colonel Butterfield, commanding Landing Team 1/28, withdrew his battered A Company from the ravine. Now it was B Company's turn to drive down into the deadly ravine in front of the hill. It, too, was stopped cold as soon as its lead elements came within range of the enemy's guns.

Meanwhile, the 2nd Battalion on the left flank of the attack stalled, so ferocious was the resistance from the front and both flanks. Colonel Liversedge now realized that neither the 1st nor 2nd Battalions could advance into the compartment between the hill and ridge until the Team was able to get tanks and suppressive fire from other weapons—machine guns and 37mm antitank guns—onto 362A's north face. That wouldn't be an easy trick, given the volume of fire in front of the hill.

★

OVIAN VON BEHREN, in Frank Wright's 1st Platoon, B Company, recollects that, on the morning of March 1, as his platoon was moving through the 27th Marines, he saw ample evidence of the terrible fighting that had been raging there for the past two days. "I knew we were really in for it."[4] When Ovian's platoon reached 362A's crest, he came across a large crevice that looked suspiciously like a cave opening. Von Behren threw a satchel charge into the crevice. This forced eight or ten enemy soldiers into the open, running northward. Several Marines in the vicinity opened up with M1 and BAR fire, killing them as they ran.

A bit later, when Lieutenant Wright ordered his platoon to attack toward the front of the hill, Von Behren recalled that things really heated up:

> I clearly recall a large shell, probably an artillery shell, passing close to my right ear. At this point, Frank Wright went down, and at the same time, there was heavy mortar and small-arms fire all around the advanced elements of Landing Team 1/28. I was very concerned about Frank Wright, as he had been badly peppered with shrapnel. I remember waving good-bye to him on a stretcher. I wasn't at all sure the lieutenant would survive his wounds. He looked pretty badly beat up.[5]

Casualties piled up fast in the ravine below the hill, but the fire was so hot that many of the wounded could not be removed. Among those hit in A Company lucky enough to be evacuated from the killing ground was a gregarious, burly sergeant, Al Eutsey:

> A mortar shell landed to my left and a piece of shrapnel cut through my pack strap. I started to bleed pretty bad from a chest wound, and within a couple of minutes, despite the fact that we were taking a whole lot of fire, Corpsman Keith Hawkins stuffed the chest wound with gauze and then a team of stretcher bearers picked me up and off we went at a trot. Well, the Japs fired at us—they always tried to get the stretcher bearers, who had no choice but to run in the open. Anyway, I think one of the bearers got shot, because he

dropped me and ran for cover. I got dumped a couple more times before I finally ended up in a jeep, and I can remember looking out the back of that jeep and seeing Jap rounds kicking up the dust. But in the end I made it back okay.[6]

While the 1st and 2nd Battalions were attempting to knock out positions in front of the hill and in its northern cliffs, the 3rd Battalion was moving forward on the far left near the coast, methodically taking out machine-gun and mortar positions. Much of the enemy fire emanated from camouflaged cave entrances. The terrain was so rough in many places that men had to claw their way on hands and knees. Some Marines had to climb rock formations fifty and sixty feet high. Cpl. Wes Plummer, an H Company machine gunner, remembered sixty years after the battle that the volume of fire coming from the east, close to 362A and Nishi Ridge, "was just tremendously loud. There seemed to be mortar and artillery rounds and machine-gun fire landing everywhere."[7]

It was only Plummer's LT 3/28 that gained significant ground that day. It pushed forward about 350 yards amid the cliffs until it was finally stopped by fire from its right flank.

As luck would have it, during that first harrowing day of CT28's fight for 362A, Colonel Liversedge became ill with excruciating abdominal pain. Lieutenant Colonel Williams quietly took command of the situation. He had the regimental surgeon, Dr. Bill Lynn, mildly sedate the colonel and had the headquarters commandant, Jack Downer, reinforce the protection around the CO's foxhole. He also told Maj. Ty Cobb, the Team's top communications officer, to route all calls and messages intended for Liversedge directly to him (Williams) until further notice. Liversedge rallied quickly and was back in the saddle about eight hours after falling ill. Those of us close to Liversedge kept the incident secret for fear that he might be relieved, which would have been a cataclysmic blow to morale.

As night approached, the attack was halted in order to tie in the lines to protect against the usual nocturnal infiltration attempts. The cries of the wounded for help could be heard all along the front. Fire teams huddled wherever they could find cover, sometimes just a few yards from Japanese spider holes. Once darkness veiled the battlefield, we pulled our wounded back within friendly lines, along with most of the dead.

Milton Gertz, a corpsman attached to the 2nd Battalion, recalled that Japanese soldiers began to imitate wounded Marines' cries for "Corpsman! Corpsman!" and that on several occasions corpsmen took the bait, rose from their foxholes, and were immediately cut down. "We told our guys to call for us using a code word, 'Tallulah,' knowing the Japanese had troubles pronouncing the letter 'L.'"[8]

Late that night, a single Japanese soldier, whose position had been overrun, scurried right past CT 28's CP, tossing a hand grenade into a foxhole en route and wounding three men badly before he was killed by a Marine sentinel near Colonel Liversedge's foxhole.

Losses during the day's fighting soared. For example, C Company of the 1st Battalion had lost ten noncommissioned officers—a terrific blow for a unit expected to engage in sustained combat after a few hours' respite. The initial assault of C Company toward the top of the hill had been halted by machine-gun fire from the southern face of Nishi Ridge. First Lt. Karl Tanner had taken command of C Company and led it into the ravine forward of 362A. Tanner performed brilliantly from the outset as a replacement company commander. He was later killed in the badlands south of Bloody Gorge on March 9 and awarded the Silver Star.

March 1 had been a rough day for the entire Team. E Company, the unit that had raised the flags over Suribachi, suffered thirty-eight casualties. Among the dead was Harlon Block, one of the Team's many former high school football stars. Block, who hailed from Weslaco, Texas, had worked in the oilfields before joining the Corps. His crouched, muscular figure is closest to the base of the flagpole in Joe Rosenthal's photograph of the second flag raising. When the photo had been initially released, Block had been mistakenly identified as "the Count," Henry Hansen of Somerville, Massachusetts. Hansen had in fact participated in the first flag raising, not the second. Harlon's mother back in Weslaco knew well before anyone else that the Marine Corps had identified the wrong Marine at the base of the flag. She had recognized Harlon's backside as soon as she saw the image in the newspaper. Hansen had also been killed in the vicious fighting between 362A and Nishi on March 1.

Hill 362A also snuffed out Sgt. Mike Strank's life that day. Strank is still spoken of with awe whenever CT 28 veterans gather. He was leading a group of Marines across open ground in front of the hill when small-arms fire erupted, pinning them down for about four hours. Strank looked around for an escape route and then seemed to drift into a private place in his mind. "You know," Strank told Pfc. L. B. Holly, an easy-going Texan, "that's going to be a hell of an experience." When Holly asked Strank what he was talking about, Strank pointed toward a dead Marine lying a few yards away. Two minutes later, a mortar round landed in the midst of the group, wounding several Marines and killing Strank. The shell literally ripped his heart out of his chest.[9]

Today, Mike Strank lies in grave number 7179 in Arlington National Cemetery, very close to the Marine Corps Memorial depicting him and five other Americans raising the flag atop Mount Suribachi.

On the east side of the hill, another hero of the Suribachi fight, Cpl. Tony Stein of A Company, was killed in action not far from where Aaron Wilkins, his commander, had fallen. Stein had volunteered to go forward of the lines, leading a patrol of twenty men in search of snipers. He had just returned to his company earlier that day after having been wounded in the arm and neck. Only seven Marines returned from the patrol. Tony Stein was not among them. His mother received his Medal of Honor posthumously, earned for his almost superhuman actions on D-day.

Early the next morning, Landing Teams 1/28 and 2/28 were ordered forward in a coordinated assault toward Nishi Ridge. At the same time, tanks and other heavy weapons would advance into the ravine, despite its tank trap, to knock out the many Japanese guns still firing from 362A's north face. Simultaneously, Marine artillery and naval guns would blast away at Nishi. Landing Team 3/28 would continue to push along the high cliffs on the west coast, protecting 2/28's left flank.

There was no "good" day, or good time of day, on Iwo Jima. But for me, the worst of the worst was around dawn of March 2. Ty Cobb had been able to get the attack order to 1/28 and 2/28 before midnight. The phone cable to 3/28 had been cut, and the radio command channel was terribly garbled. To make matters worse, a runner with the order had not made it to 3/28's CP. But about 0500, the land line was repaired. I got Karl Konover of 3/28 on the phone and told him I would meet him halfway between CT 28's CP and 3/28's with a map overlay and a frag order, clarifying his battalion's axis of attack for March 2.

As I left our dugout, the desolation and the silence, broken only by the crack of the occasional rifle round to the north, was almost overwhelming. I felt utterly alone, and I was depressed. Wilkins was dead. Liversedge was ill. And 230 more of our Marines had been killed or wounded the day before. We had lost the equivalent of about four full rifle companies in ten days of battle. Be that as it may, 3/28 had received its order; and, to borrow again from Kipling, "The gloom of the night shall die in the morning flush of a blood red sky."

March 2 proved to be a beautiful day, sunny and warm, but the battle that raged this day was devastating for us. Except for D-day, it was the worst day of the campaign. We lost 250 men.

The attack of March 2 commenced at 0800, after twenty-five minutes of preparation fire. The critical question: Would the two battalions in direct assault of Nishi take so many casualties that the attack would fail? It was by no means obvious that CT 28 would seize the ridge without reinforcements from another combat team.

In the 1st Battalion zone on the right, the story was grim. Private Von Behren of B Company found himself behind a wall with elements of his platoon. A rifleman, a replacement next to him, kept raising his head over a rock. Von Behren told him that if he kept looking up, he was going to get hit. He raised his head one more time and took a rifle round in the middle of his forehead.

In the 2nd Battalion's zone, F Company had relieved D Company in the center. A decimated E Company was still on the left. Both companies inched forward, trying to work into the draw and across it. Casualties mounted. Then came a critical development: CT 28's weapons company, under intense fire, brought up three heavy machine guns and lent their support to F Company's attack, laying a stream of .50 caliber slugs into the Japanese positions in the north face. This dampened return fire from the rear considerably, but not quite enough to ensure the success of the Team's assault on Nishi. Tanks were needed, and fast. To get the steel machines into an effective position at the base of the hill, the leathernecks had to clear a path through broken ground, and fill in the antitank ditch.

Between 1200 and 1300, an armored bulldozer cleared the way, and several Sherman tanks pushed in for the kill. The Japanese responded aggressively, as several infantrymen made suicide runs for the tanks carrying shaped charges. A number of Japanese succeeded in attaching the charges to the hulls of the tanks before being shot by covering infantry. The heavy wooden planks the tank crews had attached to the sides of their machines absorbed the blasts, and the tanks kept up their fire. The Japanese fighting positions on the north face of 362A were now the object of concentrated and effective fire from both 75mm shells and napalm, as well as the three .50-caliber machine guns.

The flame tanks quickly reduced enemy fire from the positions in and around the north face of 362A. The Japanese had no choice but to retreat deep into their tunnel networks to escape being incinerated. At the same time, our engineers were blowing up the tunnel openings on the south slope. Many of those enemy soldiers who sought refuge inside 362A never again saw the light of day.

As the tanks brought their fire to bear, Art Naylor's F Company rushed at breakneck speed across the compartment toward Nishi. His Marines reached the base of Nishi Ridge within a couple of minutes and engaged in a vicious firefight with the Japanese, while other units surged across the main compartment. We could feel the momentum of the fight begin to turn our way. We were cracking through the main defensive belt, but paying a ghastly price.

In retrospect, the terrain around 362A and Nishi was the worst that I experienced in three wars. The fighting was intensely close. Small sandstone buttes were scattered inside the compartment, providing excellent cover for snipers. Artillery, naval gunfire, and air support were available. But their use was often tightly restricted because the combat was at such close quarters.

On the afternoon of March 2, E Company charged all the way to the base of Nishi Ridge, at which point, as the regimental after action report has it, "All hell broke loose and the company suffered heavy casualties from fire coming from the cliff line on the north side of Hill 362 [Nishi], and a blockhouse on the flat ground in front of and to the east of 362."[10]

At 1530, the 1st Battalion units near the base of Nishi Ridge repulsed a counterattack in which more than 140 Japanese soldiers were killed or wounded. By 1700, only a few diehard Japanese were left in the area around 362A, and the Marines were in control of the crest of Nishi Ridge, but not its reverse slope. Nine hours after the attack of March 2 had begun, Hill 362A and most of Nishi Ridge were in CT 28's hands. The Marines had cracked the backbone of the main defensive belt in the western sector of the island, but there was still plenty of fight left in the enemy.

As the battle progressed, it became exceedingly difficult to stay focused on the dangers that lurked around every butte, hill, or ridge.

Sgt. Francis W. Cockrel, a combat correspondent with Combat Team 28, offered this revealing observation about the brutal rhythm of combat on Iwo Jima:

> I had wondered what effect it would have to see men hit, men dying, and men dead. It's no good, but it's impersonal. You see with the eye only, realize with the mind only; your emotions turn off. No human mental, nervous, and emotional structure could stand the impact of such feelings, I suppose, and so some automatic switch turns them off. It's bad, and you realize it, but you can go on with your work. . . . I had wondered what it would be like to be on the front, of course. It's hard to explain, I'm afraid, for it's difficult to imagine battle without thinking of heroics and dramatics, of dashing figures and climactic spectacles. It's even difficult for me to do now, when I have seen that it's not like that. It's like work. It is work. There are periods of urgency, certainly, demanding the right decision, made instantly, and split-second timing and desperate effort; and there are intervals when the tension is not at its peak, of course; but these are mainly parts of a whole, and the whole is no more or less than dangerous drudgery—mean, exhausting work at which men get shot and blown apart. And the only feelings evident are those of tiredness and anger, and, when a mission has been handled with a minimum of loss, grim satisfaction.[11]

Among those killed on March 2 was Lt. Col. Chandler Johnson, commander of LT 2/28. He met his end at around 1400. There have long been conflicting reports as to how Johnson was killed. Some claim he was hit by a short American artillery round. Others say it was a Japanese mortar shell. Greeley Wells, who was Johnson's adjutant, believes that Johnson was talking with F Company commander Art Naylor about the terrain and how to direct Naylor's company toward Nishi. After concluding his conference with Naylor, he headed toward the CP of E Company, against Naylor's advice. The captain had told him it was too hot in the area for him to approach. Johnson brushed off the advice and began walking away from Naylor, at which point, Naylor told Wells, the colonel stepped on an antitank mine or a booby-trapped American bomb.

In any case, no one ever disputed that Johnson was a real inspiration to his men. His fiery temper may have scared a few people out of their wits, but he was a superb leader in combat. He certainly knew how to get the best from his people. In his twelve-day campaign on Iwo Jima, Landing Team 2/28 had performed brilliantly.

Richard Wheeler remembered his battalion commander with abiding respect and admiration:

> When he was in a good mood he had a mellow, fatherly look, but when he was angry—which was often—he came closer to resembling a bulldog. He was a rigid disciplinarian. . . . But on Iwo he quickly began to earn our esteem. He strode about unflinchingly, wearing nothing on his head but a fatigue cap and carrying no gear except a .45 caliber pistol that was thrust deep into his right hip pocket. When he stopped to consult with one of his subordinates he would often stand erect, gesturing and pointing authoritatively and making no effort to keep the enemy from learning he was a senior officer.[12]

Cpl. William W. Byrd spoke for hundreds of Marines in the 2nd Battalion when he wrote, "One of my saddest memories came on about the tenth or eleventh day of the fighting. Colonel Chandler Johnson was very popular and very well liked by his troops. When we lost him, we seemed to lose part of ourselves. . . . He was a Marine's Marine. He was a hands-on type of officer. He gave everything he had when it counted most."[13]

One of the Marines in the 1st Battalion who survived the March 2 fighting unscathed was Pvt. Robert E. Allen of Thomasville, Georgia. In the sixty-plus years since the battle, Allen has always felt that a guardian angel saved him from destruction on Iwo Jima on this dark day. Death was inches away from him time and time again. Allen served in B Company, as part of a machine-gun crew. His unit had set up near the crest of 362A, pumping lead across the compartment into Nishi Ridge. Three times, Allen made one-hundred-yard dashes toward the rear to replenish his gun's ammo supply. He was zeroed in on by a Japanese mortar crew on his first trip. Several rounds landed just behind him as he ran in a low crouch.

On his second trip, a mortar round exploded just a few feet from him. The blast threw him hard against the ground. When he got back to his weapon, he discovered shrapnel had cut one of the machine-gun belts he was hauling. On his third run, he was again bracketed by enemy fire, and two Marine sergeants beckoned for him to jump into their shell hole. An instant after he did, a mortar shell exploded right in the hole, saturating Allen with the blood and flesh of his two comrades. Both Marines were killed instantly.

Later in the day, B Company advanced in assault toward Nishi Ridge. Suddenly, automatic weapons fire erupted from several directions. Allen tells the rest of the story in his *First Battalion of the 28th Marines on Iwo Jima*:

> Someone yelled "look out!" and immediately Private Allen noticed spitting sand to his left, moving in his direction. He dropped to the ground and rolled into a slight depression to his right. Instantly, he felt the . . . impact of bullets. In a state of panic and shock, he waited for the onset of pain and he moved his body parts to determine the extent of his injuries. Again, Private Allen heard the crackling of machine gun fire nearby and felt the jar of penetrating bullets on his upper back. Still, pain and the feeling of warm, oozing blood were absent. . . . Lying very still for a time, Allen sought to enlarge his refuge. Trying to remove his entrenching tool, he drew hostile fire from several directions. Abandoning this effort, he slowly deepened his shelter by scooping the loose volcanic sand with his hands. He worked his feet slowly like a female turtle digging a hole in which to lay her clutch of eggs. After a time, his exhausted body rested two to three feet below the surrounding terrain.[14]

As it happened, another Marine came under fire as he ran close to Allen, and he dove on top of him. When the Marine checked Allen for wounds, he discovered that two Japanese rounds had penetrated his pack and another had glanced off his entrenching tool. Two grenades in the pack were safe and ready for use. Allen would see another night—and plenty more combat—before departing the island.

Another young Marine from the 1st Battalion lacked Private Allen's luck. Two months after the guns had fallen silent on Iwo Jima, Pfc. Edward Gengler's parents received a poignant letter from Sgt. John F. Morrill concerning the death of their son on the afternoon of March 2. Ed had been killed while toting ammunition to his unit:

Dear Mr. and Mrs. Gengler,

I received your very nice letter and will try to relieve your minds about Edward's personal effects as much as I can. Also I will try and tell you how he met his death. I'm not very good at things like this, especially writing to the parents of one of my best friends.

The accident happened not more than 30 feet from me so I think I can tell you really what happened without going to anyone else to ask. On March 2nd around 3 or 4 o'clock p.m. there were several men carrying ammunition from our ammo dump to the front lines and Edward was one of these men. They had made several trips already and had started back up to the front again when a Jap mortar shell hit in the dump and exploded. Edward and another one of his buddies were killed instantly. Neither of the men suffered. Edward and his buddy were taken back to the 5th Division cemetery where they lay at rest now.

All of his personal effects are being sent home to you, but first they have to go to Headquarters Marine Corps, so in time you'll receive Edward's things, so please don't worry. Hoping this letter will help in some way to relieve your minds, and I regret what happened to your late son, I remain

Sincerely yours,
Sgt. John F. Morrill[15]

Late on the night of March 2, while most of the assault units were dug in around the base of Nishi Ridge, about fifty Japanese crept out of their tunnels and spiderholes and launched a cutting-in attack. A vicious melee ensued, where pistols, rocks, combat knives, and grenades proved more useful than rifles or machine guns. Virtually all the Japanese were killed within an hour, leading General Kuribayashi to issue this directive to his officers the next day: "The lookout of American forces has become very strict and it is difficult to pass through their guarded line. Don't overestimate the value of cutting-in attacks."[16]

Just before dawn on March 3, Cpl. William Byrd heard the unmistakable sounds of feet scurrying in his direction. In a couple of seconds, just as an illumination flare faded out, Byrd and a buddy were fighting for their lives. Two enemy soldiers had jumped them from behind. One of the Japanese had a pistol and the other a rifle with fixed bayonet:

> It seemed like the struggle lasted an eternity. I had one of them in a vice-like grip around the neck. I remember how he smelled. He probably didn't think I smelled very good either. My buddy . . . was cut on his hand and arm, but he was still fighting. I was hit with a rifle butt under my left eye. It was the hardest blow I ever received in my life. I still have the scar. I vaguely remember another Marine coming to help. One of the Japanese was stabbed to death, the other was shot. I remember blood running into my mouth. I was so weak, I felt lifeless. I was carried to a medical tent where they put stitches in my face. I felt guilty lying there. About 20 minutes later, I slipped out, found my rifle and helmet, and left to rejoin my company.[17]

By the time the 28th Marines were breaking through the main belt around Hill 362A, Iwo Jima had become a national fixation. Newspapers and radio broadcasts carried hundreds of stories of Marine bravery and loss back to the folks at home. Ed Gengler's parents were Wisconsin dairy farmers who had immigrated to the United States from Poland. They were highly patriotic Americans. Ed's father was by no means a wealthy man, but he had bought more war bonds than many others in their town who were far better off than he. With two sons in the Marine Corps, he felt obliged to support his boys, and his adopted country, in the big fight.

Karl Gengler fought through the Okinawa campaign and returned home to Pound, Wisconsin. After the war concluded, there was a family meeting to decide what to do with Ed's body, which then lay in the 5th Division cemetery on Iwo Jima. Karl Gengler explained what happened in a letter to the authors in 2006:

> I was for leaving Ed's body with his buddies, but my mother wanted him home and we conceded to her wishes. Ed was killed in an ammunition dump explosion. The condition of his body was unknown to us. My mother wanted to open the casket to see her son one last time. I think she thought he would be laid out as a mortician would have done it. I kept trying to discourage her. I asked the sergeant commanding the burial detail if he had to open it if she insisted. He said "yes."
>
> When we reached the cemetery my mother was insisting we open the casket. At this point I closed my eyes, bowed my head and prayed, "God, you have to help me now." My Mom was weeping, and a small white handkerchief she held was soaked with tears. Somehow I found a way to say to her, "Mom, why don't you tie the handkerchief to the casket and send it off with Ed." She walked to the casket, tied it on one of the handlebars and walked back to me. I just said to myself, "Thank you, God."
>
> My brother Ed's grave is in the Baptist Cemetery in Pound, Wisconsin. He was a real hero.[18]

★

A VERY THIN line held the front on the night of March 2. If there was ever a time for a massive banzai charge against Combat Team 28, this was it. But again, the Japanese held to their plan, ensconced underground.

The main objective of the next day was to finish off what was left of Japanese resistance on and around Nishi Ridge, then push on to the next ridgeline, gradually swinging the attack to the northwest. Progress was painfully slow—the regiment was facing the effects of attrition.

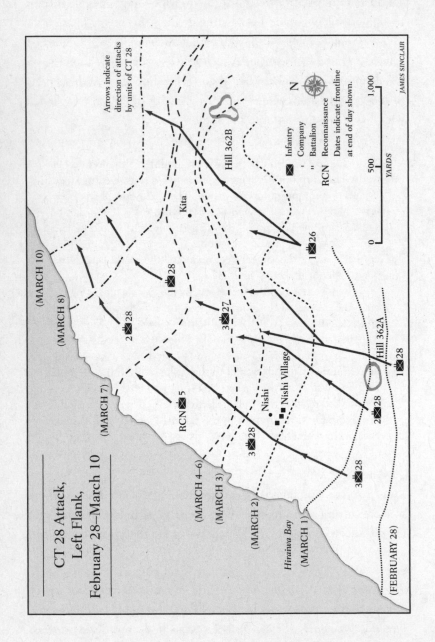

CT 28 Attack,
Left Flank,
February 28–March 10

Arrows indicate
direction of attacks
by units of CT 28

N

◻ Infantry
◼ Company
✕ Battalion
RCN Reconnaissance
Dates indicate frontline
at end of day shown.

0   500   1,000
YARDS

JAMES SINCLAIR

Hill 362B

Kita

1✕28

2✕28

3✕27

1✕26

Hill 362A

1✕28

2✕28

RCN✕5

Nishi
Nishi Village

3✕28

3✕28

(MARCH 10)

(MARCH 8)

(MARCH 7)

(MARCH 4–6)

(MARCH 3)

(MARCH 2)

(MARCH 1)

Hiraiwa Bay

(FEBRUARY 28)

Early on the morning of March 3, Colonel Williams, his runner, Wenton Yates, and I got to the top of 362A to survey the terrain ahead. Out of nowhere, a lone Japanese emerged from a cave screaming, "Banzai! Banzai!" Yates killed him with single shot from the chrome-plated revolver he carried in a shoulder holster. Where his pistol came from no one quite knew. It certainly wasn't "government issue," but it worked.

As B Company prepared to continue the attack that morning, they were hit with an enemy mortar barrage. One of Private Von Behren's comrades took a direct hit. His chest was laid open and he was begging someone to kill him. He died about half an hour later. Marine supporting artillery, recalled Von Behren, lobbed ten or more shells into the guns on the south face of Nishi Ridge, as well as bombarding the ridge's reverse slope, where the enemy mortar positions were located. "The company commander told us that we had to go across the ravine directly to our front, so we pushed off, jumping from shell hole to shell hole. We got out about a hundred yards or so and started taking small-arms fire from every direction. We felt like we were out front of everyone and alone," said Von Behren. "We were waving and hollering for the other units to leave the line of departure and join us in the assault."[19]

At this point, Von Behren himself was hit in the chest. He believes he went into shock for about fifteen minutes and then finally pulled himself together and dove into a shell hole. He felt as though half his chest had been torn out. But he calmed down when he saw the small hole with bubbles of blood oozing out as he breathed. One of the company corpsmen taped the hole and gave Von Behren a shot of morphine. "I was high as a kite, and walked back toward the CP, spitting up blood every few yards. They put me in the bed of a truck and I ended up in a long line of stretchers on the beach waiting to be evacuated."[20]

Eventually, other companies from the 1st and 2nd Battalions joined B Company, and soon Marines were swarming over the ridgeline blasting Japanese fighting positions with grenades, shaped charges, and flamethrowers. The gains for the day for CT 28 amounted to about two hundred costly yards. By 1800 on the third, Nishi Ridge had been cleansed of all but a few Japanese. They were hunkered down deep inside the ridge's tunnel network, hoping to escape that night. CT 28 platoons had cleared the ridge and moved farther north, into the ruins of Nishi village.

Another 59 Marines from the 28th Regiment had been killed in action. Total casualties for the day were recorded in the 28th Marines after action report as 240 men. From March 1 through March 3, the 1st Battalion alone suffered 389 casualties, or 100 more than it had suffered in the entire battle before its initial action against Hill 362A.

Among the dead in E Company, 2nd Battalion was Ernest "Boots" Thomas, the tough platoon sergeant who had days earlier been pulled briefly out of combat to tell the American people in his own words via radio about the conquest of Mount Suribachi. Thomas was killed on the front lines near Nishi Ridge, while on the telephone to the company CP. A single rifle round struck him in the head, killing him instantly.

★

AS THE TEAM pushed on past Nishi Ridge, Navy surgeons worked stoically at mobile hospitals close to the landing beaches, trying to save the lives of staggering numbers of casualties. Navy lieutenant E. Graham Evans, a surgeon, operated on many Marines from CT 28 and other units of the 5th Division. On the evening of March 3, he wrote a letter home to his wife: "We had 375 patients through here yesterday, to give you an idea. I've seen all the war surgery I want for a while." As for the young Marine patients, Dr. Evans reported, "They came in with wounds that make you sick to look at and all they want to do is 'Get back at those sons of bitches.' You tell them they must be evacuated and they cry."[21]

It would have been impossible for the Team to have advanced two yards let alone two hundred during the battle were it not for hundreds of acts of individual initiative by Marines, some seen by only one or two of his buddies, others seen only by the Japanese defenders. Capt. James McDermott, a Phi Beta Kappa Yale graduate, was one such individual. McDermott was the commander of G Battery of the 3rd Battalion, 13th Marines, CT 28's artillery unit. He was much admired by the Marine infantrymen, because "whenever he could," remembered his executive officer, 1st Lt. Dick Bishop, "he would take the place of a forward observer and call in artillery fire himself. I had trouble keeping him at the CP," recalled Bishop. "I'd try to get him back to the guns, and he'd say, 'I'm having too much fun up here.'"[22]

Whenever and wherever trouble loomed McDermott was there. At night, he'd call in harassing fire at irregular intervals forward of the front lines to keep infiltrators off balance. According to Pfc. Boyd Kinsey, who was himself a member of McDermott's forward observer team, "The tactic worked exceptionally well. Every morning we would find a few dead Japanese in the area where the captain had called in fire."[23]

Before CT 28 entered the hellish fight for 362A, Jim McDermott's unit was in support of the 3rd Battalion, 26th Marines. Near the end of a day of bitter fighting, that unit's right flank was pinned down and in danger of annihilation from a superior Japanese force on the verge of a counterattack. According to McDermott's Navy Cross citation,

> Captain McDermott, although surrounded by an overpowering enemy, voluntarily proceeded to the front lines of the right assault company and personally called down a brilliantly executed artillery barrage from the forward observation post to enable the line to fold back and make contact for night security. Stouthearted and indomitable in his concern for the safety of our troops, he remained steadfast in his isolated position without local security from enemy action and continued to adjust his devastating fire close to our own line, effectively thwarting an imminent Japanese counterattack and enabling our troops to re-form without casualty.

Jim McDermott was killed in the fighting near Nishi Ridge on March 3. His Navy Cross citation continues:

> Again risking his life to verify the adjustment of preparatory fire from an exposed area at dawn on 3 March, he worked skillfully and with unwavering zeal, successfully completing his perilous mission before he was fatally struck down by hostile sniper fire. By his forceful and inspiring leadership, daring initiative and great personal valor maintained in the face of overwhelming odds, Captain McDermott contributed essentially to the success of our operations against this heavily fortified stronghold and his self-sacrificing devotion to duty throughout upheld the highest traditions of the United States Naval Service. He gallantly gave his life for his country.

Sixty years after the events described in this citation, Dick Bishop, a highly successful attorney in Washington, D.C., sat with the authors of this book in his office, remembering his old commander and friend. His eyes welled up as he reflected on Jim McDermott's unflagging drive and commitment:

> If he were here with us today, he'd dismiss that Navy Cross, and say something like, "I was only doing my job." Jim was *always* doing a heck of a lot more than his job, which was only one reason we held him in such high esteem. He inspired everybody to keep going, to take the initiative. He was a class act, as a human being and as a Marine. We could not have taken Iwo Jima without men like Jim McDermott showing us the way.[24]

On March 3, two other members of CT 28 would perform feats of heroism that were extraordinary, even for Iwo Jima. Both men's actions earned them the Medal of Honor. One, Jack "Arkie" Williams, was a Navy corpsman. "I don't care how damn much fire there was, they came running," remembered H Company's Pfc. Clay Coble as he described these angels of mercy on the battlefield.[25]

Pharmacist's Mate 3rd Class Williams of H Company, from the

Ozark Mountains of Arkansas, ran directly into the line of Japanese fire to provide aid to a severely wounded Marine, Pfc. Jim Naughton. Naughton, it just so happened, was Arkie's tent mate at Camp Tarawa, and the two men were close friends. As his citation tells it, Williams

> went forward on the front lines under intense enemy small arms fire to assist a Marine wounded in a fierce grenade battle. Williams dragged the man to a shallow depression and was kneeling, using his own body as a screen from the sustained enemy fire . . . when he was struck in the abdomen and the groin three times by hostile fire. Momentarily stunned, he quickly recovered and completed his ministrations before applying battle dressings to his own multiple wounds. Unmindful of his own urgent need for medical attention, he remained in the perilous fire swept area to care for another Marine casualty.

After tending to the second wounded Marine, Williams was shot and killed by a sniper as he attempted to return to friendly lines. It was the fourth time the Japanese had found the mark on Arkie Williams, and the last.

Close to the base of Nishi Ridge, near dawn on March 3, Sgt. William G. Harrell of Rio Grande, Texas, shot two infiltrating Japanese with his M1 carbine when the harsh yellow light of a star shell silhouetted their crouching forms as they approached Harrell's foxhole. Another enemy soldier lobbed a grenade toward Harrell. It exploded a couple of feet from him, fracturing Harrell's thigh and severing his left hand, but he remained conscious. Minutes after this blast, a Japanese officer charged the Texan's foxhole, with saber at the ready. Harrell shot him with his .45 Colt.

Still another Japanese ran toward the sergeant, this time with a grenade in hand. Harrell, already drenched in his own blood as well as that of his attackers, shot him with the .45, killing the attacker, but the grenade detonated, tearing off Harrell's right hand. In the morning, twelve Japanese bodies were found around the semiconscious Harrell, but he ultimately survived the battle, learned to use artificial forearms and hands, and became a rancher back in Texas after the war.

For the entire 5th Marine Division, March 3 had been a costly day but also a triumphant one, for the division had succeeded in clearing the primary defensive belt at last. In total, the 5th Marine Division suffered 518 casualties on March 3, including 135 men killed. Five men of the division earned Medals of Honor for their actions on this day. To the best of our knowledge, this feat has never been duplicated by an American infantry division, Army or Marine, in any conflict.

Yet the enemy had fared far worse. According to reports filed by General Kuribayashi to Major Horie on Chichi Jima, 65 percent of his officers had been killed, and he had only 3,500 men effectively under his command as of March 3.[26] Perhaps another 2,000 Japanese were still alive and fighting, but they were out of communication with their unit commanders, operating essentially as small, roving bands.

★

FROM MARCH 4—D plus thirteen—until battle's end, the Team would find itself engaged in a torturously slow and highly lethal type of combat in which dog-tired Marines plodded ahead yard by painful yard against individual, but often mutually reinforcing, Japanese fighting positions. CT 28 was punching its way into extremely broken terrain of rocky lanes and tiny ravines, most of which contained Japanese-infested caves and spider holes. These were virtually impossible to detect until the enemy opened fire. Here sulfur fumes and vapors, mixed with the smell of decaying flesh and cordite, cast a white haze over parts of the barren landscape.

There was something inexorable about our drive through the main enemy defenses around 362A and Nishi Ridge. We weren't going to be stopped by fire. The deaths of so many men, so many close friends, tough as that was to take, wasn't going to stop us. We put aside our grief for another time, if we were lucky enough to be granted that time, and kept moving forward, sometimes only a few yards a day. If one squad or fire-team leader went down, a unit on the line didn't pick up a telephone and call the company CP to ask for replacements or ask, "What do we do now?" The guys just adapted to the situation at hand and made do, which is something the Marines, I think, train you to do very well. When a platoon lost its lieutenant or its platoon sergeant, as most of them did, the most experienced man left in the unit took over. And it worked like that day after day, even two weeks after we'd taken Nishi Ridge and were in Bloody Gorge. At that point, with just a handful of exceptions, all the original squad and platoon leaders had been killed or wounded. Many of the wounded guys protested vehemently about leaving their buddies to go to the aid stations or the hospital ships. They wanted to stay, to be there when it was done. The resolve was just fantastic to witness.

Bad weather, coupled with the exhaustion resulting from the last few days' fighting, meant that March 4 was essentially a stand-down in the 28th Marines' sector and most places along the front line. A few yards were gained here and there, but very few.

A welcome break from the monotony—and a boost to morale—was the sight of a B-29 Superfortress lining up from the northwest for a rough landing on Airfield No. 1. This was the airfield adjacent to the landing beaches that had been bought and paid for in Marine blood during the first few days of the campaign. *Dinah Might* had successfully dropped its load of five-hundred-pound bombs near Tokyo, but its bomb-bay doors were stuck in the open position, and a fuel valve problem meant that its commander, 1st Lt. Fred Malo, had a difficult decision: chance a landing on Iwo under Japanese fire, or go into the drink and hope that the crew would be rescued at sea. He chose the former.

After making two passes, he brought the plane down on the runway, which the Seabees had just lengthened to three thousand feet, barely enough room for a safe landing. On the way in, *Dinah Might's* wings trimmed off a couple of telephone poles along the runway; the plane rolled to a hard stop just a few feet from the runway's end. Fred Malo's airplane was the first of more than two thousand B-29s to land on the island. "To the Marines," wrote *Time* correspondent Bob Sherrod, "Iwo looked like the ugliest place on earth, but B-29 pilots who made emergency landings there called it the most beautiful."[27] On April 12, after the Marines had seized the entire island and departed for happier climes, *Dinah Might* was back on Iwo, making its second emergency landing after being heavily damaged in a low-level incendiary raid over Tokyo.

Bob Sherrod knew what he was talking about. Just before the landing, he had been on Saipan along with the 5th Division photo chief Norman Hatch. An Army Air Forces lieutenant colonel told them that twenty young officers were "in hack"—confined to their quarters—for threatening not to fly their B-29s. Their reasons: no fighter escorts accompanied them on the long and dangerous trip, the air-sea rescue efforts were poor, and they resented having to fly a dogleg around Iwo Jima, thus using precious fuel. P-51s began to fly from Iwo Jima as escorts on March 7 and the dogleg was eliminated. Morale soared among the flight crews. They even renamed one B-29 for each of the three Marine divisions that were fighting on Iwo Jima. The P-51s on Iwo ultimately flew 4,172 sorties against the Japanese home islands. They escorted B-29s as well as conducting sweeps over Honshu and Kyushu, and were credited with destroying or damaging more than one thousand Japanese aircraft in the air and on the ground by war's end.

Down on the ground, Iwo was getting uglier all the time. The statistics tell the story. Through March 4, the combat teams of the 5th Marine Division had suffered casualties that defied imagination: the 26th Regiment landed with 3,256 Marines; 1,644 had been killed or wounded. Col. Thomas A. Wornham's team, the 27th, had lost 1,319 officers and men thus far, or about 40 percent casualties. The 28th

Marines suffered worst of all with 1,952 casualties or almost 60 percent of its original complement.

General Kuribayashi knew full well that this was his last mission and that he would soon die with his men "in glorious sacrifice for the emperor. I shall fight to the best of my ability, so that no disgrace will be brought upon our family. I will fight on as a son of Kuribayashi the samurai and will behave in such a manner as to deserve the name of Kuribayashi. May my ancestors guide me."[28]

Not long before the American invasion, he had written to his son Taro that "the life of your father is like a flicker of flame in the wind. It is apparent your father will have the same fate as the commanders of Saipan, Tinian and Guam. There is no possibility of my survival."[29] On March 4, he sent a rambling message to Tokyo through the communications station on Chichi Jima:

> Our forces are making every effort to annihilate the enemy, but we have already lost most guns and tanks and two-thirds of officers. We may have some difficulties in future engagements. Since our headquarters and communication center are now exposed to the enemy's front line, we fear we may be cut off from Tokyo. Of course, some strong points may be able to fight delaying battles for several more days. Even if all the strong points fall, we hope the survivors will continue to fight to the end. . . . We are sorry indeed we could not have defended the island successfully. Now I . . . believe that the enemy will invade Japan proper from this Island. . . . I am very sorry because I can imagine the scenes of disaster in our empire. However, I comfort myself a little, seeing my officers and men die without regret after struggling in this inch-by-inch battle against an overwhelming enemy with many tanks and being exposed to indescribable bombardments.[30]

While the Japanese commander was thinking the end was near, his American counterpart, scanning the casualty sheets, reached a different conclusion. The three Marine division commanders received the following order from General Schmidt's headquarters around 1700 on the fourth: "There will be no general attack tomorrow. Except for limited adjustment of positions, each division will utilize the day for rest, refitting, and reorganization in preparation for resumption of action on 6 March."[31]

A bit before noon on March 5, Colonel Williams and I went forward along the coastal road. When we arrived in the 2nd Battalion's area, I asked the colonel's permission to go up in the LT 2/28 observation post (OP) and see what the terrain looked like ahead of us. He told Yates, his runner, to accompany me. I climbed up what was essentially a pinnacle on a spur that jutted to the north of Nishi Ridge. I waited just outside the OP until the 2/28 scout completed his work there. While I was waiting, a sniper began to take aim at the OP. I could not hear the report of the rifle, but I could hear the splat of the bullet. It was impossible to tell what direction it was coming from at the time. Finally, I moved into the OP proper, and using a pair of binoculars, I was able to get a pretty good view of the terrain on our immediate front. While I was in the OP, Yates took my place just outside. When I finished my view of the terrain ahead and stepped out of the OP, I found that Yates had been hit in the leg by the same sniper and had been evacuated.

Meanwhile, late in the afternoon of March 5, Fred found himself near Nishi Ridge, bought and paid for with the lives of so many of his comrades in Combat Team 28, including his best friend in the Marines, Gove Wilkins, and other men, like Col. Chaney Johnson, Mike Strank, and Arkie Williams. He cast his gaze to the south, across the corridor of flat ground between the ridge and 362A, and into the ravine where Wilkins had met his end.

My thoughts drifted back to a fall day when I'd been studying at the SMU library for an exam. I took a break and was strolling in the stacks to clear my head. One book's title caught my attention. It was Fix Bayonets! by Capt. John Thomason, USMC. I hadn't a clue about it at the time, but the book is a classic history of the Marines in combat in World War I. I browsed its pages. Halfway through the book's introduction, I came to Thomason's description of the Marines who had fought with such ferocity and steadfastness in the wheat fields and forests of Belleau Wood:

> In the big war companies, 250 strong, you could find every sort of man, from every sort of calling. There were northwesterners with straw-colored hair that looked white against their tanned skins and delicately spoken chaps with the stamps of the eastern universities on them. There were large-boned fellows from the Pacific lumber camps and tall, lean southerners who swore amazingly in gentle, drawling voices. There were husky farmers from the corn belt and youngsters who had sprung, as it were, to arms from the necktie counter. And there were also a number of diverse people who ran curiously to type, with drilled shoulders and bone-deep sunburn and a tolerant scorn of nearly everything on earth. Their speech was flavored with navy words and words culled from the folk who live on the seas and ports where our warships go. Rifles were high and holy things to them, and they knew five-inch broadside guns. They talked patronizingly of war and were concerned about rations. They were the leathernecks . . . the old breed of American regular, regarding the service as home and war as an occupation; and they transmitted their temper and character and viewpoint to the high-hearted volunteer mass that filled the ranks.[32]

It was one of those moments in life when a door opens and changes everything. I wanted to be one of those guys Thomason described. I wanted to be a U.S. Marine. As I gazed back over the killing ground near 362A, that day in the SMU library seemed like ancient history. It suddenly occurred to me that Thomason's description fit the 28th Marines to a tee.

And then came a more sobering reflection—that sometime during the past day or two, in the killing ground near and in front of the hill, the Combat Team had lost so many fine men that it no longer even remotely resembled the superb fighting organization it had been when we landed on February 19. It was running on empty. It was running, what was left of it, on spirit and sheer guts alone. Colonel Liversedge that day estimated the combat efficiency of the unit at 40 percent. And there was nothing for me to do now but get back to the game and begin to prepare the plan for the next day's attack.

8

DRIVING NORTH
TOWARD KITANO POINT

ith casualties spiking at a perilous rate among all eight combat teams on the island, General Schmidt, commander of VAC, first requested to land the 3rd Marine Regiment—the only fresh infantry regiment available to join in the battle—as early as February 28. Admiral Turner demurred. With more than the thousand men per square mile already on the island, Turner argued that the battlefield was too crowded for Schmidt to use additional troops effectively. Unless Schmidt was willing to say he could not take the island *without* a fresh combat team, Schmidt would have to make do with what he already had.

On March 4, Schmidt, increasingly concerned about the staggering casualty rates among the assault battalions, again requested that the 3rd Marines enter the fight. He put this request to Lt. Gen. Holland Smith, who asked the same question to Schmidt that Turner had previously. Schmidt grimaced, but he was honor-bound to answer Smith just as he had Turner: Yes, he *could* take the island without additional forces. So there would be no fresh Marine landing teams to help reduce the considerable enemy force still defending the northern third of the island. Combat Team 3 sailed for Guam on March 5.

VAC's top operations officer throughout the campaign, Col. Edward Craig, thought the decision wrongheaded. In a letter to the Historical Branch of the Marine Corps after the war, he wrote, "It was my considered opinion . . . having visited all parts of the island in our hands, that the 3rd Marine Regiment could have landed without in any way overcrowding the island. Commitment of this well trained and experienced regiment would have shortened the campaign and saved us casualties."[1]

The decision to refrain from using CT 3, with its three fresh infantry battalions, was to have a profound effect on the rhythm of the fight ahead for CT 28 and, indeed, for the entire Marine force on the island. In retrospect Craig was certainly correct: the battle would have ended more quickly and with fewer casualties had the 3rd Marines' battalions been thrown against what remained of Japanese resistance. There was no question that the replacements who did more and more of the infantry fighting for CT 28 and the other combat teams after March 5 lacked the small-unit assault skills of the 3rd Marines.

A 5th Marine Division intelligence report described the spooky terrain faced by the men of the 28th Marines as they attacked into the badlands south of Kitano Point on March 6:

> In the final defensive area north of Nishi the increased natural defensive strength of the ground and the subterranean defensive features compensated for the reduced amounts of concrete and steel used by the Japanese. . . . Volcanic eruption has littered the whole northern end of the island with outcrops of sandstone and loose rock. The sandstone outcrops make cave digging easy for the Japs. . . . Our troops obtained cover only by [hunkering down in] defilade or by piling loose rocks on the surface to form rock-reveted positions. A series of irregularly eroded, crisscrossed gorges with precipitous sides resulted in a series of compartments of various shapes. These were usually small but some extended for several hundred yards. The compartments

were lined with a labyrinth of natural and artificial caves which covered the approaches from all directions. Fields of fire were usually limited to 25 yards and an unusual characteristic of the Japanese defensive positions in this area was that the reverse slopes were as strongly fortified as were the forward slopes.[2]

To a far greater extent than around Suribachi or on the Motoyama plateau, where the airfields were situated, the northern sector of the island was honeycombed with natural caves. The Japanese had made good use of these, in addition to digging scores of man-made caves and spider holes. Concrete pillboxes were well concealed by sand, rocks, and other natural terrain features. One American five-hundred-pound bomb that was dropped into a cave entrance near Kitano Point blew white smoke out of a cliff four hundred yards away; another fighter dropped a bomb in a nearby cave entrance, causing a ring of smoke and dust to emerge from numerous exits in the ground for a radius of two hundred yards from the blast.

The fighting during the second and third weeks of March for the ever-more exhausted men of CT 28 was conditioned by several factors. First, by the time the Team had cracked the main defensive belt, all the rifle platoons had suffered casualty rates in excess of what military commanders consider the maximum number an infantry unit can withstand. Experienced infantry lieutenants, noncommissioned officers, and the enlisted men who comprised the original platoons of the three infantry battalions were in painfully short supply. The shortage of well-trained manpower would get much worse as the drive toward Kitano dragged on.

Scores of replacements sent into these units lasted less than two days before being wounded or killed. In an effort to identify the newcomers, a white stripe was painted on the backs of their helmets, and the experienced members of their squads were told to keep a close eye on these men. This precaution did help, but it hardly compensated for the lack of thorough small-unit infantry training among the replacements.

The shrinking body of fully trained combat veterans who had landed on D-day or shortly thereafter were suffering increasingly from exhaustion. By the second week in March, many men who had been on the line since the beginning were reaching their breaking point. We were in great physical shape when we landed, but after two weeks of steady fighting with little sleep, our senses were dulled and it took enormous reserves of willpower just to get up each morning and keep going. The battle took on the coloration of a marathon run with no clear finish line in sight.

The maiming and killing of friends carried an enormous emotional strain. Many men fought in a murky half-awake state, too tired to remain attuned to their surroundings. This was a grave problem, because on Iwo Jima, vigilance could not guarantee survival, but its absence all but ensured death or serious wounding. Among the frontline veterans, one often saw men who had lost a great deal of weight. Their eye sockets appeared hollow, and there was a strange disjunction between the movement of the head and the eyes. Many very tough Marines were approaching the point where we officers could not expect them to continue fighting indefinitely.

Exhaustion, the large number of replacements without sufficient infantry training, and the dreadful terrain made the attack discouragingly slow after about March 9. From the sixth through the eighth, our three landing teams were able to move as much as five hundred yards a day against resistance that was quite light compared with the Hill 362A days. This was surely because the Japanese had opted to concentrate what remained of their garrison farther north. As we got into the approaches of Bloody Gorge around the tenth—the deep gash in the earth that proved to be the final pocket of organized resistance—the happy story of five-hundred-yard daily gains came to an abrupt end. On several days between the tenth and fifteenth, our assault battalions gained no ground at all—not a single yard, so ferocious was the resistance.

The combat between Nishi Ridge and the gorge was extremely tough on company commanders. On March 9, one of our best company COs, Karl Tanner of C Company, was killed. I'd been up at the front the night before Karl was killed. He and I were quite close. In fact, his sis-

ter had gone to high school with my wife back in Texas. I had asked him if he needed anything. He said, "Fred, could you spare a few cigarettes?" I happened to have a full pack of Camels with me, and I gave him the pack. He was very grateful. That was the last time I ever saw Karl Tanner. He earned a Silver Star for leading a number of successful assaults from the front. The 1st Battalion executive officer, Maj. William Wood, took command. He single-handedly attacked a key pillbox with a bazooka and some shaped charges, enabling C Company to gain substantial ground in the nightmarish terrain.

On the same day we lost Karl, Capt. Russ Parsons, who had led A Company after Gove Wilkins was killed, received a wound so severe the surgeon had to amputate his leg. LT 1/28's "utility infielder," 1st Lt. Charles Weaver, took command.

Capt. Carl Bachman of I Company was killed on the fourteenth. One of his close friends, Capt. Bob Spangler, the operations officer of the 3rd Battalion, recalled that, a few days before he was killed, Bachman had led a raiding party of sixty volunteers. They were caught advancing in the open and were badly chewed up by mortars and machine-gun fire. Only a handful of Marines returned alive and unwounded. After the disastrous raid, Carl was mentally shattered. From then on, he led his company with total disregard for his own life. A sniper killed him.

Despite the close presence of a burgeoning military base and airfield in the south of the island, the enemy-held northern end cast a spell of foreboding and desolation. Everyone knew the battle had been won. But we also knew that the enemy holed up in the north would fight—and fight with desperate tenacity. This realization wasn't exactly a boost to morale.

Another significant characteristic of the fighting after the Team moved into the rugged terrain of the north was a spike in enemy night activity. The Japanese waged a costly struggle each night, attempting to infiltrate the Marines' lines, desperate for water or to seek a quick, honorable death in the name of the emperor, hoping to take one or two leathernecks with them in the process. Marines waged frequent hand-grenade duels with infiltrators, and incidents of hand-to-hand combat were frequent.

Combat Team 28 survivors of the fighting from the second week of March on also recall their dread of being shot at by seemingly ubiquitous snipers. Even the most seasoned Marines were unnerved by their number and their accuracy. Some men—Carl Bachman was a prime example—just gave up caring about their own safety. The effect of the snipers on the replacements was different: quite a number of them froze up with fear, and a few lapsed into shock after witnessing the deadly effects of the unseen enemy riflemen.

Most snipers used standard bolt-action service rifles, although some had telescopic sights. Also, the Japanese rifle round was virtually smokeless, but, in close quarters, the discharge had an unmistakable odor. Many of the snipers used spider holes or rocky outcroppings for their primary positions. They would fire one round and then wait for one to three hours before they fired again. There were underground passages as well as trenches that connected spider holes with caves, which were used as living quarters.

On the night after the most powerful Japanese counterattack of the entire battle—almost one thousand Japanese attacked the 23rd Marines of the 4th Division near the main airfields, resulting in the death of at least six hundred enemy soldiers—the Pacific War took on a shocking, new level of destructiveness. Gen. Curtis LeMay on March 9 sent more than three hundred B-29 Superfortresses from the Marianas on a low-level night raid over Tokyo. Incendiary bombs set sixteen square miles of the city ablaze, knocking out twenty-two key industrial and military targets and killing more than eighty thousand people, the vast majority of them civilians.

★

WHILE TROOPS OF the 3rd and 4th Divisions were starting to clear out the last pockets of resistance in their zones of action on March

11, the 28th Marines got a bitter foretaste of the stubborn resistance they would encounter each day for the rest of the campaign. Their attack in the direction of the ridgeline running along the southern lip of Bloody Gorge was prefaced by fifty minutes of heavy preparation fire, including the guns of twelve artillery battalions. This thunderous barrage seemed to have little effect on the action that transpired. The 3rd Battalion's after action report summarizes the frustrations of this merciless day:

> The enemy was too close to our front lines to use heavy supporting weapons [in the infantry attack]. G Company at 1330 [more than five hours after the attack commenced] was still pinned down by heavy sniper and knee mortar fire [small-caliber mortars capable of being fired and moved quickly by individual Japanese soldiers] and so far had been unable to move but a few feet. The enemy were so well concealed that it was almost impossible to see them. By 1630 the situation was still the same although both companies had suffered heavy casualties trying to move. Whenever a man showed himself in the lines it was almost certain death due to the uncanny accuracy of the enemy riflemen and machine gunners.[3]

On the night of the eleventh, the Japanese conducted scores of infiltration attempts along the Team's front lines. Around 2100, a company or so of enemy soldiers was spotted organizing itself for an attack into the 28th's positions. A highly accurate artillery barrage broke up the attack before it commenced. In the morning, twenty-six Japanese corpses were counted as Marines warily approached.

Capt. James Blackwell, the 13th Marine regimental intelligence officer, recalled that "our artillery was probably the most lethal when it fired directly into the Suribachi defenses. The defensive positions in the north proved far more difficult for us to destroy. However, up in the north, our forward observers were often able to keep the enemy off balance by calling in extremely close fire to our front lines at irregular intervals. This tactic was particularly effective in breaking up night infiltrations and mini-banzais."[4]

Since the Japanese habitually crawled up close to the Marine lines during the preassault bombardments, Colonel Shepard, commander of 3/28, called off the preliminary artillery and naval gunfire on March 12. His infantry units advanced in the half-light of dawn, hoping to surprise the defenders. After gaining but twenty yards, two companies were stopped cold. By 1230, "the conditions had not changed, except the enemy had annihilated two [Marine] machine gun crews and had taken over the guns and were using them against us. . . . Several of our men were hit and could not be evacuated due to the heavy fire which prevailed all along our front."[5] The next day, none of the 28th's assault companies gained more than a few yards, so accurate and sustained was Japanese machine-gun and sniper fire.

Our frontline units were so depleted by March 13 that Colonel Liversedge directed Capt. Jack Downer to pick fifty men from the Combat Team headquarters and service company to reinforce Landing Team 2/28. Downer called for volunteers, of which there were probably a total of ten, so the remainder were chosen in each section using the straw method: the men who had the short straws went to 2/28 along with the volunteers. Jim Scotella drew straws with his message-center buddies. His luck held. With the longest straw, he got to stay with headquarters. The name of the individual in the message center who drew the shortest straw has disappeared into history. We do know from Scotella that he met his end about three days later, probably not too far from the southern ridge overlooking Bloody Gorge.

By this point, we were fighting under tremendous pressure from the top brass to clear out the remaining area of organized resistance. The 3rd and 4th Divisions' battles were essentially over. We of the 5th Division had the most ground to cover, and the terrain up near the gorge was worse than anywhere else on the island. In any case, Capt. Sidney Woodd-Cahusac, a Yale man and a good friend who was General Rockey's senior aide throughout the battle, told me that General Schmidt, the V Corps commander, had called Rockey and told him that

if his division did not advance immediately and take the final ap-
proaches to the gorge, Schmidt would have to relieve Rockey of his
command.

Rockey told Woodd-Cahusac to get Colonel Liversedge on the phone,
which he did. Rockey said, "Harry, I just finished a conversation with
General Schmidt, and he told me that if your men didn't move imme-
diately, he was going to relieve me of my command." Liversedge ex-
plained that his men were exhausted, his assault teams were chock-full
of replacements, and the enemy resistance was showing no signs of
slackening, but the 28th would complete its mission as fast as it could.

At that point, General Rockey paused for a moment and said,
"Harry, I know you and your men are doing the best you can. God
bless." And he hung up. Woodd-Cahusac, who after the war became an
Episcopal priest, said that he had never heard a more courageous state-
ment at a more crucial time. And that it had reminded him, when he
thought back on it, of St. Paul's second letter to the Corinthians, "For
we walk by faith, not by sight." Faith in our commanders, faith in our
fellow Marines, faith in God to see us through.

Over the next two days, March 14 and 15, CT 28 pushed forward
slowly and methodically, cleaning out bypassed positions with the
help of flame tanks around the southern ridgeline overlooking the
gorge. The 5th Marine Division intelligence report captured the
essence of the fighting here:

> In attacking these positions, no Japanese were to be seen,
> [hidden as they were] in caves or crevices in the rocks, and
> [positioned in such a way] as to give an all-around interlock-
> ing, ghost-like defense to each small compartment. Attacking
> troops were subjected to fire from the flanks and rear more
> than from their front. It was always difficult and often impossi-
> ble to locate where defensive fires originated. The field of fire
> of the individual Japanese defender in his cave was often lim-
> ited to an arc of 10 degrees or less; conversely he was protected
> from fire except that coming back on this arc. The Japanese

smokeless, flashless powder for small arms was of particular usefulness here.[6]

Unremitting combat continued for CT 28's rifle companies each day. Charlie Shepard's 3rd Battalion had come ashore last on D-day, but it had taken a terrific pasting—the worst among the three line battalions. We assigned one hundred artillerymen whom General Rockey sent as replacements on March 12 to the 3rd Battalion in order to keep it functioning as a unit. Sixty of them would be dead or wounded by battle's end. That's a pretty fair barometer of the lethality of the struggle for replacements as we staggered toward the battle's conclusion.

Pfc. Gordon Byrum, Liversedge's radioman, who was on the scene when Shepard was reassigned, said, "The battalion CO had had enough. With tears coming down his face, he told the colonel he could no longer send his men to attack. He kept saying too many were being killed for nothing. . . . The colonel talked to him, and Shepard seemed relieved. The next thing I know we had a new CO."[7]

Shepard was teetering near total collapse. Colonel Liversedge decided to assign him to Maj. Oscar Peatross's position as operations officer— Peatross at the time was serving as executive officer of one of the infantry battalions. First, Shepard was given a heavy sedative by our regimental surgeon, Bill Lynn. After a few days of rest, he recovered nicely, and he made some excellent contributions to the operations work. Before the battle ended, Liversedge gave a much rejuvenated Shepard his battalion back. In so doing, of course, he saved the colonel's Marine career. It was typical of Liversedge's decency and compassion.

On March 14, the top brass gathered a couple of hundred yards north of Suribachi around a demolished Japanese bunker. Admirals Turner and Hill were there, as were Lt. Gen. H. M. Smith and the three Marine division commanders. This was the "official" flag-raising ceremony marking the seizure of Iwo Jima by the Americans. A decree written by Adm. Chester Nimitz was read.

> I, Chester William Nimitz, Fleet Admiral, United States Navy, Commander in Chief Pacific Fleet and Pacific Ocean Areas, do hereby proclaim as follows:
>
> United States forces under my command have occupied this and other of the Volcano Islands. All powers of government of the Japanese Empire in these islands so occupied are hereby suspended. All powers of government are vested in me as military governor and will be exercised by subordinate commanders under my direction. . . . All persons will obey promptly all orders given under my authority. Offenses against the forces of occupation will be severely punished.
>
> Given under my hand at Iwo Jima this fourteenth day of March, 1945.[8]

As the flag ascended over the bunker, the notes of "To the Colors" issued forth from a single bugler. The flag on Mount Suribachi was lowered as the new flag was raised up an eighty-foot pole. The event was not without irony, especially for the Marines still fighting and dying for yards of ground in the north. This was also the day when the first Marine units prepared to depart the island. Over the next few days, most elements of the 3rd and 4th Marine Divisions would clean out the last pockets of resistance in their zones, pack up their equipment, and prepare to depart Iwo Jima.

Not so for the 5th Division's Marines. It fell to them to reduce the final pocket of organized resistance on the island.

As we reached the approaches to the gorge, we were still taking significant losses each day. Marine bodies were strewn all over the place, and an important job for sanitary as well as morale reasons was to remove these remains from the field and get them down to our cemetery where they could be appropriately interred. Our two chaplains were, as always, very busy comforting the wounded and praying over the dead.

Chaplains Glenn Bauman and Paul Bradley were of invaluable help during the entire battle.

By March 17, there were still perhaps 2,500 Japanese alive on the island. Of this number about two thousand were scattered in small groups. Many were wounded or too weak for lack of food and water to do much more than hide deep inside their underground lairs, suffering amid the heat and stench. They only dared to venture aboveground at night in search of a bit of food and water. There was only one place left where the defense was strong, well-manned, and organized: Bloody Gorge.

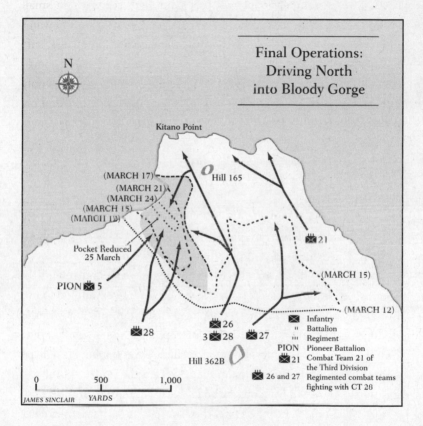

Final Operations:
Driving North
into Bloody Gorge

N

Kitano Point

Hill 165

(MARCH 17)
(MARCH 21)
(MARCH 24)
(MARCH 15)
(MARCH 12)

Pocket Reduced
25 March

21

(MARCH 15)

PION 5

(MARCH 12)

28

26
3 28   27

Infantry
" Battalion
Regiment
PION   Pioneer Battalion
21   Combat Team 21 of
the Third Division
26 and 27   Regimented combat teams
fighting with CT 28

Hill 362B

0   500   1,000

JAMES SINCLAIR   YARDS

9

BLOODY GORGE

loody Gorge ran along a southeast-northwest axis, about five hundred yards south of Kitano Point. It opened onto a small beach on the west coast and extended inland for about seven hundred yards. Its width varied from two hundred to five hundred yards. This cavernous ravine was itself cut into many minor draws, most at odd angles. Rocky outcroppings, some standing like forty-foot primitive statues, offered excellent cover for snipers. All avenues of approach into the main gorge—from the north, south, and east—were covered by scores of machine-gun, mortar, and rifle positions. The only good news was that the Japanese had no artillery left.

It would be hard to conceive of better terrain for a last stand. General Kuribayashi had chosen the ideal locale for the final phase of his defense. The attack into Bloody Gorge commenced on March 17, shortly after the 26th Marines, with Landing Team 3/28 attached, cleared out Kitano Point and pivoted down from the north toward its eastern mouth. That entrance was very close to both the Japanese naval headquarters cave and Kuribayashi's main command post. As

CT 26 and 3/28 pushed methodically toward the sea, the remaining two infantry battalions covered their advance by firing into enemy positions from the southern ridgeline; in the process, they cleared that area of scores of enemy positions.

By coincidence, March 17 also marked the date that Tokyo announced Kuribayashi's promotion to four-star general. According to a March 15 telegram sent to Major Horie on Chichi Jima, the general planned to lead what remained of the force directly under his control in a final banzai charge on the night of March 17. However, no such charge materialized; nor did Horie hear anything further from Kuribayashi until the twenty-first, when the general reported that he and his remaining force had instead opted to head out from his main command post during the night of the sixteenth into a large cave 150 yards northwest of his former CP to continue the battle of attrition against the Americans. That telegram read in part: "We have not eaten or drunk for five days. But our fighting spirit is still running high. We are going to fight bravely till the last."[1]

It must have been around the seventeenth, too, when Kuribayashi, sensing the end was near, filed a briefing for the chief of the Imperial General Staff in Tokyo, offering trenchant insights into the factors leading up to the loss of the island. The briefing itself has never been recovered, but Horie wrote a summary of the general's insights at the behest of the U.S. government shortly after Japan surrendered, in the appendix to his "Explanation of the Japanese Defense on Iwo Jima." Among the key points were these:

1. Too much time and too many resources had been wasted trying to extend and repair the airfields. These resources could have been better used shoring up major defensive positions far from the beaches.
2. The power and accuracy of American supporting fire, particularly naval gunfire, was so great that it could destroy any kind of defensive position set up near a landing beach. The only

way to stop U.S. Marines in an amphibious assault was to attack their ships before they commenced landing.

3. Much of the success of the American attack on Iwo was due to
their extensive array of aircraft and superior tanks. The Japanese military needed better tanks and planes if it was to win future land battles.

4. Dummy pillboxes should have been used extensively to draw
fire away from real defensive positions.

5. The Marines had two or three flamethrower operators for
every fifty to sixty infantrymen. It was "extremely urgent" to
neutralize these men as fast as possible if a position was to be
held for any length of time.[2]

The Japanese had now run out of wiggle room. Each day of
the fight, from the seventeenth through the twenty-fifth of
March, the ground they called their own shrank by sixty or seventy yards. And each day, the casualty lists for the 28th Marines
grew longer.

The decision to attack from east to west, down the main compartment formed by the two ridgelines that comprised the gorge's southern and northern boundaries, had its origins, at least in part, in a
reconnaissance flight Fred had taken on around March 10.

*Bob Williams and I went up Hill 362A to get a good feel for the terrain
ahead. It appeared that if we continued attacking directly north, more
murderous cross compartments, replete with mutually reinforcing enemy defenses, stood in the way. On our way back to the CP, I suggested
to Colonel Williams that I make an aerial reconnaissance of our likely
zone of action toward Kitano Point. The purpose would be to determine
if we could somehow make better use of the terrain by attacking down
the corridors.*

*Colonel Liversedge agreed. So we arranged for a Grasshopper, a
small observation plane from our Marine Observation Squadron 5
(VMO 5), to take me up to get a clear view of the situation. With a*

Marine pilot at the controls, I flew north over Kitano Point, thence west to seaward for about a mile. We then did a "one-eighty" over Kangoku Rock, dropped down to about four hundred feet, and flew east toward the area between Kitano Point and our front line. The terrain was a jumble of shallow, rocky draws and rugged, poorly defined ridges.

One feature stood out, however: the gorge. To attack across this deep gash from south to north would almost certainly have proved as costly as our fight for 362A and Nishi Ridge. So after talking with Williams and Liversedge, we agreed to press Division for an attack down into the eastern mouth of the gorge rather than across it.

Unfortunately, between our front and the gorge, there were a number of smaller draws and ravines, very irregular in shape. We simply could not change the direction of attack in this area. The fire from the high ground on our right flank was too intense. Nor did we have sufficient troops left to support attacks down these compartments with fire from the ridgelines that framed them. This is the most effective way to clear out low, broken ground—to bring supporting fire to bear from the high ground while infantry and demolitions men assault the enemy dug into the low ground and the surrounding cliffs.

However, by the fifteenth, the 27th Marines and 21st Marines on the division's right flank had successfully cleared out the enemy positions in the northeastern sector of the island. This had the salutary effect of all but eliminating enemy fire on our right flank. On the sixteenth, CT 26, with our 3rd Battalion attached, cleared Kitano Point and began to pivot down from the north to join us in the fight to clean out Bloody Gorge. Together, the two combat teams had sufficient infantry forces to "shoulder" their way down into the gorge from east to west, while covering the attack by fire from the ridgelines.

Each cave and pillbox, once silenced by flame tanks and infantry, had to be sealed by the engineers before we could move deeper into that deadly canyon. The contorted terrain made it impossible for tanks to operate effectively until armored bulldozers had cleared a road for their advance. We were too close to the enemy to use artillery, naval gunfire, or air support, so the infantry advanced warily to draw fire, thereby *identifying enemy positions. Then, armored bulldozers under cover of infantry had to clear the broken ground of rocks, ditches, and mines, allowing flame tanks to roll in and to burn out the caves.*

Demolition squads armed with bazookas and shaped charges followed closely. Engineers closed the larger caves. Only flame tanks seemed to scare the Japanese into fleeing their fighting positions inside the gorge and its approaches. All other forms of attack were met with fierce resistance until the defenders had been silenced. Where it was impossible to bring flame tanks to bear, the only heavy fire support for the infantry and demolitions squads were 37mm antitank guns, manhandled into position in the cliffs by teams of weary, struggling Marines. It was tough going all the way.

The gorge was indeed an eerie and desolate place, the last bit of the island to be conquered, the hardest place to spot and kill the enemy. Here Japanese fire was more sporadic than it had been around Suribachi or Hill 362A. Enemy soldiers would appear in the most unlikely places just long enough to fire a single round, and all too often a single rifle shot resulted in another dead or wounded Marine. Robert Coster, a replacement drawn from the headquarters company of the 28th Regiment and the Marine who had purchased Roscoe back at the Los Angeles Zoo, went into the line around March 20. As Coster recalled,

I joined about 50 Marines, all of us of different trades. Some cooks, plumbers, etc. We weren't trained as line men [infantrymen], but we were still Marines. At last we started toward the front with ten thousand thoughts in our minds. . . . We were going forward when we came to a clearing. We stopped for a minute and sent the first man across. We were expecting sniper fire and we got it. They let the first man go through, but they opened up on the second. The bullets hit around his feet but he was lucky. There was no way we could cover ourselves because we didn't know where the shots were coming from. The third man started across, but he was hit in the leg. I was next and I knew the Nip would open up as soon as I crossed his sights. It was like shooting fish in a barrel, just standing by and waiting until the next man tried to make a dash.[3]

Coster was lucky. His squad leader grabbed him by the arm and decided to maneuver around the clearing. Just as the squad leader pointed out the route of advance, another shot rang out, whining past Coster's ear and hitting the squad leader in the right arm, splattering blood on everyone.

Pfc. Don Traub recalled the loss of one of his buddies to the ubiquitous snipers in the gorge:

> After we had finally taken out an enemy mortar position in the gorge, we advanced to an open area strewn with remnants of Japanese artillery. I dove into a shallow revetment where an enemy gun had been knocked out, and landed on top of a fellow Marine. I had seen him once before, when he was trying to run for cover while pulling up his pants after relieving himself during a sudden bombardment. I don't recall his name today. He had a lilting Irish brogue and had often recounted the history of his family's struggle against the British during the Black and Tan Rebellion. We joked and laughed together until the order came for us to move out. I had gone about twenty yards before looking back. The Irishman was draped over a destroyed gun emplacement, killed by a sniper's bullet.[4]

The nights in the gorge area were chock-full of nasty surprises. Danger was not restricted to the front because of the peculiarly broken terrain and the enemy's desperate effort to infiltrate into and behind Marine lines. Pfc. John Lyttle, the Bougainville veteran who had landed with the 3rd Battalion on D-day, received the welcome news that his squad was leaving the line on the edge of "Death Valley"—another sobriquet for the gorge—on March 16 to take up a position three hundred yards behind the front. Lyttle and his men yearned for sleep, and the new position held out its promise: the base of a sheer bluff around some large rock outcroppings. There they found a number of foxholes, several of which contained the bodies of Marines who had been killed in the past few hours. The men were too tired to do anything else but remove the corpses, set up watch, and doze, with their backs to the cliff. Suddenly, there was firing toward their front, Lyttle recalled:

> We heard the Japs talking. They were yelling something that was hard to understand. We finally realized they were saying, "Roosevelt eats shit!" Of course, we replied, "Tojo eats shit too!" The Gunny called for illumination, and a flare lit up our area so we could see what we were up against. The Japs were coming from the cliffs behind us. They were hiding behind a wall and our foxhole was directly in line with the gap in the wall. We started firing at them and we stopped their charge. The Japs lit their grenades by striking the fuse on something hard, like a rock or a helmet. We heard them hitting their helmets, and then I saw a grenade flying over us into Hambrick's hole. Hambrick thought he'd been hit in the family jewels. To reassure him, a corpsman had pushed Hambrick's hand far enough down his pants to verify for himself that everything was in place. . . . [Another Marine] took the full blast from the grenade and was clearly dying.
> When the second charge started, before we could start shooting, a machine gun went off a few feet behind us. The gunners had the wall opening well covered, and it was quite a relief. I always marveled in knowing that these machine gunners must have been green replacements but still had enough ingenuity to realize what started out to be our rear was now our front line, and they took it upon themselves to change their position and save the day. That is what being a Marine is all about.[5]

The day after Carl Bachman was killed and Shepard was transferred to regimental headquarters—March 15—the entire 5th Pioneer Battalion was attached to CT 28 to shore up its lines as they approached the gorge's southern rim. Since D-day the Pioneers had been unloading ammo, water, and other supplies from LSTs and other naval craft and loading the wounded for evacuation. They were also attached to the graves registration people, handling the paperwork for the steady flow of the dead into the 5th Division cemeteries. Now, they were outfitted with a plentiful supply of BARs and light machine guns, given a crash course in assault tactics, and funnelled into the front lines.

Among the Pioneers who led a platoon into the gorge was 1st Lt. Bob Hansen. Hansen would survive the battle but not before being shot in the leg in the very last gasp of Japanese resistance early in the morning on March 26. On the march up the west coast toward the front lines, Hansen recalled, "We came upon an arm sticking up out of the sand, and someone had put a lighted cigarette between the fingers. This was a little battlefield humor, and we thought it pretty funny."[6]

Hansen was apprehensive when he was ordered on the seventeenth to deploy his platoon into the gorge:

> I was so scared I had to stand up and walk around, because I felt if I just sat still, my men would see me shaking and be demoralized. When I finally got over the shakes, I sat back down. The front lines were where the action really happened. Stretcher bearers brought the wounded back from the front line past our bivouac area, with the guys on the stretchers covered with bloody bandages, smoking cigarettes, and smiling![7]

Hansen's platoon took its first casualty immediately, but it was not inflicted by the Japanese. At dusk, as his men moved along in a crouch to tie in with the unit on their left, a Jap grenade suddenly plummeted into their midst. The men hit the ground, but it turned out to be a dud. "We got up and moved a little bit more and a shot rang out, and one of my squad leaders was killed—by a Marine on the right flank of the unit we were tying into. The Marine thought he was a Jap. I yelled at him and he said, "Anybody moves around here this time of night gets shot!"[8]

Hansen's unit spent several harrowing days on the line in the gorge. His unit's initial position put him directly in front of a well-camouflaged Japanese cave that seemed indestructible. Even after heavy machine guns and an additional demolitions squad were called up to support the assault, the Japanese kept up a steady rain of fire. Finally, one of Hansen's men climbed into a flame tank from the hatch on the tank's bottom to show the gunner where to fire napalm into the cave entrance. That spelled the end for the enemy in the cave, but Hansen's unit's troubles were hardly over:

> I called my squad leaders to my foxhole and laid out my plan for the advance. We hadn't moved out very far when we were subjected to sniper fire. I was hunkered down behind a rock, and Pfc. White was in back of me behind another rock. White evidently got tired of all this nonsense, so he peered over the rock with his rifle at the ready. He was going to get that Jap who had been shooting at us, wherever he might be. I started to motion to him to get back down behind the rock when a shot rang out. The bullet went through White's helmet and head, killing him instantly. So I lost one of my men when my platoon was moving into position at the front, and another man when we started the attack. They were not more than five or six feet from me when they were shot.[9]

Hansen's harrowing experiences were typical of the Marines who struggled near the gorge.

Pfc. Don Traub remembered the replacement selection process and the "training" he and his men received before heading off into the hell of frontline combat:

> Of the two hundred Marines of the 13th Artillery Regiment to be sent to the front, forty-nine were to be selected by my battalion CO, Maj. Carl Hjerpe and his subordinates. I had little opportunity as a lowly private first class to get to know him in training, but he was a dignified, consummate Marine who later became a good friend. I discovered after the war that Hjerpe knew the background and personality of almost every man in his charge. I can only imagine the despair that they must have felt when they had to choose among us for the risky assignments; officers later said that they felt they were sending us to certain death. Yet some of us survived, remembering to "keep your head

down," "don't lose touch with the man next to you," and "when
you get the order to move out, run forward like hell in a zigzag
pattern, then hit the deck while rolling away from the spot
where you landed and find some sort of cover." These inspiring
words were supposed to turn us into seasoned infantrymen![10]

The official company and battalion after action reports for CT 28
during the battle, housed in the National Archives in College Park,
Maryland, are chock-full of entries marking changes of command at
squad, platoon, and company levels resulting from the death or serious wounding of commanders. Tom Lambe, a Guadalcanal veteran,
was one of many such men who stepped into the breach just as the
gorge fight was escalating. A sergeant sent up to the line to command
a platoon of men from the regimental headquarters and service company, Lambe found his first night as a platoon leader a busy one. His
unit was assigned the hazardous duty of filling a gap in the line at
night. Lambe managed to get his men in place just as a reinforced
platoon of Japanese attacked into the gap. The sergeant and his men
then repelled seven Japanese assaults before dawn. Lambe gave a
good account of himself, as his Silver Star citation indicates:

> Throughout the night he repeatedly exposed himself to intense
> hostile fire to move among his men, reassuring them, distributing
> hand grenades and directing machine-gun and rifle fire in a bit-
> ter struggle to disrupt the attempted break-through. By his initia-
> tive, leadership and courage, he aided in the annihilation of over
> thirty Japanese and in holding a vital road until relieved by flank-
> ing troops. His heroic devotion to duty was in keeping with the
> highest traditions of the United States Naval Service.

Bob Coster's makeshift replacement unit was told it would be
spending one night in support of E Company, on the front line. That
first night was an eventful one:

> Altogether there were four foxholes, four men to a hole. The line
> of foxholes stuck out into the enemy's area like a large finger.

We dug ourselves in as best we could. Then, the Nips came. We drove them off with grenades and tried to dig in. The ground was like rock and by morning we only had a hole large enough for one man. We all four got into it somehow. As morning came we tried to enlarge our little home. It was about seven in the morning when one of our fellows in the next hole let out a scream. He had shown himself and it cost him his life. We were all in one pile trying to keep four men out of the line of fire in a hole large enough for one. The fellow who was killed was "Nick." He was married with three children, one of whom he had never seen.[11]

Coster and his comrades ended up spending seven nights in the vicinity of that same hole. By that point,

we were at each other's throats. It didn't make much difference what any of us would say; someone would pick it up and then we would all fight amongst ourselves. It would soon stop and each one would tell the other we were sorry. Each night and every morning we would thank God we were still alive and make a few promises on how we would live if we came out of the battle alive. I am sure we prayed and dug more in those seven long days and nights than we ever did before in our lives. There are thousands of things that go through your mind when you believe you are going to die. It so happened the Good Lord brought us out alive and we never will forget it.[12]

Pfc. John H. Harrison, another replacement from the artillery, saw action in the gorge as an infantryman. He recalled one night around March 18 when his platoon had settled down. The men had carved out foxholes a few yards apart from one another, with three men in each foxhole. Harrison was on watch at about 0200 when he heard a noise in front of his foxhole. At the same time, a man from the foxhole on his left threw out an illumination grenade. Not fifteen yards from the front of Harrison's foxhole, two Japanese officers lurked. Harrison fired his M1, killing one officer with a shot to the head. He then swung the rifle toward the second officer, hitting him in the cheek of his buttocks. He fell to the ground and rolled behind the rock, so I couldn't get a decent shot at him. I didn't have a grenade, so I called over to the next foxhole, "Throw one out and we'll get this guy." Someone threw a grenade out and they killed the Japanese. The next morning, around six o'clock, several of the squad members were up and out where the Japanese officers laid. They yelled over to me, "Come out here and see what you've got."[13]

Harrison picked up the sword and pistol of a Japanese colonel. The other Japanese officer was a major. They were apparently trying to sneak through the Marines' lines to create confusion and to destroy men and supplies.

Death was as common as dust, blood, and Japanese spider holes in the gorge. In their exhaustion, some men were broken by the gorge's excruciating demands—you could see a faraway, haunted look in the sleepless, darting eyes, and sometimes tremors in the hands. These men were removed from the line. It was a tribute to the Team's training and spirit that so few were relieved. During the entire campaign, for example, only thirty-six men from the 1st Battalion, which, including replacements, consisted of about twelve hundred men, were evacuated for combat fatigue and other psychological disturbances.

As Pvt. Robert Allen, himself of B Company, 1st Battalion, recounted, "Some Marines developed erratic behavior, and their presence endangered the lives of their comrades. . . . Some cracked under the constant pressure. A few needed to be restrained and forcibly removed from the lines to prevent them from doing themselves or others bodily harm. Others developed a syndrome called 'the bulkhead stare' and ceased to function responsibly."[14]

I had the opportunity to observe virtually all the assault companies in action toward the end of the battle. The vast majority of men, including the replacements, managed to draw on reserves of moral and physical strength they never imagined they possessed. They kept on with the grim business at hand, becoming inured not only to the ghastly sights of destruction, death, and hordes of bloated, blue-green flies, but to the stench of swollen bodies heated by the warm volcanic earth.

Amid all the suffering and exhaustion, the lingering effects of death would seep into the Marines' consciences, eroding their hardened veneer. Such was the case with Pfc. John Lyttle, surely by the time of the gorge one of the Team's most trusted and experienced small-unit leaders. He saw action steadily on the front from D-day until March 20, when the modest Californian was shot through the neck while rushing with a stretcher to save the life of a seriously wounded Marine. A couple of days before he was shot, Lyttle had a grim encounter with several enemy corpses, prompting him, then and there, to reflect on the meaning of death:

On our way down we passed a lot of dead, both ours and theirs, but the three Japs lying near [our new position] were grossly bloated, to say the least. Someone had told me that men who had died by concussion would swell up to unbelievable proportions. These three must have suffered that fate. One guy looked like he was ready to float down the streets of New York in the Macy's Thanksgiving Day Parade. This bloating was not limited to the stomach, but every arm, leg and finger as well. Even his head was swollen, with the exception of his nose, which was hidden in between large swollen cheeks. A purple tongue forced its way outward toward the sky. The scene was unbelievably horrid, but it held us for some unknown reason.

One Marine reached over and plucked his wallet out, giving it to me saying, "What the hell. He won't be using it anymore." There were some bills neatly folded, which I removed and pocketed. It was then that I saw a small photo which had been pasted on the inside flap. It showed a small Jap soldier sitting with what appeared to be his bride, who stood partly behind him. She was wearing what must have been her wedding dress, with all the bows and stuff that only made her look smaller. Her round white face showed no expression. This hit hard. It gave this ghastly corpse a soul. "They" also had loved ones back home who would never see them again or know how they died. . . . The enemy had just taken on a new face for me. Why don't they make the Tojos of this world fight their own wars?[15]

The gorge was also a venue of the bizarre. After a fierce firefight smack in the middle of Bloody Gorge, Pfc. Don Traub checked enemy corpses for booby traps:

I came upon a neatly arranged bier with long poles staked at the four corners. The top was lightly covered with thatch supported by twigs and small branches. Under this was a raised catafalque, upon which lay a dead Japanese officer outfitted immaculately in full-dress uniform, his arms crossed over his bloodied chest. I gazed at the body for ten minutes, struck by the care his men provided for him. I could only think that this person had been a revered leader and that before their own inevitable deaths, they had made this tribute as a last measure of devotion to a highly respected officer.[16]

While Marines toiled in the gorge, just four miles to the south, under the shadows of Mount Suribachi, the graves registration people labored to prepare dead Marines for interment. "At one point, we had four hundred or five hundred bodies stacked up, waiting for burial," recalled Lt. Gage Hotaling, a Navy chaplain. He continued:

I am not a smoker, but I found the only way I could go around and count bodies was to smoke one cigarette after another. . . . I was addicted to smoking for 26 days. Once we had the bodies lined up, I would give a committal to each one, with Marines holding a flag over the body. And I said the same committal words to every Marine, because they were not buried as Protestants or Catholics or Jews. They were buried as Marines.[17]

Around the same time John Lyttle was grappling with death's tragic consequences in Bloody Gorge, 1st Lt. John McLean, the

Japanese language officer, nearly lost his life when he tried to coerce a wounded enemy officer in a cave to surrender. The Japanese was clearly booby-trapped with a hand grenade. He looked up at the Marines several times, offering "a faint grin, but said nothing. From time to time, he would pick up a handful of sand in his hand and let it sift through his fingers."[18]

McLean ordered his Marines to shoot the soldier when all his pleading came to naught. He hadn't wanted to do it but had had no choice. There were potentially valuable maps and documents nearby on a table. When the party of Marines reached the table on which the documents were placed, several Japanese hiding in the cave sprung their trap, unleashing a fusillade of machine-gun and rifle fire that killed three Marines instantly and wounded two others. McLean himself was unscathed, yet he could not dart from the cave's entrance without exposing himself to the enemy's field of fire. Acting on instinct more than calculated thought, McLean hugged the wall and inched toward the cave's mouth, where he saw a lone Marine with an M1 rifle aimed right at him. McLean identified himself and asked the rifleman to toss him a grenade so he could cover his own dash toward the cave opening.

It worked. When McLean finally reached the regimental CP, he startled his comrades—one of the wounded Marines who had escaped the cave had reported the lieutenant killed in action.

The slow but inexorable attack by 3/28 and the 26th Marines pressed past General Kuribayashi's huge command post near the eastern mouth of Bloody Gorge on March 18, but the general and his much-diminished staff had already vacated west on the night of the sixteenth, toward the sea, into a deep cave that served as the commander's last command post on Iwo. Even though Kuribayashi had gone west, the approaches to his former CP remained staunchly defended. It took two full days of assaults by tanks, flamethrowers, and infantry to clear the protective network of cave and spider-hole positions.

The command and communications blockhouse was about 150 feet long and 70 feet wide. It contained three underground chambers, two for communicators and one for the commanding general himself. The walls of were composed of reinforced concrete five feet thick, and the roof was no less than ten feet thick.

The Marines attempted to blow up the CP. It proved all but indestructible. Satchel charges had no effect on its structural integrity. Finally, engineers sealed a huge door on the north side of the complex and destroyed the structure with five separate charges, totaling 8,500 pounds of explosives. "When they blew up that blockhouse, I thought the world had come to an end. I'd been in the midst of heavy fighting since D-day," recalled Cpl. Wes Plummer, who was involved in the assault on the complex, "and it was the loudest damned explosion I'd ever heard."[19]

Kuribayashi continued to send radio communiqués to Major Horie on Chichi Jima until March 23. On the twenty-first, he wrote a terse summary of the situation in the gorge. Clearly his own fighting spirit had remained strong until the last: "At midnight of the seventeenth, I went out from my cave and gathered all survivors of the 145th Regiment, as well as men from the northern, eastern and western [defense] sectors, and we are continuing our fighting. I have four hundred men under my control. . . . They [the Marines] advised us to surrender through a loudspeaker, but we only laughed at this childish trick."[20]

We had indeed used a loudspeaker to implore the remaining Japanese to surrender. We had learned the whereabouts of the general's headquarters from a very well-informed Japanese noncommissioned officer who had surrendered to Lt. Candy Johnson of H Company at first light on March 17. Master Sgt. Taizo Sakai was Kuribayashi's chief code clerk. As such, he had been responsible for encoding his commander's communications to Chichi Jima. From there, the general's communiqués were passed on to Tokyo. Sakai provided not only very detailed information about the enemy order of battle on Iwo Jima, but also about what Tokyo knew of the American order of battle and her planned future operations. Sakai knew quite a bit about the impending invasion of Okinawa.

The most important prisoner taken by CT 28 during the battle had only narrowly missed being killed as he surrendered. Just as he approached Lieutenant Johnson, a sniper had shot a round through the lieutenant's helmet. Remarkably, it missed Johnson's head, rattled around the steel pot, and fell to the ground. Johnson was momentarily shaken up but otherwise fine. He might very well have suspected Sakai of a ruse, but he kept his cool and radioed his company commander, 1st Lt. Fio Lopardo. Lopardo couldn't raise a language officer immediately, so he tried his hand at interrogating the prisoner. Lopardo spoke no Japanese, and Sakai no English. But remarkably enough, both men were proficient in French, and they struck up an immediate rapport.

"While we were waiting for it to turn light," said Lopardo, "I used Sakai to help me blast caves. You could hear them [the Japanese] in the caves. Sakai said, 'They're going to banzai,' and I said, 'If they are going to banzai, we're going to kill them.' And so we set up a machine gun at the mouth of the cave aimed right into the thing. They accommodated us real well. Just about the time we got all set up, Sakai said, 'They're coming.' And out they came. We just let go and got them all. Sakai turned his back and said, 'They're all fanatics.'"[21]

The following day Sakai told Lt. John McLean he knew the whereabouts of Kuribayashi's cave. The two men, joined by a team of Marines with loudspeakers, headed up to the site of the cave. McLean recounted what happened next:

> We took Sakai [to the gorge] and had him pinpoint the location. We proceeded down a series of gullies and ravines toward a clearing beyond which several hundred yards away was the general's headquarters. Along the way there were bodies of dead Marines and Japanese soldiers killed earlier that day in a bitter skirmish. Spider traps in niches along the wall of the narrow valley had inflicted a terrible toll on our forces. There was simply no way to see the enemy until he saw you first, as Marines rounded the numerous bends. Now silence reigned amidst the various bodies.

We set up our loudspeakers and began our surrender appeal with little expectation of success. We knew there wasn't a chance in a hundred that Kuribayashi would surrender, but we wanted to give him one last chance. For a good part of a day, I took Sakai around the front lines to call out to any Japanese survivors to surrender. In one place the Marines had surrounded a cave, and knew there were Japanese inside. From a cliff overhanging the cave, Sakai called out to his comrades to surrender, lest the cave be blown up with them inside. Some Marines were waiting for a response, their rifles at the ready. When the defenders heard the message, they came charging out in one of their famous banzai charges. But there was no one in front of them to confront, and they were easy targets for the Marines above them.[22]

Sakai was a true rarity among the soldiers defending Iwo Jima. A graduate of the prestigious University of Tokyo, over time he had gradually realized the futility of continuing to fight the Americans. I recall he told McLean that his comrades were down to a half cup of rancid water and a hard biscuit a day and that morale had plummeted. Men no longer blindly trusted their officers, and some men were losing faith in the emperor. Sakai's goal, it seems, was to help end the fighting as soon as possible and to live in peace. He wanted to live for Japan's future— not die in vain for a lost cause. In a very real sense, Sergeant Sakai's attitude anticipated the sea change among the Japanese people as a whole that helps explain the great postwar success story of that country. Sakai had made a choice for his own salvation. When I went with the 28th Marines to Sasebo, Japan, for occupation duty, I witnessed this change firsthand. I must say, it came as a big surprise, and not only to me. Within a few years, most of his countrymen would follow in Sakai's footsteps. It was a choice well expressed in an editorial in the Nippon Times *right after the Japanese surrender in August:*

If we allow the pain and humiliation to breed within us dark thoughts of revenge, our spirit will be warped and perverted into a morbidly based design. . . . But if we use this pain and this humiliation as spur to self-reflection and reform, the motive force for great constructive effort, there is nothing to stop us from building, out of the ashes of our defeat, a magnificent new Japan free from the dross of the old which is now gone, a new Japan which will vindicate our pride by winning the respect of the world.[23]

Before Sakai was flown back to the United States for further interrogation, he gave two pictures of himself and his family to Lieutenant Lopardo, remarking that he'd rather Lopardo have them than to surrender them to his interrogators. After the war, Lopardo graduated from Harvard Law School and became a superior court judge in California. Until his death in 2004, Judge Lopardo made strenuous efforts to locate Sakai and members of his family so that he could return the pictures. Lopardo's son, Stephen, has continued in this quest. And so at least one of the legacies of Iwo Jima has passed from father to son.

Only one other Japanese prisoner among the sixteen men captured by CT 28 seemed to have shaken off the cultural taboo of surrender. When John Lyttle was fighting with the 3rd Battalion in the gorge, an unusually tall Japanese soldier came down from a ridge waving a dirty white blouse, with the clear intention of giving up. In his pigeon Japanese, Lyttle shouted, "Surrender! I will take you prisoner." The enemy soldier didn't seem to understand what the Marine was trying to say. The Japanese soldier then announced in clear English with a decidedly American accent: "I don't go for this hara-kiri shit!" It turned out he knew English perfectly, had grown up in Chicago, and had been visiting his grandparents in Japan when war broke out. He had been forced to join the army or face incarceration. He chose the army.[24]

On the twenty-first, several hundred American servicemen—soldiers and sailors as well as Marines—attended the dedication ceremony of the 5th Marine Division Cemetery. There Rabbi Ronald Gittelsohn, a chaplain of the 5th Division, gave a moving address that has often been recited when Iwo Jima survivors and their families gather in remembrance:

> Somewhere in this plot of ground there may lie the man who could have discovered the cure for cancer. Under one of these Christian crosses or beneath a Jewish Star of David there may now rest a man who was destined to be a great prophet—to find the way, perhaps, for all to live in plenty, with poverty and hardship for none. Now they lie here silently in this sacred soil, and we gather to consecrate this earth in their memory.
>
> It is not easy to do so. Some of us have buried our closest friends here. We saw these men killed before our very eyes. Any one of us might have died in their places. Indeed, some of us are alive and breathing at this very moment only because men who lie here beneath us had the courage and strength to give their lives for ours. To speak in memory of such men as these is not easy. Of them, too, it can be said with utter truth: "The world will little note nor long remember what we say here. It can never forget what they did here."[25]

Even as the rabbi spoke, the killing raged on four miles to the north. On the night of March 22, all was quiet in the 1st Battalion zone, but sixty Japanese soldiers made a suicide charge up a ravine about two hundred yards behind where both D and F Companies of the 2nd Battalion had their command posts. The Marines around the perimeter held their ground. At this late stage, suicide charges were expected, even welcomed, for they hastened the end of the deadly horror show the Marines had endured now for more than a month. Most of the Japanese were shot by rifle- and BAR-wielding sentries; a few were killed in hand-to-hand fighting.

That same night, Lt. Emery D. H. Friend of Denver, Colorado, a platoon leader in A Company, stealthily led a volunteer demolition squad over the southern ridge of the gorge into the heart of the enemy's remaining defensive network. Working with great speed and efficiency, the squad destroyed twelve enemy emplacements inside the gorge. Friend then led the squad back to the 1st Battalion's lines before dawn without suffering a single casualty. The lieutenant earned himself a Silver Star for the raid.

By March 23, the Marines in the gorge could sense the end was near. Yet this day proved to be the worst of the entire campaign for the company commander of the Suribachi flag raisers, Capt. Dave Severance. He had come to be quite friendly with one of his replacement platoon commanders, Cpl. David C. Bowman. Bowman's wife was pregnant. So was Dave Severance's wife. The two Marines had talked on occasion about impending fatherhood and what it would be like to return home to a new baby. Severance was at the front with Bowman's unit on the twenty-third, just as it was due to be relieved by a platoon from another battalion. Bowman had just received a telegram informing him that his wife had given birth to their first child, a girl.

While Severance, Bowman, and his platoon waited together at the front for the relieving unit's commander, a sniper snuffed out David Bowman's life instantly with a single shot. Severance, bone tired and weary, was deeply affected by the loss. He returned to his CP. There he received a letter from his wife: their baby, a boy, had not survived. "I went off to an area all by myself and cried."[26]

Pfc. Jim Buchanan told me at the fifty-fifth reunion of the Combat Veterans of Iwo Jima that he and Bowman had narrowly missed being shot by a well-camouflaged sniper on March 16 as E Company had approached the gorge. A few days later, Bowman had approached Buchanan, clearly dejected and upset. He had just shot a Japanese sitting on the edge of a road, dressed only in a loincloth, and Bowman discovered after killing the man that he was unarmed. "I didn't have an alternative," said Bowman, plaintively. "He was there in the road, and I had to shoot him." Buchanan told me, "I believe this affected him for the rest of his short life, since he was such a compassionate and good man. It has been fifty-five years, but I still miss him."

It took two more days to finish off the Japanese positions in Bloody Gorge. There was no quit in the 150 or so hard cores holed up in the final pocket. Dog-tired Marines, some almost sleepwalking, pressed forward, yard by yard, reducing one enemy position, and then another. Cpl. Wes Plummer was one of only a handful of men in H Company who had been on the line since D-day. On March 24, Plummer exposed himself to enemy fire for almost two hours, laying down suppressive machine-gun fire so his company could make its final advance toward the sea. His Silver Star citation reads:

> Corporal Plummer, a machine gun squad leader, set up his weapon, single-handedly, while subjected to deadly fire from concealed enemy riflemen. The company advance had been halted by fire from enemy emplacements. Disregarding his personal safety, Corporal Plummer placed his gun on elevated, open terrain upon which a short time earlier, one machine gun had been demolished, killing one man and wounding two. For almost two hours he delivered supporting fire for the advancing troops. Though he was a constant target for . . . enemy rifle fire, Corporal Plummer . . . unaided, kept his gun in action. He managed to neutralize the enemy fire and thus assured his company of only light resistance in the advance. His courageous conduct was in keeping with the highest traditions of the United States Naval Service.

One of the most powerful photographs we have of the entire battle (see photo insert) shows Plummer blasting away with a .30-caliber machine gun during the fight for Mount Suribachi. His position is surrounded by thousands of spent cartridges and more than a dozen boxes of ammo. In the photo, Plummer seems a man possessed—we only see his profile, but he wears a look of iron determination—as if he couldn't be displaced by a direct hit from a large-caliber artillery shell. By all accounts this soft-spoken Oklahoma native lost neither his vigilance nor his desire to take the fight to the enemy. A few days before he earned the Silver Star, he had been dug in for the night when he suddenly found himself in a wrestling match with a Japanese infiltrator. Plummer killed the attacker with his K-bar knife.

Though wounded early in the battle, Plummer quickly returned to his unit and was lucky enough to sail from Iwo Jima with what was left of the 28th Marines on March 26. Plummer was one of only a handful of men who had landed on D-day with the assault teams of the 3rd Battalion and left on his own two feet.

On the morning of March 25, Wes Plummer's battalion, along with the 3rd Battalion of the 26th Marines, attacked into a pocket about fifty yards square and cleared the gorge of resistance all the way to its western mouth at the edge of the sea.

Still, the fighting and dying dragged on. During the Combat Team's final night on the island, fourteen enemy infiltrators were killed attacking the Team's command post. Then, at 0400 on March 26, about three hundred Japanese soldiers, many armed only with swords, moved stealthily down from the north along the west side of Airfield No. 2. Undetected, they commenced a savage and well-organized attack on the Army Air Forces tent camps and the 38th Army Field Hospital, the last organized Japanese assault. Wild hand-to-hand fighting ensued. Many pilots, maintenance-crew members of the Army's 7th Fighter Command, and badly wounded Marines in hospital beds were killed by marauding enemy soldiers.

Among the units hit was C Company, 5th Pioneer Battalion, which recently had performed so valiantly on CT 28's front line. The last Medal of Honor earned on Iwo Jima went to 1st Lt. Harry L. Martin of that company. Martin killed several marauding enemy soldiers with his .45 pistol while rallying a diverse group of Americans, including black Marine service troops and soldiers from the 147th Infantry, to break the back of the last attack. In this final fight, 44 Army Air Forces men were killed and 88 wounded. The Marine Pioneers also took heavy casualties: 9 men killed and 31 wounded. More than 250 Japanese corpses littered the battleground. All was quiet by about 0800 that morning.

Tom Cox of C Company, 5th Engineers, spent the night of the twenty-fifth in the bottom of Bloody Gorge. He and his partner had planted a number of antipersonnel mines in front of caves there.

Before midnight they heard several of the mines explode, followed by much yelling and general commotion. To this day, Cox thinks that many of the participants in the last banzai were survivors of the gorge.

According to the 28th Regiment's War Diary, the unit had suffered 140 men killed in action or died of wounds and 388 wounded in action between March 11, when the Team began to fight through the approaches to the gorge, and March 25, when the fighting ceased.

The fate of B Company's platoon leadership during the last phase of the battle, commencing on March 11, illustrates what happened to the rifle platoons in all three infantry battalions of CT 28. On the opening day of the drive toward the gorge, Franklin W. Fouch, a second lieutenant from the 27th Replacement Battalion, assumed command of the 1st Platoon. He was the unit's seventh commander since the landing. Three days later, Fouch assumed command of the 2nd Platoon as well, when its eleventh commander, Pvt. Dale O. Cassell, was killed. Cassell had commanded the 2nd Platoon twice—before and after Gunnery Sergeant Julius Wittenberg had led the unit for all of a few hours before being seriously wounded and evacuated.

When Fouch took over the 2nd Platoon, it consisted of three Marines. None of those three men—two privates and a corporal—had been in the original platoon of forty-two men that landed on D-day. Every one of those Marines had been killed or evacuated with wounds. Two days later, both privates in the 2nd Platoon were killed by friendly fire when a bazooka round fell short, landing directly in their foxhole.

By the day the battle ended, Fouch was also in charge of the 3rd Platoon, which had been led for eight days by Pfc. G. C. Burk Jr. Burk had been wounded in the gorge by shrapnel in his belly, and he could not stand up straight, but he refused evacuation until the final pocket was cleaned out and the victors could walk freely on the beach at the western mouth of the gorge. Burk had landed on D day, and he was not going to quit until the battle was well and truly over.[27]

Early on the next day—March 26—Private Burke joined the remnants of Regimental Combat Team 28 in a solemn route march from the gorge to the southern end of the island, under the shadow of Mount Suribachi. Cpl. William W. Byrd recalled that on the morning of March 26

> Martin Anderson from Salt Lake City and I walked up a hill and looked out across the vast Pacific Ocean. We looked to the north in the direction of Japan and wondered what lay ahead. We shook hands, and he said, "Man, you need a shave." Lt. Armstrong sent word to the other two companies in the 2nd Battalion that he had gotten word from the Command Post of the 28th Regiment to have our troops move out in about an hour. We were headed for the beach area near Mt. Suribachi, four miles away. . . . Everyone got their gear together. My rifle was just about all I had. Lt. [Edwin] Armstrong looked around and was worried that some of the weary, dirty, twice-wounded Marines might not be able to make the hike. We formed two lines for our march back to the south end where we first landed thirty-six days earlier. As we walked down the single-lane road parallel to the beach, it seemed that everybody was looking down and not looking to the left, at all the hellish places where so many of our comrades had died.[28]

Shortly after dawn on March 26, Combat Team 28 left the gorge in route march, headed for the 5th Marine Division Cemetery for a brief memorial ceremony prior to leaving Iwo. Colonel Liversedge and Major Peatross went ahead by jeep. Williams and I brought up the rear. As we watched the passing column from a rocky outcrop near Nishi Ridge, I told Williams that I was reminded of Kipling's "Route Marchin'," a poem I had learned as a young teenager, and I recited a verse for the colonel's benefit:

> *"There's a regiment a-comin' down the Grand Trunk Road,*
> *With its best foot first*
> *And the road a-slidin' past,*
> *An' every bloomin' campin'-ground exactly like the last. . . ."*

Williams nodded and said simply, "The next camp for us will be in Japan!"

The 28th Marines marched down to the 5th Division Cemetery in the flatland between Suribachi and the Motoyama plateau. There was a short memorial service, after which the men dispersed into small groups and began to walk, slowly and deliberately, through row after row of white crosses and Stars of David, in search of their fallen comrades, to say a last good-bye. Many Marines wept openly. Combat correspondent Sgt. Francis W. Cockrel was on the scene to witness the unit as it prepared to leave the island:

> I landed with the 28th Marines and had good friends among them. Theirs had been the task of taking Suribachi at the first, the key to the operation, and they took it. Then, with a few days' rest, they were on the front lines almost steadily until the very end, and it fell to their lot to hit that deep gorge with its hive of caves, which the Japs chose for the final stand. And chose well. I was on the beach when the 28th came down to re-embark. They had finished the Gorge only the day before. They were cheerful, for they were getting off the island now, but they were quiet men. They would smile instead of laugh. You couldn't distinguish officers from men—all dusty, all weary, nearly all heavily bearded.
>
> A battalion sergeant major stopped to pass a word with a sergeant I was talking to. The sergeant said he was looking forward to getting back into camp and coming over to the battalion's sergeants' mess for a good meal once again. A battalion's normal complement of sergeants is sixty-nine. "Well, I got six now," he said. Six from sixty-nine.[29]

EPILOGUE

rom Iwo Jima, the remnants of Combat Team 28 sailed eastward, back to the port of Hilo. Then they returned to their old stomping grounds at Camp Tarawa, where they took on new Marines, equipment, and weapons and inaugurated another training cycle. The next campaign slated for the Team was Operation Olympic, the invasion of Kyushu. It was to have been the largest amphibious operation in history, but Olympic never happened. It was precluded by the Japanese surrender following the dropping of the atomic bombs on Hiroshima and Nagasaki in August 1945.

In the wake of Japan's defeat, the 28th Marines sailed to Sasebo, Japan, arriving on September 22, 1945. They joined the rest of the American occupation force in anticipating a hostile reception from the civilians and a difficult, complex mission. Instead, they encountered smiling children and a war-weary population, eager to cooperate with their conquerors.

Three months later, they sailed back to Camp Pendleton. On

January 23, the unit was deactivated as part of the great drawdown in the American armed forces following World War II.

★

EVEN BEFORE THE men of CT 28 boarded ships and took to the sea, they began to reflect on the meaning of their ordeal. For survivors of the unit, for Fred, for John Lyttle, Ovian Von Behren, Wes Plummer, and all the rest, the reflection persists even today.

Putting together this book has been a remarkable experience and an education in the meaning of brotherhood, sacrifice, and the resilience of the human spirit. For more than four years, with the help of my CT 28 comrades, James Warren and I have been reconstructing the seminal event of my life and one of the greatest battles of the twentieth century. It has been an unusual privilege. Men who shaped my understanding of what it means to be a Marine and an American—Liversedge, Williams, Peatross, Wilkins, Tanner, Strank, and so many others—have become, through memory and reflection, my daily companions once again. The spirit of CT 28 lives on!

My respect and admiration for all young men who fought in the whirlwind of death has brought tears to my eyes many times. Thoughts of what they endured and sacrificed have strengthened my resolve to, in the words of my CT 28 comrade Barber Conable, "make a contribution to the future beyond my own individual, normal, daily duty" on their behalf.

I was recently given a letter by Mark Kleber, written by his father, Victor, the CO of the reconnaissance platoon of CT 28, shortly after we returned to Camp Tarawa. It might have been written by any of us who survived the battle:

Dear Folks,

I hardly know where to begin, as the events of life since the 19th of February cover a million lifetimes—plus the fact that my handwriting is shaky and I find it extremely difficult to sit down and write, let alone concentrate my thoughts. This, I am told, is the normal reaction to sustained combat. . . .

My health is excellent, my spirits are on the way up, because I am now back at our old camp. After a little acclimation, we will settle down in preparation for what the future holds. . . . Before going to our ships on Iwo, we marched to our cemetery—the largest Marine burial ground in the world—the regiment, or what remained of it, followed into the grounds to stand at attention between the white crosses. I was the last man to enter, as I was the Company Commander of the last Company in the order of the march. As I stood there among my comrades— bearded, dirty (we hadn't bathed for over 30 days) and very tired—I felt like sobbing because I remembered the day in our tent camp, amidst the mountains of California, we proudly passed in review after receiving our regimental colors. We were more than 3,000 strong—the world's best and we were damn proud of it—but now, just a handful remain. Our Colonel, 6'4 and 240 pounds and 54 years old, was respected and loved by all who knew him. His speech was short and simple, but it hit home. While he spoke, newly arrived P51s cavorted in victory rolls overhead. Yes, "Harry the Horse," the famous leader of the First Raider Regiment, known for his courage and drive, gave the word to his men as a patriarch speaks to his children. He looked tired—oh, so tired—but his posture was erect and head high, as he mentioned in closing that our job now was to rebuild the regiment, and go on as those we would be leaving behind would go on: as United States Marines.

As we went to the ships, the air was filled with B29s taking off for Tokyo and with them, fighter escorts—the Army's best—for the first time in WWII. I thanked the Almighty for answering my constant prayers for strength to carry on, and to keep as many of my men as possible from dying. Death was around every corner. The Regiment landed 3,200 strong and had taken 2,900 casualties. I landed with 27 picked men and had 17 casualties. I had no idea what effect such an experience has on a person. Through the grace of God, I was not wounded, my escapes were miraculous, and in the hands of God. For some reason, He saw fit to keep me safe.

Returning to the same camp we left, we were given a wonderful welcome. Roscoe, our lion mascot, now weighed 160 pounds, licked the bald head of one of my sergeants (the only one I had left) to show his approval of our return.

More mail from me coming up. Yes, my dearest possessions, it's great to be alive.

Love, Vic[1]

More than sixty-three years have passed since the 28th Marines and their comrades in arms departed Iwo Jima. The survivors of the battle and their families continue to meet at annual reunions, where they renew close friendships and talk of the bad old days on Iwo and what they have done with their lives since they left the island. Being Marines, they gather in pride to honor their departed comrades in arms.

A 5th Division veteran of the battle who later became an Episcopalian priest, Sydney Woodd-Cahusac, spoke eloquently about the meaning of such commemoration in a homily before fellow veterans and family members at the National Cathedral in Washington, D.C., on the fifty-fifth anniversary of the battle:

> I call these remarks "May Our Light Shine Before Others" because in the Sermon on the Mount, Christ told his followers, in words fitting the thought of many faiths, "You are the light of the world. A city built on a hill cannot be hid."
>
> Nor can a flag, raised on a hill called Mount Suribachi fifty-five years ago. That event was captured forever in a remarkable photograph which lives in the minds and hearts of not just us here, but of an entire nation. This is because what was done on Iwo Jima fifty-five years ago has indeed been a light shining before those who follow us. It was a piece of work "well done," to use the old understated Marine phrase, which, freely translated, means "done extraordinarily well." For as was said at the time, "Uncommon valor was a common virtue."
>
> Six thousand eight hundred men who landed on Iwo Jima did not leave with us when the task was done. They were mostly young men in their late teens and early twenties in the prime of their virile and healthy youth. But they were denied, in the most abrupt fashion, the chance to live a life—mistakes and all—as you and I have been privileged to do for the fifty-five years since we last saw them. Only the Lord knows what they might have accomplished—for friends, family, community and country—had they lived.
>
> Now I ask you to put names as well as faces to the men you knew. Remember, that in the eyes of God, as the Book of Wisdom of Solomon assures us, they are full of immortality. Immortality is

not our gift to give, but we can pay them the highest tribute that is in our power to give, and that is to recall them individually, as human beings, as friends and not just as numbers.[2]

The Lions of Iwo Jima was written in large measure as a call to contemporary and future generations to remember a terrible battle, fought at a crucial time in history; to remember the cruel demands and sacrifices that war requires of men. And finally, this book is a call to remember the men of Iwo Jima, living and dead, by name.

APPENDIX 1

COMBAT TEAM 28: ORGANIZATION

The 28th Marines, an infantry regiment consisting of three infantry battalions and about 3,250 individuals, was the principal fighting element around which the Combat Team was formed. The World War II combat team was a very flexible organization. It could vary in strength from day to day, even from hour to hour, depending on the mission and the type of enemy opposition. The total number of men of all services who at any given time were supporting CT 28 is impossible to determine. For example, at several junctures, whole battalions of the 27th Marines were under Colonel Liversedge's command. And quite often, the Team had a Navy cruiser and several destroyers providing fire support exclusively to its units.

A snapshot of CT 28's composition for the Battle of Iwo Jima is shown below. The numbers of personnel listed are not exact "Table of Organization" (T/O) numbers as set by Marine Corps headquarters for a World War II Marine combat team. Rather, with a few minor exceptions, they are the actual numbers of men in the units as of D-day, February 19, 1945.

COMBAT TEAM 28

Col. Harry Liversedge, commanding officer (CO)
Lt. Col. Robert Williams, executive officer (XO)

Headquarters and Service Company: Liversedge's staff and essential support components:

- Operations
- Supply
- Maintenance
- Manpower
- Motor transport
- Communications
- Medical and dental
- Intelligence
- Reconnaissance

Strength: 38 officers, 290 enlisted

Weapons company: Four 75mm half-tracks; twelve 37mm antitank guns, distributed among the landing teams as the combat team CO sees fit.

Maj. Henry Rolph, CO
Maj. James Finch, XO
Strength: 8 officers, 165 enlisted

Landing Team 1/28: A reinforced infantry battalion
Lt. Col. Jackson Butterfield, CO
Maj. William Wood, XO

1st Battalion, 28th Marines:

- 81mm mortars
- Three infantry companies
- 60mm mortars

- Machine guns

Strength: 37 officers, 895 enlisted

Platoon, 5th Engineers: Mine warfare, demolitions
Strength: 1 officer, 45 enlisted

Forward Observer Team: Control of artillery fire
Strength: 2 officers, 12 enlisted

Detachment, 5th Joint Assault Signal Company (JASCO): control
of naval gunfire and air support
Strength: 3 officers, 15 enlisted

Collecting Section, 5th Medical Battalion: Casualty handling
Strength: 14 enlisted

Detachment, 31st Replacement Draft: Litter bearers
Strength: 12 enlisted

Liaison Party, C Company, 5th Tank Battalion: Tank support
Strength: 3 enlisted

Landing Team 2/28. A reinforced infantry battalion
    Lt. Col. Chandler Johnson, CO
    Maj. Thomas Pearce, XO
    Same composition as Landing Team 1/28
Strength: 43 officers, 996 enlisted

Landing Team 3/28: A reinforced infantry battalion
    Lt. Col. Charles Shepard, CO
    Maj. Tolson Smoak, XO
    Same composition as Landing Team 1/28

Strength: 42 officers, 945 enlisted

C Company, 5th Tank Battalion: Fourteen to sixteen Sherman
medium tanks
Strength: 5 officers, 120 enlisted

C Company, 5th Pioneer Battalion: Stevedores, shore party teams,
logistic support
Strength: 7 officers, 170 enlisted

3rd Battalion, 13th Marine Regiment: Artillery: twelve 105mm
howitzers
Strength: 23 officers, 600 enlisted

APPENDIX 2

COMBAT TEAM 28 SURVIVORS: WHAT THEY DID AFTER THE WAR

This is only a partial list of postwar activities of survivors who were touched by the spirit of CT 28 during the battle. Many of the survivors have passed away, and many of the living have been impossible to find. Many survivors we found had, after the battle, pledged to themselves to do something of value with their lives in honor of those we left on Iwo. Many of these men were active in civic affairs—schools, church, and government.

Name	Duty on Iwo	Postwar
Abbatielo, Al	Engineer, demolitions	Construction superintendent, New York and Puerto Rico
Antonelli, Tony	Infantry battalion CO, CT 27	Brigadier general, USMC
Armstrong, Ed	Infantry company CO, LT 2/28	Lawyer, Chicago
Beech, Keyes	Marine combat correspondent	*Chicago Tribune*; Pulitzer Prize for Korean War reporting
Bishop, Richard	Artillery battery CO, 3/13	Lawyer, Washington, D.C.

Name	Duty on Iwo	Postwar
Bradley, John	Corpsman	Director, funeral home
Bulkowski, Len	Clerk/runner, CT 28	Benedictine monk
Caldwell, Frank	Infantry company CO	Colonel, USMC; director, USMC History and Museums
Carney, Robert	Infantry company CO, CT 28	Brigadier general, USMC
Conable, Barber	Artillery battery CO, 4/13	Minority leader, U.S. House of Representatives; president, World Bank
Cox, Thomas	Engineer, demolitions	CIA
Daskalakis, John	1st Sgt, E Company, Infantry, LT 2/28	Colonel, USMC; treasurer, Combat Veterans of Iwo
Dike, George	Artillery battery CO	PhD, college professor
Finch, James H., "Bill"	XO, weapons company; XO, LT 2/28 (also commanded an infantry battalion in Korean War)	Architect: designed Coca Cola headquarters and BellSouth Tower, both in Atlanta, also many sports complexes and stadiums; professor, Georgia Tech
Gillespie, Kyle	Aerial observer	Head of major automobile agency, Houston
Hammond, Ivan	JASCO Air Support	Principle engineer, Union Carbide
Hatch, Norman	Photo officer	Major, USMC; photo archivist, author
Haynes, Fred	Operations officer, CT 28	Major general, USMC; commanded two marine divisions; chairman, American Turkish Council; executive, LTV Aerospace; Council on Foreign Relations
Henderson, Wm.	Operations officer, LT 1/28	Leading developer, North Carolina; president, Jr. Chamber of Commerce, North Carolina
Holes, Floyd	Communicator, CT 28	Chief engineer, radio station
Hooke, Walter	Mortars	Teaching; Veteran Affairs
Huffhines, John	Communicator, artillery, 3/13	Head of energy company; president, 5th Marine Division Association

Name	Duty on Iwo	Postwar
Jacobs, Ray	Radioman, LT 2/28	TV news anchor, San Francisco, California
Kleber, Victor	Recon, CT 28	Colonel, USMC; Korean War and Vietnam War veteran
Leader, Robert	Infantry, LT 2/28	Art professor; art museum director, Notre Dame University
Liversedge, Harry	CO, CT 28	Brigadier general, USMC; director Marine Corps Reserve
Lopardo, Fiorenzo	Company CO, LT 3/28	Harvard Law; superior court judge, California
Lowery, Lou	Combat photographer	Photo editor, *Leatherneck* magazine
Lyttle, John	Infantry, LT 3/28	Construction management, southern California; expert trout fisherman
McCain, Jinx	Infantry, CT 28	Colonel, USMC; Korean War and Vietnam War veteran
McLean, John	Language officer, CT, 28	CIA; financial manager, broker
Meisenheimer, Bill	Infantry, LT 1/28	National union representative for several leading U.S. companies
Miller, Richard	Infantry, LT 1/28	Leading trial lawyer, Houston
Naylor, Art	Company CO, LT 2/28	National representative for leading pharmaceutical company
O'Hara, James	Infantry/artillery	New York businessman
Padavano, Carl	Infantry, CT 28	Superintendent of city schools, New Jersey
Peatross, O. F.	XO, LT 3/28	Major general, USMC; noted sculptor of Carolina waterfowl
Plummer, Wes	Infantry, machine gunner, LT 3/28	Senior executive, Shell Oil
Roach, Phil	Company CO, LT 1/28	Football coach, Texas Christian University

Name	Duty on Iwo	Postwar
Rolph, Henry	CO, weapons company, CT 28	Stanford Law School; superior court judge, California
Russell, Gerald	Battalion CO, CT 27	Special assistant to the president, University of Pennsylvania
Schrier, H. George	Company CO, LT 2/28	Major automobile agency, Florida
Severance, Dave	Company CO, LT 2/28	Colonel, USMC; Marine fighter pilot
Shriver, James	Infantry, LT 3/28	CPA; established Arthur Anderson accounting offices in much of South America
Spangler, Robert	Operations officer, LT 3/28	Farmer, Arizona
Thomey, Tedd	Operations officer, LT 1/28	Broadway playwright; author of *Immortal Images*; newspaperman, *San Francisco Chronicle*
Veronee, Marvin	Naval gunfire spotter, LT 1/28	University of Chicago, administration
Von Behren, Ovian	Infantry, LT 1/28	Police lieutenant, Florida
Waterhouse, Charles	Engineer, demolitions	Colonel, USMC; combat artist; sculptor
Wells, G. Greeley	Infantry, LT 2/28	President, Sanborn map company; mayor of N.J. town; real estate developer
White, Richard	Language officer, CT 28	Lawyer, Seattle
Williams, Robert	XO, CT 28	Brigadier general, USMC; consultant, Brookings Institution; author
Wood, William	XO, LT 1/28	Colonel, USMC; senior industry executive, Texas
Woodd-Cahusac, Sydney	Headquarters, 5th Marine Div.	Treasurer, Rockefeller University; Episcopal priest, Connecticut
Wright, Frank	Infantry, LT 1/28	College professor

NOTES

Introduction

1. V Amphibious Corps, USMC, "Estimate of the Enemy Situation, 5 March 1945" (typescript, Fred Haynes collection), 3.

2. Holland M. Smith and Percy Finch, *Coral and Brass* (New York: Scribner's, 1949), 254.

3. Ibid., 255.

4. Task Force 56 Intelligence Report, quoted in Whitman S. Bartley, *Iwo Jima: Amphibious Epic* (Washington, DC: USMC, 1954), 30.

5. Robert S. Burrell, "Did We Have to Fight Here?," Iwo Jima special issue, *World War II Magazine* (Leesburg, VA: Weider History Group, 2006): 66.

6. Smith and Finch, *Coral and Brass*, 238.

1: Forming Up at Camp Pendleton

1. This description of the formation of the 5th Division and the 28th Marines draws extensively on H. M. Conner, *The Spearhead: The World War II History of the 5th Marine Division* (Washington, DC: Infantry Journal Press, 1950), 1–10.

2. Readers looking for more detail on the development of amphibious doctrine should consult the definitive work on the subject, Jeter A. Isely and Philip A. Crowl, *The U.S. Marines and Amphibious War: Its Theory, and Its Practice in the Pacific* (Princeton: Princeton University Press, 1951), 1–71.

3. Quoted in Victor H. Krulak, *First to Fight: An Inside View of the U.S. Marine Corps* (1984; repr., Annapolis, MD: Naval Institute Press, 1999), 157.

4. John K. McLean, "World War II Reminiscences and the Battle of Iwo Jima" (typescript, n.d., Fred Haynes collection), 4–6.

5. Ibid., 5.

6. Alice Tuckerman Williams, letter to Fred Haynes, n.d., Fred Haynes collection.

7. United States Marine Corps, *Warfighting: The U.S. Marine Corps Book of Strategy* (1989; repr., New York: Doubleday, 1994), 12–13.

8. This and all subsequent citations for medals awarded to individuals during the Iwo Jima campaign were obtained from the Department of the Navy, Navy Historical Center, Washington Navy Yard, Washington, DC, or the USMC Awards Branch, Quantico, VA.

2: The Adversaries Prepare for Battle

1. Marvin D. Veronee, *Sailor on the Beach: A Memoir of Naval Service in World War II* (self-published, 2005), 56.

2. Wayne H. Bellamy, interview by Charles Petterson, July 1996, transcript, Fred Haynes collection, 21.

3. Robert Snodgrass, interview by Alice Clark, July 1996, transcript, Fred Haynes collection, 6.

4. John B. Lyttle, "If I Should Die Before I Wake: One Marine's Experiences on Iwo Jima" (typescript, 2002, Fred Haynes collection), 5.

5. Snodgrass interview, 9.

6. Japanese Operation Order A, No. 3, dated December 1, 1944, quoted in Whitman S. Bartley, *Iwo Jima: Amphibious Epic* (Washington, DC: USMC, 1954), 12.

7. Isely and Crowl, *U.S. Marines and Amphibious War*, 483–85.

8. Unidentified battalion commander of the 28th Marines, quoted in ibid., 484.

9. Kuribayashi letter, quoted in Richard F. Newcomb, *Iwo Jima* (New York: Henry Holt, 1965), 8–9.

10. Smith and Finch, *Coral and Brass*, 255.

11. Ibid., 259–60.

12. Snodgrass interview, 17.

13. Isley and Crowl, *U.S. Marines and Amphibious War*, 440.

14. Ibid., 586–87.

15. "Courageous Battle Vows," quoted in Newcomb, *Iwo Jima*, 50.

16. McLean, "World War II Reminiscences," 8.

17. William W. Byrd, *By the Dawn's Early Light* (self-published, 2005, Fred Haynes collection), 11.

18. Ted White, Marine Corps History Division Veteran Questionnaire about the Battle of Iwo Jima, 1995, Fred Haynes collection.

19. Robert H. Williams, "Morale and Esprit de Corps," *U.S. Naval Institute Proceedings* (January 1961): 137.

20. White questionnaire.

3: The Assault

1. Turner and Smith, quoted in Newcomb, *Iwo Jima*, 72, 75.

2. Suver, quoted in Newcomb, *Iwo Jima*, 103–4.

3. Jerry Seright, quoted in Floyd O. Holes, "The Iwo Jima Communicators" (typescript, n.d., Fred Haynes collection), 43.

4. Snodgrass interview, 14.

5. John P. Marquand, "Iwo Jima Before H-Hour," *Harper's* (May 1945): 496.

6. Richard Wheeler, *The Bloody Battle for Suribachi* (1965; repr., Annapolis, MD: Naval Institute Press, 1994), 20.

7. Ray Jacobs, interview by authors, August 2006, transcript, Fred Haynes collection.

8. Holes, "Iwo Jima Communicators," 44.

9. Carnara Carruth, interview by Fred Haynes, July 2007, transcript, Fred Haynes collection.

10. Newcomb, *Iwo Jima*, 99.

11. Byrd, *By the Dawn's Early Light*, 15.

12. Liversedge radio message, quoted in Bill D. Ross, *Iwo Jima: Legacy of Valor* (New York: Vanguard Press, 1985), 65.

13. Greeley Wells, typescript of recollections, n.d., Fred Haynes collection, 3.

14. Ray Jacobs, interview by authors, July 2006, transcript, Fred Haynes collection.

15. Stanley Drabowski, quoted in Lynn Kessler, ed., *Never in Doubt: Remembering Iwo Jima* (Annapolis, MD: Naval Institute Press, 1999), 46.

16. Albert D'Amico, quoted in Kessler, *Never in Doubt*, 61.

17. Veronee, *Sailor on the Beach*, 92–93.

18. Unidentified Marine, quoted in Isely and Crowl, *U.S. Marines and Amphibious War*, 488.

19. Anthony Visconti, interview by Alice Clark, July 1996, transcript, Fred Haynes collection, 4.

20. Ibid., 6.

21. This account of Wright's platoon is drawn from two key sources: Frank Wright, interview by James Warren, February 2005, and Robert E. Allen, *The First Battalion of the 28th Marines on Iwo Jima* (Jefferson, NC: McFarland, 1999), 30–32.

22. Ovian Von Behren, interview by Fred Haynes, July 2007, transcript, Fred Haynes collection.

23. Dick Miller, interview by Fred Haynes, July 2007, transcript, Fred Haynes collection.

24. Dick Young, interview by James Warren, March 2006.

25. Dollins story recounted in Newcomb, *Iwo Jima*, 107.

26. William Meisenheimer, interview by Fred Haynes, June 2007, transcript, Fred Haynes collection.

4: The Assault, Part II

1. Lyttle, "If I Should Die Before I Wake," 14.

2. Alvin T. Josephy Jr. et al., "Iwo: The Red-Hot Rock," in *Semper Fidelis: The U.S. Marines in the Pacific, 1942–1945*, eds. Patrick O'Sheel and Gene Cook (New York: William Sloane Associates, 1947), 93–94.

3. T. Grady Gallant, "The Friendly Dead," in O'Sheel and Cook, *Semper Fidelis*, 745–46.

4. Wheeler, *Bloody Battle for Suribachi*, 35.

5. Wayne H. Bellamy, interview by William Petterson, transcript, Fred Haynes collection, 11–12.

6. John Lardner, "A Correspondent at the Battle," in O'Sheel and Cook, *Semper Fidelis*, 729–30.

7. George Dike, interview by Fred Haynes, August 2007, transcript, Fred Haynes collection.

8. Ibid.

9. Anthony Visconti, interview by Alice Clark, July 1996, transcript, Fred Haynes collection, 8.

10. This account of the actions of the 3rd Platoon, E Company, 2nd Battalion, 28th Marines is drawn largely from Wheeler, *Bloody Battle for Suribachi*, 65–67.

11. Unnamed officer, quoted in Josephy, "The Red-Hot Rock," 90.

12. James Bradley with Ron Powers, *Flags of Our Fathers* (2000; repr., New York: Bantam Books, 2006), 73.

13. Wheeler, *Bloody Battle*, 56–57.

14. Francis W. Cockrel, "How It Was on Iwo," O'Sheel and Cook, *Semper Fidelis*, 101–2.

15. Wheeler, *Bloody Battle*, 59.

16. Dick Bishop, interview by the authors, August 2006, transcript, Fred Haynes collection.

5: The Fight for "Hot Rocks"

1. Robert Sherrod, quoted in George W. Garand and Truman R. Strobridge, *Western Pacific Operations*, vol. 4, *History of U.S. Marine Corps Operations in World War II* (Washington, DC: USMC, 1971), 527.

2. Robert Leader, "The Killing Fields of Sulphur Island," *Notre Dame Magazine*, Winter 2002–03, nd.edu/~ndmag/w2002–03/contents.html.

3. Don Traub, "Thirty-four Days on Iwo: A Personal Account" (typescript, n.d., Fred Haynes collection), 5–7.

4. Byrd, *By the Dawn's Early Light*, 19–20.

5. Allen, *First Battalion of the 28th Marines*, 180.

6. Conner, *Spearhead*, 57.

7. Kuribayashi directive, quoted in Newcomb, *Iwo Jima*, 142.

8. Harry Lloyd, interview by Alice Clark, July 1996, transcript, Fred Haynes collection, 6.

9. Lyn L. McCormick, "Iwo Jima Revisited" (typescript, n.d., Fred Haynes collection), 5.

10. Garand and Strobridge, *Western Pacific Operations*, 641.

11. Quoted in Michael E. Young, "Four Ever Young, Brave," *Dallas Morning News*, May 24, 2003, 24A.

12. Robert Snodgrass, interview by Alice Clark, July 1996, transcript, Fred Haynes collection, 16.

13. Leader, "Killing Fields of Sulphur Island."

14. Bernard Link, interview by Fred Haynes, July 2007 transcript, Fred Haynes collection, 9.

15. Josephy et al., "The Red Hot Rock," 95.

16. Quoted in Richard Wheeler, *Bloody Battle for Suribachi*, 108.

17. The account of this firefight draws heavily from Wheeler's narrative. Keith Wells, quoted in ibid., 121.

18. William E. "Gene" Bull, "A Monument to Guts" (typescript, n.d., Fred Haynes collection), 8.

19. Shozo Matsumura, quoted in Newcomb, *Iwo Jima*, 158.

20. 3rd Battalion, 28th Marines, after action report, 14–15.

21. Bull, "Monument to Guts," 9–10.

22. Lowery's quote of Johnson in transcript of interview with Arnold Shapiro, 1985, Arnold Shapiro Productions, Hollywood, CA, 3.

23. Severance, quoted in Bradley, *Flags of Our Fathers*, 202.

24. Raymond Jacobs, "Iwo Jima: February 23, 1945: First Flag Raising" (booklet, Fred Haynes collection, n.d.), 11.

25. Ibid., 15.

26. David Severance, letter to Fred Haynes, July 31, 2003.

27. Note that Harlon Block was not officially identified as a flag raiser until two years after the event. Initially, the Marine Corps wrongly identified Sgt. Hank "the Count" Hansen of Somerville, Massachusetts, as the man at the base of the pole.

28. *Time*, "Story of a Picture," March 26, 1945, 60.

29. Smith and Finch, *Coral and Brass*, 261.

30. *Life* writer quoted in Karal Ann Marling and John Wetanhall, *Iwo Jima: Monuments, Memories, and the American Hero* (Cambridge: Harvard University Press, 1991), 74.

31. Lou Lowery, letter to Raymond Jacobs, September 17, 1947, Fred Haynes collection, courtesy of Raymond Jacobs.

32. John Ripley, e-mail message to Fred Haynes, November 21, 2005. Ripley was at the time the head of the History and Museums Division, USMC.

33. 3rd Battalion, 28th Marines, after action report, 24.

34. Wayne D. Bellamy, interview by Charles W. Petterson, September 1995, transcript, Fred Haynes collection, 18.

35. 5th Marine Division Intelligence Journal, quoted in McLean, "World War II Reminiscences," 54.

36. 5th Marine Division Language Section Report, quoted in McLean, "World War II Reminiscences."

6: The Enemy

1. Toshihiko Ohno, "A Japanese Remembers Iwo Jima," *New York Times Magazine*, February 14, 1965, 26.

2. Ibid., 69.

3. Robert Mueller, interview by James Warren, February 2005.

4. Unidentified Marine enlisted man, interview by James Warren, February 2005.

5. Josephy, "The Red-Hot Rock," 97.

6. Unidentified Marine, quoted in Meirion and Susie Harries, *Soldiers of the Sun: The Rise and Fall of the Imperial Japanese Army* (New York: Random House, 1991), 440.

7. Satoru Omagari, as told to David McNeill, "Even the Dead Were Forced to Fight," in Iwo Jima special issue, *World War II Magazine*, 50.

8. Ulrich Straus, *The Anguish of Surrender: Japanese POWs of World War II* (Seattle: University of Washington, 2003), 249.

9. Ibid., 252.

10. Ibid., 255.

11. Ibid., 477.

12. Harries, *Soldiers of the Sun*, 475–76.

13. Ibid., 478.

14. John Keegan, *The Second World War* (New York: Penguin, 1989), 241.

15. Dower, *War Without Mercy*, 215.

16. Ibid., 247.

17. Ibid.

18. E. B. Sledge, *With the Old Breed, at Peleliu and Okinawa* (New York: Oxford University Press, 1990), xiii.

19. Donald S. Griffin, quoted in Herman Kogan, "These Nips are Nuts," in O'Sheel and Cook, *Semper Fidelis*, 221.

20. Harries, *Soldiers of the Sun*, 6–7.

21. John Keegan, *A History of Warfare* (New York: Random House, 1993), 41–42.

22. Harries, *Soldiers of the Sun*, 481.

23. Ibid., 325.

24. Saburo Ienaga, *The Pacific War: World War II and the Japanese, 1931–1945* (New York: Pantheon Books, 1978), 48–49.

25. Alvin M. Josephy Jr., "Some Japs Surrendered," in O'Sheel and Cook, *Semper Fidelis*, 238.

26. H. Minami, "Psychology of the Japanese People," Translation Series 36 (Honolulu: East-West Center, 1970), 12–13.

27. Gerald P. Averill, *Mustang* (Novato, CA: Presidio Press, 1987), 3.

7: Breaking Through the Main Belt: The Battle for Hill 362A and Nishi Ridge

1. Eugene Hubbard, interview by Charles Petterson, September 1995, transcript, Fred Haynes collection, 40.

2. Harold Keller, quoted in Richard Wheeler, *Iwo* (New York: Lippincott & Crowell, 1980), 177.

3. Ernest Thomas, quoted in Wheeler, *Iwo*, 186.

4. Ovian Von Behren, interview by Fred Haynes, July 2007.

5. Ibid.

6. Al Eutsey, interview by James Warren, February 2005.

7. Wesley Plummer, interview by James Warren, March 2007.

8. Milton Gertz, untitled typescript, Fred Haynes collection, 4.

9. Mike Strank, quoted in Bradley, *Flags of Our Fathers*, 350.

10. 2nd Battalion, 28th Marines, after action report, 27.

11. Cockrel, "How It Was on Iwo," in O'Sheel and Cook, *Semper Fidelis*, 104.

12. Wheeler, *Iwo*, 58–59.

13. Byrd, *By the Dawn's Early Light*, 27.

14. Allen, *First Battalion of the 28th Marines*, 123.

15. John F. Morrill, letter to Edward Gengler's parents, July 13, 1945, Karl Gengler collection.

16. Kuribayashi directive, quoted in Yoshitaka Horie, "Explanation of Japanese Defense Plan and the Battle of Iwo Jima" (typescript, 1946, Fred Haynes collection), 11.

17. Byrd, *By the Dawn's Early Light*, 28.

18. Karl Gengler, letter to Fred Haynes and James Warren, n.d., transcript, Fred Haynes collection.

19. Ovian Von Behren, interview by Fred Haynes, July 2007.

20. Ibid.

21. E. Graham Evans, quoted in Newcomb, *Iwo Jima*, 226.

22. James McDermott, quoted in Richard Bishop interview by Fred Haynes, March 2007.

23. Boyd Kinsey, interview by Fred Haynes, April 2007.

24. Richard Bishop, interview by Fred Haynes and James Warren, August 2006.

25. Clay Coble, quoted in "The Boys of H Company," DVD, directed by Joe Weicha (New Dominion Productions, 2004).

26. Summary of Kuribayashi reports in Newcomb, *Iwo Jima*, 224.

27. Robert Sherrod, quoted in Ross, *Legacy of Valor*, 277.

28. Kuribayashi letter, quoted in ibid., 20.

29. Kuribayashi letter, quoted in John Toland, *The Rising Sun: The Decline and Fall of the Japanese Empire, 1936–1945* (New York: Random House, 1970), 647.

30. Kuribayashi cable, quoted ibid., 661.

31. Schmidt order, quoted in Ross, *Legacy of Valor*, 284.

32. John W. Thomason, *Fix Bayonets!* (New York: Charles Scribner's Sons, 1926), ix–xiii.

8: Driving North Toward Kitano Point

1. Edward Craig letter, quoted in Garand and Strobridge, *Western Pacific Operations*, 608.

2. 5th Marine Division Intelligence Report, n.d., quoted in Bartley, *Amphibious Epic*, 140.

3. 3rd Battalion, 28th Marines, after action report, 24.

4. James Blackwell, interview by Fred Haynes, July 2007.

5. 3rd Battalion, 28th Marines, after action report, 25.

6. 5th Marine Division Intelligence Report, n.d., quoted in Bartley, *Amphibious Epic*, 190.

7. Gordon Byrum, quoted in Holes, "The Iwo Jima Communicators," 67.

8. Nimitz decree, quoted in Newcomb, *Iwo Jima*, 277–78.

9: Bloody Gorge

1. Yoshitaka Horie, "Explanation of Japanese Defense Plan and Battle of Iwo Jima" (typescript, 1946, Fred Haynes collection), 14.

2. Horie, "Japanese Defense Plan," Appendix, 1–2.

3. Robert Coster, letter to Gloria Coster, March 25, 1945, Fred Haynes collection.

4. Don Traub, "Thirty-four Days on Iwo: A Personal Account" (typescript, n.d., Fred Haynes collection), 15–16.

5. Lyttle, "If I Should Die Before I Wake," 34–35.

6. Robert B. Hansen and Barbara Hansen Harris, "A Grateful Nation Remembers Iwo Jima" (typescript, n.d., Fred Haynes collection), 21.

7. Ibid., 21.

8. Ibid., 22.

9. Ibid., 23.

10. Traub, "Thirty-four Days on Iwo," 8–10.

11. Coster, letter to Gloria Coster, 5.

12. Ibid., 6.

13. John H. Harrison, interview by Fred Haynes, January 2007, transcript, Fred Haynes collection.

14. Allen, *First Battalion of the 28th Marines*, 180.

15. Lyttle, "If I Should Die Before I Wake," 32–33.

16. Traub, "Thirty-four Days on Iwo," 22.

17. Gage Hotaling, quoted in Donald L. Miller, "Deathtrap Island," in Iwo Jima special issue, *World War II Magazine*, 15.

18. McLean, "World War II Reminiscences," 22.

19. Wesley Plummer, interview by James Warren, February 2007.

20. Horie, "Japanese Defense Plan," 13.

21. F. V. Lopardo, quoted in "Four Marines Remember Iwo Jima," videotape no. 2 ("Document It" on Video, a Multimedia Company, 1996).

22. McLean, "World War II Reminiscences," 28–29.

23. *Nippon Times* quoted in Toland, *Rising Sun*, 870.

24. Lyttle, "If I Should Die Before I Wake," 38.

25. Roland B. Gittelsohn, "Memorial Address at the Fifth Division Cemetery at Iwo Jima," in O'Sheel and Cook, *Semper Fidelis*, 167.

26. Dave Severence, quoted in Wheeler, *Iwo*, 230.

27. This information on command changes in B Company is found in Conner, *Spearhead*, 180–82.

28. Byrd, *By the Dawn's Early Light*, 35–36.

29. Francis W. Cockrel, "How It Was on Iwo," in O'Sheel and Cook, *Semper Fidelis*, 104–5.

Epilogue

1. Victor Kleber, letter to his parents, April 16, 1945, Fred Haynes collection.

2. Sydney Woodd-Cuhusac, "May Our Light Shine Before Others," in program for the fifty-fifth anniversary commemoration of the Battle of Iwo Jima, 2000, Fred Haynes collection.

SELECTED BIBLIOGRAPHY

A Note About Primary Sources Consulted

All the various units that comprised Combat Team 28 and the 5th Marine Division, of which CT 28 formed a major part, produced after action reports, war diaries, intelligence reports, and intelligence journals during and after the Battle of Iwo Jima. Many of these reports have been quoted directly in the text and are cited in the endnotes. Many others provided specific bits of information on casualties, dates, or unit engagements that proved indispensable in helping us shape the narrative. Virtually all of these documents may be obtained from Record Group 127, the operational records of the Marine Corps in World War II, National Archives, College Park, Maryland. There are far too many of these reports relevant to CT 28's battle to be listed individually here. Nor do we include below individual citations for the welter of typescripts, letters, and self-published works by members of CT 28 that are cited in the endnotes as belonging to the Fred Haynes collection.

This bibliography cites the major works consulted that are readily available collections of primary source accounts from participants and correspondents on the scene, as well as the best secondary sources on the Battle of Iwo Jima.

Alexander, Joseph. *Closing In: Marines in the Seizure of Iwo Jima*. Washington, DC: USMC, 1994.

———. *Sea Soldiers in the Cold War*. Annapolis: Naval Institute Press, 1995.

Allen, Robert E. *The First Battalion of the 28th Marines on Iwo Jima: A Day-by-Day History*. Jefferson, NC: McFarland & Co., 1999.

Averill, Gerald P. *Mustang*. Novato, CA: Presidio Press, 1987.

Bartley, Whitman S. *Iwo Jima: Amphibious Epic*. Washington, DC: USMC, 1961.

Bradley, James, with Ron Powers. *Flags of Our Fathers*. New York: Bantam Books, 2000.

Burrell, Robert S. "Did We Have to Fight Here?" Iwo Jima special issue, *World War II Magazine*, 2006.

Conner, Howard M. *The Spearhead: The World War II History of the 5th Marine Division*. Washington, DC: Infantry Journal Press, 1950.

Dower, John W. *War Without Mercy: Race and Power in the Pacific War*. New York: Pantheon Books, 1986.

Garand, George W., and Truman R. Strobridge. *Western Pacific Operations*, vol. 4, *History of U.S. Marine Corps Operations in World War II*. Washington, DC: USMC, 1971.

Harries, Meirion, and Susie Harries. *Soldiers of the Sun: The Rise and Fall of the Imperial Japanese Army*. New York: Random House, 1991.

Haynes, Fred E. "Left Flank at Iwo." *Marine Corps Gazette* (October 1951): 48–53.

Heinl, Robert Debs, Jr. *Soldiers of the Sea: The United States Marine Corps, 1775–1962*. Annapolis: Naval Institute Press, 1962.

Ienaga, Saburo. *The Pacific War: World War II and the Japanese, 1931–1945*. New York: Pantheon Books, 1978.

Isely, Jeter A., and Philip A. Crowl. *The U.S. Marines and Amphibious War: Its Theory, and Its Practice in the Pacific*. Princeton: Princeton University Press, 1951.

Keegan, John. *A History of Warfare*. New York: Random House, 1993.

———. *The Second World War*. New York: Penguin, 1989.

Kessler, Lynn, ed. *Never in Doubt: Remembering Iwo Jima*. Annapolis: Naval Institute Press, 1999.

Krulak, Victor H. *First to Fight: An Inside View of the U.S. Marine Corps*. Annapolis: Naval Institute Press, 1984.

Leader, Robert. "The Killing Fields of Sulphur Island." *Notre Dame Magazine*, Winter 2002–03, nd.edu/~ndmag/w2002-03/contents.html.

Leckie, Robert. *Strong Men Armed: The United States Marines Against Japan*. New York: Random House, 1962.

Lambert, John W. *The Pineapple Air Force: Pearl Harbor to Tokyo*. St. Paul, MN: Phalanx Publishing Co., 1990.

Lindsay, Robert. *This High Name: Public Relations and the U.S. Marine Corps*. Madison, WI: University of Wisconsin Press, 1956.

Marling, Karal Ann, and John Wetenhall. *Iwo Jima: Monuments, Memories, and the American Hero*. Cambridge: Harvard University Press, 1991.

Marquand, John P. "Iwo Before H-Hour." *Harper's* (May 1945).

Mersky, Peter B. *U.S Marine Corps Aviation: 1912 to the Present*. Baltimore: Nautical and Aviation Publishing Co. of America, 1983.

Miller, Donald L. "Deathtrap Island." Iwo Jima special issue, *World War II Magazine*, 2006.

Millett, Allan R. *Semper Fidelis: The History of the United States Marine Corps*. Rev. ed. New York: Free Press, 1991.

Moskin, J. Robert. *The U.S. Marine Corps Story*. 3rd ed. Boston: Little Brown, 1992.

Nalty, Bernard C. *The Right to Fight: African-American Marines in World War II*. Washington, DC: USMC, 1995.

Newcomb, Richard F. *Iwo Jima*. New York: Henry Holt and Co.,1965.

Omagari, Satoru, as told to David McNeill. "Even the Dead Were Forced to Fight." Iwo Jima special issue, *World War II Magazine*, 2006.

Ono, Toshihiko. "A Japanese Remembers Iwo Jima." *New York Times Magazine*, February 14, 1965.

O'Sheel, Patrick, and Gene Cook, eds. *Semper Fidelis: The U.S. Marines in the Pacific, 1942–1945*. New York: William Sloane Associates, 1947.

Ricks, Thomas E. *Making the Corps*. New York: Simon & Schuster, 1998.

Ross, Bill D. *Iwo Jima: Legacy of Valor*. New York: Vanguard Press, 1985.

Shaw, Henry I., Jr., and Ralph W. Donnelly. *Blacks in the Marine Corps*. Washington, DC: USMC, 1975.

Simmons, Edwin H. *The United States Marines, 1775–1975*. New York: Viking Press, 1976.

Sledge, E. B. *With the Old Breed at Peleliu and Okinawa*. New York: Oxford University Press, 1990.

Smith, Holland M., and Percy Finch. *Coral and Brass*. New York: C. Scribner's Sons, 1949.

Smith, S. E., ed. *The United States Marine Corps in World War II*. New York: Random House, 1969.

Spector, Ronald H. *Eagle Against the Sun: The American War with Japan*. New York: Free Press, 1984.

Straus, Ulrich. *The Anguish of Surrender: Japanese POWs of World War II*. Seattle: University of Washington Press, 2003.

Thomason, John W. *Fix Bayonets!* New York: Charles Scribner's Sons, 1926.

Thomey, Tedd. *Immortal Images*. Annapolis, MD: Naval Institute Press, 2006.

Tibbetts, Paul. *Return of the Enola Gay*. Columbus, OH: Mid Coast Marketing, 1988.

Toland, John. *The Rising Sun: Decline and Fall of the Japanese Empire*. New York: Random House, 1970.

United States Army Air Forces. "Statistical Summary, 7th Fighter Command" (1945). College Park, MD: National Archives.

United States Marine Corps. *Warfighting: The U.S. Marine Corps Book of Strategy*. New York: Doubleday, 1994.

Vandegrift, A. A. *Once a Marine: The Memoirs of General A. A. Vandegrift, United States Marine Corps*. New York: W. W. Norton, 1964.

Warren, James A. *American Spartans: The U.S. Marines: A Combat History from Iwo Jima to Iraq*. New York: Free Press, 2005.

Wheeler, Richard. *The Bloody Battle for Suribachi*. New York: Crowell, 1965.

———. *Iwo*. New York: Lippincott & Crowell, 1980.

Williams, Robert H. "Morale and Esprit de Corps." *U.S. Naval Institute Proceedings* (January 1961): 135–37.

ACKNOWLEDGMENTS

FRED HAYNES

In early December 2003, James Warren and I had agreed that we would coauthor *The Lions of Iwo Jima*, but on December 19, 2003, I was stricken by a near-fatal blood disorder. Most of the attending physicians felt that my case was hopeless. My wife, Bonnie, had faith that I would recover, and through her superhuman efforts my life was saved. She is the most remarkable human being that I have ever known and I love her dearly. The completion of this book must be attributed to her indomitable spirit.

There were a number of people who joined with her to ensure my survival. They include Dr. Paul Mayo and all of Beth Israel Hospital's Medical Intensive Care Unit in New York City, Dr. Stephen Bernstein, Dr. Mike Colin, Dr. Todd Linden, Dr. William Haynes, Dr. Mike Arnold, Linda May Arnold, and Sam Shirakawa. Many others were involved in my hospitalization and long recovery: Ian Sanmiguel, Gibby and Andy Haynes, and the Haynes tribe—Karen, Fred, Bill, Mark, Nancy, and Kristen as well as Alexandra Traimont and Matteo Mauri.

In May 2004, after five months of hospitalization, we were finally able to move ahead with the book. We were assisted by many people, some veterans, some historians, and some individuals who for one reason or another were keenly interested in the story we wanted to tell. Special mention includes Colonel Frank "Butch" Caldwell (USMC-ret) and Colonel Tom Fields (USMC-ret) for information concerning Combat Team 26 and the battle in general; Colonel Gerry Russell (USMC-ret) for information on Combat Team 27; and John Huffhines, Burt Clayton, and George Cattelona, all 5th Marine Division Association presidents at one time or another, for their help in tracking down members of Combat Team 28 who were still with us.

T. J. Donleavy and Dr. Mary Hayden, both members of the Haynes tribe, and Colonel John Ripley (USMC-ret), were kind enough to review the original manuscript. Major Norm Hatch (USMC-ret) provided access to most of the photographs that appear in the book and was very helpful in developing certain key points in the manuscript. Thanks also go to Colonel Walt Ford (USMC-ret), editor of *Leatherneck*, for photo support and help. Dustin Spence's photo "sleuthing" led to an accurate identification of all the men who participated in the first flag raising on Suribachi. General Lawrence Snowden (USMC-ret) and Iwo Jima veteran Bill Gallo, now a columnist with the *Daily News*, gave us excellent information on the 4th Marine Division at Iwo, as did the always supportive Cyril O'Brien and Colonel George Carrington (USMC-ret) on the 3rd Marine Division. Mrs. Alice Williams and Mrs. Sarah Fenno Lord provided extensive biographical information about Combat Team 28's executive officer, Lieutenant Colonel Robert Williams.

Ivan Hammond and Marvin Veronee were a tremendous help in developing our understanding of the role that naval gunfire and air support played in the battle. Veronee became "Mr. Naval Gunfire" to us. He has one of the best collections of data on the Joint Assault Signal Company detachments that supported Combat Team 28. Ann Neary provided background information concerning her father, the Reverend Sidney Woodd-Cahusac. Bill Henderson filled in the blanks on Landing Team 1/28. Greeley Wells was an excellent source on Landing Team 2/28. He also provided many insights into the two flag raisings of February 23, 1945. Jim Shriver and Jim Miles were excellent sources for the operations of Landing Team 3/28.

Stephen Lopardo provided invaluable information about Taizo Sakai, the Team's most important Japanese POW. My brother, William "Doc" Haynes, who was flying antisubmarine patrols in the Mediterranean when we were fighting on Iwo, gave us useful technical background on naval air as well as Army Air Corps fighters. Alice and Bee Clark provided invaluable information on Camp Tarawa and the Parker Ranch. William Jordan was our primary source on the role of DUKWs in landing and servicing our artillery. Bill Fowler, a boat officer on the USS *Talledega*, provided excellent information on the role LCVPs and LCMs played in the assault landing. Colonel Frank Seabeck sent us excellent vertical aerial photographs of the island. Pat Mooney and Jim Adams dug up a variety of helpful facts about training as well as the battle itself. Thanks go to Bill Taylor for research material on our CO, Colonel Harry Liversedge.

We owe a special debt of gratitude to our splendid agent, John Thornton. John kept us going when the going got tough and provided excellent editorial advice from the very start of the project.

The people at Henry Holt, especially Jack Macrae, senior editor; Supurna Banerjee, associate editor; Kelly Lignos, publicist; Chris O'Connell, production editor; Victoria Hartman, designer; Meryl Levavi; and James Sinclair provided excellent support, advice, and encouragement. Hamilton Cain did a superb job editing the manuscript. Throughout the development of the book Mariko Carpenter attended to the typing, the many e-mails, and was a source of excellent advice on manuscript format.

I have been sustained and encouraged throughout not only by the support of Bonnie and the skills of my coauthor, James Warren, but also by the spirit of the men of Combat Team 28. Special thanks go to Colonel Warren Weidhahn (USMC-ret), now president of Military Historical Tours. Weidhahn made it possible for us to visit Iwo

Jima—trips that were absolutely indispensable in writing the book. Tom Cox and Al Abbatiello were key sources with respect to the accomplishment of CT 28's mission. Jack Lambert, former historian of the 7th Fighter Command, provided detailed information on the important role Army Air Force fighters, based in Iwo, played in the air war on Japan.

JAMES WARREN

First and foremost, I want to express my enduring gratitude to my good friend Fred Haynes for inviting me to coauthor the book. I had never envisioned coauthoring any book, but sharing the burdens and the joys of discovery and creation with Fred has been one of the most rewarding experiences in my life. His faith in me, and his constant encouragement over the past several years, proved essential to the completion of the book.

Thanks to Bonnie Haynes as well for her cheerful moral support, as well as her invaluable creative input.

A very special thanks to all the survivors of CT 28 who agreed to share their experiences with us. Fred has named many of them above. I want to add two who were especially helpful and insightful: Dick Bishop and Ray Jacobs. Sadly, neither Dick nor Ray lived to see the book in print. It was a rare privilege to get to know so many of the brave Marines of CT 28.

Without the cheerful help of the research staff at the Marine Corps Historical Division and the librarians of Columbia University and Brown University, the book would never have been completed. Finally, sincere thanks to several close friends for unstinting moral support: Cliff Chappel, Erin Connole; Craig Crawford and Tom Ginnerty; Helen and Peter Flynn; Carol Hoyem, who also helped us a great deal with the art program for the book; Lance King; Amy Lipman and her son, Michael Golden; and Patrick Tracey.

INDEX

ABOUT THE AUTHORS

MAJOR GENERAL FRED HAYNES (USMC-ret), a veteran of three wars, commanded the Second and Third Marine Divisions and the Fifth Marine Regiment. He is the last living officer of the 28th Marines who participated in the planning and conduct of CT 28's assault on Mount Suribachi and subsequent combat on Iwo. The first Marine officer elected to the Council on Foreign Relations, General Haynes is chairman emeritus of the American Turkish Council. He holds degrees from SMU and George Washington University and is a distinguished graduate of the U.S. Air War College. He lives with his wife, Bonnie Arnold Haynes, in New York City.

JAMES A. WARREN is the author of a critically acclaimed history of the Marines, *American Spartans* (Free Press, 2005), as well as books on the Vietnam War and the Cold War. For more than twenty years he was an acquisitions editor of nonfiction and reference books for New York City book publishers. Warren is a magna cum laude graduate of Brown University and lives in Narragansett, Rhode Island.